NATIONAL ACCLAIM FOR CONNIE FLETCHER'S FASCINATING BOOKS

BREAKING AND ENTERING

"Connie Fletcher has committed her own B&E on precincts around the country and has absconded with no less than the truth. Gritty and eye-opening reading for anyone interested in the criminal justice system."
—Lisa Scottoline, author of *Running from the Law*

"Good dish and chilling war stories. . . ."
—*Los Angeles Times*

"What makes Fletcher's book compelling is that, despite its long catalog of insults and slights and hazing, the women she interviews don't come across as whiners or victims. They are cops, who wanted into the brotherhood badly enough to endure the idiocy of some of the brothers."
—*Newsday*

"Candid . . . informative. . . . [A] well-organized compendium of the experiences of 106 female officers."
—*Publishers Weekly*

WHAT COPS KNOW

"A lively, intelligent, amazingly well-informed look at cops from the inside out!"

—Joseph Wambaugh

"Great, the real stuff . . . fascinating."

—Elmore Leonard

"For anybody who ever wondered what it's like behind a badge, this is the book. *What Cops Know* pulls no punches."
—*San Francisco Chronicle*

"May just be the finest book on police work ever published. When one is through reading it, one understands what it's like to be a cop—how fascinating, how discouraging, how addictive, and how terrifying. . . ."

—Father Andrew Greeley

"A rare and engrossing insider's look into police work . . . a fast and fascinating read."

—*Chicago Sun-Times*

"Every policeman, whether he is small-town or big-city, has said at least one time in his career: 'With everything I've seen and everything I've done, I ought to write a book.' Connie Fletcher has let us do just that."
— Captain Tom Cronin, Research and Development, Chicago Police Department

"Connie Fletcher tells 'what cops know' in scary but colorful detail. . . . *What Cops Know* is plenty entertaining, and is probably as close to the gruesome realities of being a cop as most of us want to get."
— *New City* (Chicago)

"An engrossing piece of oral history . . . uncensored."
— Cleveland *Plain Dealer*

"Not a book for the queasy. . . . It offers insight into the significant crime problem from the perspective of our first—and last—line of defense."
— *The Record* (Hackensack, NJ)

"Fast and hard-hitting reading . . . fascinating—and frightening."
— *Dallas Morning News*

Books by Connie Fletcher

Breaking and Entering*
What Cops Know
Pure Cop
Who Runs Chicago? (with Michael Kilian
    and F. Richard Ciccone)

*Published by POCKET BOOKS

BREAKING
AND
ENTERING

WOMEN COPS BREAK THE CODE OF SILENCE
TO TELL THEIR STORIES FROM THE INSIDE

CONNIE FLETCHER

POCKET BOOKS

New York   London   Toronto   Sydney   Tokyo   Singapore

POCKET BOOKS, a division of Simon & Schuster Inc.
1230 Avenue of the Americas, New York, NY 10020

Copyright © 1995 by Connie Fletcher

Published by arrangement with HarperCollins

ISBN: 0-671-00086-1

First Pocket Books printing February 1997

10 9 8 7 6 5 4 3 2 1

POCKET and colophon are registered trademarks of Simon & Schuster Inc.

Cover photo by Frank Siteman/The Picture Cube

Printed in the U.S.A.

To Trygve, Bridget, Nick
and Spiffy
with Love

"We're a very closed society. We have so many secrets, so many secrets. We build walls. And the walls are starting to crash in on women and minorities."

—Detective Stephanie Roundtree,
Philadelphia Police Department

ACKNOWLEDGMENTS

I value the candor and courage of all the women who spoke with me. The trail of contacts and referrals started with Sergeant Pattie McConnell of the Winnetka, Illinois, PD, who introduced me to Assistant Commissioner Carolen Bailey of the Minnesota Department of Public Safety and former president of the International Association of Women Police. Commissioner Bailey was unfailingly helpful and gave me contacts all over the country who gave me more contacts and more insights. Among the women who went the extra mile in helping me are Julia Thompson of the NYPD; Monica Smith of the Dallas PD; Deborah Sibilia, DEA, Houston; Penny Harrington, former police chief of Portland, Oregon; Debbie Montgomery of St. Paul; Adrienne Hilliard of Philadelphia; Cindy Tallman of the Seattle PD; Kim Anderson of the Chicago PD; Roberta Reddick and Diane Harber of the LAPD; and Sherry Schlueter of the Broward County Sheriff's Office Animal Abuse Unit.

Women in law enforcement are almost unanimous in saying that while the system fails to protect male or female against individual enemies or harassers within the organization, most male officers have been neutral or even extremely encouraging to their women counterparts. Male officers were helpful to me, too, in my gaining interviews. I'd like to especially thank Herb Timm, former chief of the Winnetka PD, currently police chief of the Burr Ridge, Illinois, PD, and lieutenant Joe Sumner (retired) of the Winnetka PD; chief George Carpenter of the Wilmette, Illinois, PD;

inspector N. L. Hendrix of the San Francisco PD; Mike Vadnal of the Broward County Sheriff's Office; detective Jim Dyment of the Seattle PD; and detective Ed Carmody of the Metro-Dade County PD, who all led me to remarkable women with remarkable stories.

This book never would have been completed were it not for Loyola University Chicago, which granted me a research leave in order to conduct interviews and write the book. The chair of my department, W. Barnett Pearce, gave me his support for my research leave and has always broadened my research scope. All my colleagues at Loyola are superb in their support and enthusiasm. My gratitude, as always, to Ed Rooney.

My family gives me strength and joy. My daughter, Bridget, is a wonderful writer and gives truly helpful suggestions; my son, Nick, gives me lots of company and advice while I write, and my husband, Trygve, has probably listened to more tales of cops than any man alive. And with a good will, too. And none of this would be possible without my sister and reality check, Julie.

CONTENTS

PREFACE xv

CHAPTER 1 **THE ALLEY** 1

CHAPTER 2 **THE UNIFORM** 29

CHAPTER 3 **THE ACADEMY** 53

CHAPTER 4 **THE HOUSE** 93

CHAPTER 5 **THE LOCKER ROOM** 119

CHAPTER 6 **THE CAR** 137

CHAPTER 7 **HOME** 165

CHAPTER 8 **THE CLUB** 183

CHAPTER 9 **THE CODE** 223

EPILOGUE: THE ALLEY 251

CONTRIBUTING OFFICERS 253

PREFACE

I'm on the phone with a male police lieutenant. "Whoa! Whoa! Wait a minute!" he says. "I can't concentrate. This rookie just walked in and she's got the cutest little ass. What a nice tight ass! God! These rookies! They're not like the lady lard-asses we usually see around here. You're driving me crazy! Yeah, honey, just leave those reports on the desk. And let me watch you walk that cute little ass out."

It's 1994.

Women have been in policing throughout the U.S. since 1910, when social worker Alice Stebbins Wells became the first full-fledged policewoman in the LAPD (the NYPD hired women as jail matrons as early as 1845). Until the mid-seventies, when the application of civil rights legislation to policing put women on patrol, policewomen were largely confined to one of two assignments: Youth Division or Jail. According to Captain Diane Harber, who joined the LAPD in 1957, "We had two choices: Go to the Youth Division or to the jail. Most of us went directly to jail." As policewomen, they did what male officers couldn't do (conducting searches on female suspects, prisoners, or corpses, working as decoy prostitutes or girlfriends) or didn't want to do (typing reports, changing diapers, dispensing baby bottles, baby-sitting). They weren't eligible for promotions or the same pay as male officers. They were trained separately from the men. They were barred from roll call. They were banned from the "elite" units, like Homicide (though some women did work Homicide, unofficially, and at policewoman pay). Many of them had to use their own cars or take public transportation to their assignments outside the station house. If they were black women, they couldn't work with white women.

In the seventies, Dallas police wives showed up at a Police Association meeting, protesting the presence of women officers "who will either get our husbands killed or cheat on us with them." In Miami, a uniformed woman officer running to the aid of her partner in the projects broke up a fight just by showing up—"They took one look at me and just fell on each other, laughing." In Portland, Oregon, a rookie in the newly legislated same-sex Police Academy successfully performed a jujitsu move in which she threw a male rookie over her head. On the way down, he pulled her Portland Police Bureau sweatshirt over her head. Everyone applauded.

All this was in response to legislation requiring police forces to hire and treat women as equals. By the mid-seventies, following passage of the 1972 Equal Employment Opportunity (EEO) Act, which applied Title VII (prohibiting employment discrimination on the basis of race, color, religion, sex, or national origin) of the 1964 Civil Rights Act to state and local governments, and following a host of legal skirmishes and delaying tactics, women police had been legislated into equality with male officers. Same training. Same uniforms. Same duties. Same pay.

Many outsiders assume that that was the end of the story, that women officers climbed into squad cars and rode off into a sunset crime-red with job security. But reports and cases of the past few years point to another story, one that is only now starting to be told.

The story is partially told by statistics. The FBI's *Uniform Crime Reports* puts women police at only 9.1 percent of the country's 544,309 police officers, a figure that has grown by a mere 4 to 5 percent since departments and agencies were mandated to hire women in the mid-seventies. Yet of the 204,521 civilian employees in policing, fully 63.5 percent are female. The Police Foundation's latest survey-analysis, *On the Move: The Status of Women in Policing,* states that women are in the minority in midlevel managerial positions and are "virtually excluded from command positions." The stats could mean that very few women want to become police officers and that only a tiny percentage apply or perform well enough to promote. Or the stats could mean that something beyond enforced equality is at work here.

Another part of the story is untold, but it walks into the lieutenant's office with the rookie officer, the one who was hung up on a meathook and described to another woman over the phone. The rookie is learning something. She's learning that whatever she thought this job was—whatever she was trained for in four months of Defensive Tactics and Community Policing and Sensitivity Training in the Police Academy—it isn't. The rookie will learn more, depending on what she does next. She'll keep learning throughout her career.

What really happens when women join what many describe as "the biggest Boys' Club in America" is best illuminated by the testimony of women officers themselves. Women police have been traditionally tight-lipped about their careers, at first for fear of nonacceptance, later for fear of retribution, though I discovered in writing two previous books about policing, *What Cops Know* and *Pure Cop,* that the format of anonymous storytelling allows people in this most closed and secretive of cultures to speak freely.

Narrative is more revealing than survey or statistic. It is one thing to read a statistic saying that 87 percent of women police officers have experienced, at one time or another, a hostile work environment. It is quite another to hear an officer talk about coming into her first roll call, in 1980, a union rep strewing rose petals before her, and the roll-call lectern festooned with sanitary napkins and tampons, or to hear an officer talk about her first locker room, a janitor's closet with holes cut in the walls and a shotgunned dead rat awaiting her one night. It is one thing to read survey results saying that women face opposition as they advance. It is another to hear a SWAT officer, the first female on the team, talk about attending a 1990 SWAT banquet that culminated in a homemade porno film or the first woman in a Canine Unit tell of the men always setting the biggest dogs on her in training. Statistics and surveys reveal that women officers keep quiet lest they're ostracized or hung out to dry on the street. Narratives detail what it's like to be shunned in the station house or when you need backup.

The truest picture of women in policing is found in the voices of women themselves—in their stories. Yet, many times, women's voices are silenced or discounted in policing. The stories they tell each other about what actually goes on in this world are, except for a few individual accounts, virtually unknown to the public. And since policing can be both a demanding and isolating experience, these stories seldom travel beyond a woman's closest circle of friends. Unless a woman is involved in a professional organization, such as the International Association of Women Police (IAWP) or the National Organization of Black Women in Law Enforcement (NOBWLE), she can believe that the problems she encounters, rather than being systemic and part of police culture, are unique to her. Stories that are untold and stories that are unheard perpetuate abuses.

I sought out these stories by interviewing more than one hundred women in U.S. law enforcement. Because the largest representation of women is on big-city forces, the majority of my interviews were with women cops in New York, Los Angeles, San Francisco, Seattle, Portland, Chicago, Boston, Dallas, Houston, Miami, Cleveland, San Jose, and Minneapolis–St. Paul. I interviewed women in federal agencies: the FBI, DEA (Drug Enforcement Agency), ATF (Bureau of Alcohol, Tobacco, and Firearms), and the U.S. Marshals Service. I spoke with women in the Broward County Sheriff's Office and in state agencies. I spoke with state troopers, suburban cops, county cops, and rural cops.

I tried to get a cross section of views. Some of the women I spoke with began policing in the forties and fifties (the woman interviewed with the longest policing experience is an African-American who joined the LAPD in 1947); a few were new on the job, like the NYPD officer who joined in 1992 and wears her mother's old badge, and the Texas Ranger, one of the first two women ever to become a Ranger, in 1993. I tried to represent ranks and levels of experience, from the first woman police chief of a major U.S. city (Penny Harrington, former police chief of Portland, Oregon) and the NYPD's highest-ranking female officer (now retired inspector Julia Thompson), through SWAT Team members, hostage negotiators, Homicide detectives, Defensive Tactics instructors at police academies, Youth Division officers, jail workers, and patrol officers. And I sought the experiences of women who have encountered extra obstacles in policing: African-Americans, Latinas, and lesbians.

My interviewing MO was simple. I asked these women officers to walk me through their careers, taking detours into topics as they saw fit. I also asked them about different places common in police careers: the Academy, the squad car, the station house, the locker room, the roll-call room. I did this, first of all, so that I wouldn't be fitting them into prefabricated topics ("Have you experienced discrimination?" "Have you experienced harassment?") and distorting the material before it was even spoken. I've also discovered that the best way to have people remember things is to get them thinking about the places in which their lives, or their working lives, have been enacted.

I was surprised by the almost universal picture of police work that emerged from these very diverse sources: Policing is a club for men; this club has a strict hierarchy (white males first, then black and other minority males, then white females, black females, and finally, gay males); the club still operates in a culture of socializing and informal contacts impervious to legislation; people who are not wanted in the club may be harassed, ostracized, denied desired assignments, days off, shifts, or promotion; speaking or "grieving" (filing a grievance) about what happens within the club breaks the code and, thereafter, breaks the officer. This is a club where harassers can get away with virtually anything because no one, male or female, can afford the punishments that follow ratting on a fellow cop. And this is a club where you can get killed if people don't like you.

At the same time, another near universal report from these 106 women is that many male cops have been neutral about women in police work, adopting a wait-and-see attitude toward them, and some have been extremely supportive. Women police also report that working with male officers usually makes a convert of the male, at least as regards that *one* female officer. But the club atmosphere permeates all of police culture so that, while a man is automatically accepted into the club, a woman must prove herself over and over again, from assignment to assignment, before she gains respect, if not total acceptance. And the system supports the lone jerk, the lone harasser, who can make any male or female officer's life miserable and still be supported, or at least overlooked, by the other club members.

The format for this book is to let the women in law enforcement speak for themselves in a way police culture has never let them. They can do this only if they speak anonymously. So, in each chapter, after a brief introduction, the experiences of these women are given in their own words without their names attached and usually without their agencies or departments identified, unless the reference is neutral—or the woman *asked* that the department or agency be identified. This method both enables women to speak freely without fear of retribution and demonstrates the universality of the challenges women face in policing. However, in order that credit be given to the women who courageously came forward to tell their stories in this book, and so that the reader can see the width and breadth of experience represented in these stories, brief biographies are given, in alphabetical order, at the end.

This book is organized, like the interviews themselves, primarily by place, to show how biases and prejudices are played out in locker room, roll-call room, station house, patrol car.

This oral history, extending from the forties to the present, but concentrating on that most volatile of all periods for women in policing, from the early seventies on, has much to say about discrimination, how protean and multifaceted it is and how it has changed, in the past two decades, from blatant and overt to subtle and insidious. It also shows how women have coped and sometimes failed to cope—an oft-repeated complaint among women is that women in law enforcement are their own worst enemies, failing to organize and support each other. Finally, the testimony of these women shows the ways in which women have changed policing itself.

My hope is that this oral history will not only acquaint the reader with the obstacles, both physical and psychological, women in policing have encountered, but will also acquaint them with a new model of police heroism, operating both on the streets *and* inside. I also hope that this book can help break the isolation and hopelessness many women police still feel when they encounter the ever-changing obstacles of discrimination by sparking discussion and action.

BREAKING
AND
ENTERING

CHAPTER 1

THE ALLEY

*T*he one major thing that came up endlessly, endlessly, endlessly, and I still have to answer this sometimes, starts: "Women on the job. I have nothing against women on the job. But what would you do if you found yourself in an alley with a big 250-pound man comin' at you? What would you do?"

Always. It's always that guy in the alley. Every day, that same scenario. Every day.

Always. Always. Always. They say this: "You're there. You have no gun, no radio, no club. And you're at the end of a dead-end alley. And some huge 250-pound raving maniac is coming after you. What would you do?"

And I always say, "I'd fall in love. What are you, crazy?"

—Chicago Police Department officer

*T*he alley thing comes up constantly. It's one of those urban folk legends.

It's always . . . "What are you gonna do if you face a criminal and you're alone? You're gonna have to use your gun."

—LAPD officer

*W*hat we get—it's a 250-pound Finlander. A Finlander drunk. Who just came out of the woods after all week cutting wood. A woodsman. A 250-pound drunken woodsman. But most of the time it is a Finlander.

You arm yourself with a pastie and a beer and throw it at him. That'll change his mind about you.

—Two officers from Michigan's Upper Peninsula

The 250-Pound Man in an Alley" story is part of cop folklore, encapsulating, in almost fairy-tale terms, the belief that policing is a matter of strength, a heavyweight contest between giants and giant killers. To the extent that it's believed, men and women cops and the public are blinded to the complicated realities and skills of policing.

What is startling about this story is not so much its content, even though it sets up a ludicrous no-win situation. What is most startling about this story is that it appears everywhere: while not all women police have heard this story, many have (and many have heard it ad nauseam throughout their careers). It's been circulating in police departments in every part of the country for the past twenty-plus years, and while there are different spins on the woman cop's degree of vulnerability, she always comes up short against a big guy in an alley. And this guy almost always weighs in at 250 pounds.

It's a dangerous story. And, for many cops and civilians, it just won't go away.

What follows in this chapter, as in all the chapters of this book, are the anonymous stories of women cops around the country, given in their own words . . .

The alley imagery is neat . . . in the way that I think of being a police officer and a woman.

Alleys are traditionally . . . they're incredibly connected to the way our society thinks about rape: it's always in an alley a woman gets raped by a stranger.

It's been fascinating to me, talking with the guys who came on the job when I came on . . . And they've had to learn to deal with the constant threat of physical danger, whereas we women have always had it. Little girls are molested, or raped, or physically abused. Women are not safe in their own homes. Over fifty percent of all women are battered by their husbands or boyfriends. Seventy percent of all female homicide victims are killed by husbands or boyfriends. So, for women, physical safety, physical harm, is a way of life. For men, they're not used to that—they're not used to fearing for their physical safety—till they come on the job.

For me, it's been empowering. When I'm . . . a civilian, and it's three in the morning and I'm walking down the street by myself—if I see a group of men on the street, I have to watch, I have to constantly watch. If I cross the street and they cross with me—you know.

Now, it's three in the morning and I have a radio, I have a gun. I see that same group of men on the street—they have to watch *me.* They have to worry about what *I'm* going to do.

So the alley imagery is really good. It goes from—*before,* when I was in that alley, as a civilian, I didn't have a chance. Now I'm a *cop* and I'm in that alley and the odds have been evened—I've been given a gun, I've been given the power of arrest, I've been given society's approval to be here—whereas, before, at three in the morning, boy, you had it coming to you. Now I have the approval to be here. I have that acceptance. I'm not asking for it. And I have a radio.

So, to me, that alley really shows what it's like to go from being a woman civilian to a cop.

I became a cop because I was teaching school and I needed a safer job than teaching school. I mean to tell you, I needed a job that allowed me to carry a gun because where I was teaching, a large, overcrowded, inner city, two hundred kids in this elementary school, and I mean to tell you I was almost raped, I was regularly spit upon, had rocks thrown at me every single night as I left for my car.

I was dragged into a first-floor washroom by a seventh-grade boy, dragged me in there, pulled up my skirt . . . it was a tough school. They'd stand up on the stairs and spit on top of my head. I had a chair broken over my back. It was

3

a combat zone. I was dating at the time the man who would be my husband, and he told me of a test offered for policewomen.

I needed a safer job, that's what it was.

The Joe Public—when they think of danger on this job, they may be thinking of a Caucasian female; they think that she's not gonna handle it. They're not gonna think that way about a black female police officer unless somebody has inside knowledge. They're not gonna think about a black female on the job; they're gonna think about a *Caucasian* female on the job. They figure she would be in more danger than a black woman would. They figure a black woman can handle herself. All right? It's a real perception.

They think . . . well, a black woman . . . she has to go to a rough neighborhood and she has to deal with those gang members. They're gonna think about a blond little lady—they're gonna think, "Oh my *God!*" They're gonna think of Charlie's Angels–type women or something. But they're not gonna think about—SISTER SOULJAH!—with her *braids* and stuff—they're not gonna *think* about her.

A black female officer can be in as much danger as the white female officer. But people think we black women are warriors anyway, so we should be able to take care of it.

In my own personal experience—and not to divide the sexes—but there were a lot of times when I felt more comfortable on the street with a female than with a male. And the reason for this is that some males are not challenged—their fear level is not challenged as much as a female's fear level. And when that fear kicks in—it takes a whole hell of a lot of thinking to get control of yourself. And if you can't get control of yourself, you're gonna lose the battle. Bottom line.

And some males have actually turned and run because of that fear. I've seen it happen. They don't understand their fear. Whereas a lot of women have been placed in many fearful situations to where you're constantly practicing getting control of your fear.

When I teach Defensive Tactics at the Academy, I try to

explain that to the cadets. It's a matter of conditioning. If you're female, you've been *conditioned* to be aware because of the threat of harm coming to you. Say you're standing at a bus stop alone. The minute somebody says boo, you're gonna jump and react. So as a woman you're—most of the time—aware of your surroundings. And there are times, more than with men, that you are placed in fear. Joe Blow may come up and start talking to you and he's lost. You might think that's just an in for him to approach you, so you're gonna start to step back and prepare yourself the best way you know how without literally coming out and attacking the person before you know what he wants.

But with some men, when they get in a fearful situation, it overwhelms them. It overwhelms them. That's what I've seen. I've seen them literally shut down.

The biggest thing when you're out there is controlling your fear. I don't care if you're on a disturbance or what, I mean, a lot of people overreact because they're afraid—*that* the general public doesn't understand—when you've got an officer that strikes out at somebody, sometimes it's because they are in fear and not because they're mean or hateful; it's that they're in fear and they want that fear to stop. They want that threat to go away. So they strike out or they overreact or they say something that escalates a situation.

The supervisor in my old building always used to say that anybody who has *not* been on the job for ten years—and *any woman*—is not in the department. They're not cops.

This was a big, fat slug. He'd been in the building for years. And when he was on the street, he was a slug. But he was always mouthing off about how no one with less than ten years could be a cop—and no woman could ever be a cop.

During the Rodney King riots, he was the biggest coward of all. You could see him shaking out there; he couldn't make any decisions. And there were others like him—the men who did the most bitching and the most griping were the most scared.

In some ways, men have the advantage, especially if you're bigger, because the threat of you is pretty inherent, just by how you look. With women, I mean, really, if somebody wanted to . . . a lot of them, they could hurt you and hurt you bad even before you can get backup there.

So you really rely on being smart and verbal and presenting things in a way that's acceptable for everybody. And admitting—"Hey! You're right. You can kick the shit out of me, no doubt about it. But my friends are on their way and there's no reason to take it that far and you're not in that much trouble now, but then you'd be in *real* trouble. This is no sweat."

It's constantly feeling that you need to prove yourself. I mean, I had a partner, nice guy—didn't like drunks. Well, the district we had was nights and it was a big bar district downtown, so all we're gonna run into was drunks. And he was like, he was tall, but he was a skinny little guy, and at the time I was 5'5" and 130 pounds and he's 6' and 170 pounds.

When you go to a bar call, kind of the standard way to handle it, you know, some drunk refusing to leave, is to sort of not rush to the call. Give the guy—you know, some of these drunk people, it takes them a while to assimilate what's happening. So, you kind of like take your time getting there, not that you dog it too much, but it's not a hot call. Ninety percent of the time the guy's gone by the time you get there and the problem's solved; you don't have to have the confrontation with a drunk person and the people are happy that you showed up. And even if you see the guy sort of standing there, and you're on your way in, and you see the guy, but he's on the way out, it's like—you didn't see him. You like walk in and go to the bartender, "What's the problem here?" What is it worth hassling some drunk for not leavin' when he's leavin'?

Well, this partner took his job a little seriously. We're going into the bar and the guy that fits the description is on the way out and instead of letting him go—he didn't notice he had Popeye forearms and huge biceps—*I* did; I noticed that—but he stops and starts dressing the guy down for not doing what the bartender asked him to do.

Drunk people don't make sense out of these little talks.

They don't. Anyway, he stops this guy, and next thing I know I see this guy starting a fight that didn't need to be started. And I see my partner flying through the air and I'm just like, "Ohhhh. I'm gonna get hurt and I have to do this." And for no good reason. We didn't have to be in this fight. But now, because my partner's been hit, *I* have to go and get hit by this guy who just sent somebody who weighs thirty pounds more than I do thataway. Now I have to go and get hurt or my reputation is ruined.

So then I go, I go, and somehow I get behind him and I try to put a choke hold on him but he's bigger and he tosses me, he throws me over his back and my partner's back up and they're fighting . . . Finally, I got up and I looked at both of them, so I just tackled both of them and went to the ground. Least on the ground, we're all sort of equal size. It was like . . . tables were flying; it was like the movies . . . it's weird how your mind, I mean, you're in it, but you're catching the other stuff too.

I just remember . . . finally I saw him in this fight and then I saw a gun. Oh, this isn't good. So I grab the gun and my mind goes, "So if you grab the gun and if you have time to get your radio, we might get more police here." So I got on the radio and asked for more police, and actually a citizen came in and helped us and we finally got the guy under control.

It was all okay, but it was all because we didn't walk in and ignore the drunk guy walking out.

A woman up against a man, a man will wait and see where a woman's coming from. He's kind of curious. Now, man to man, they'll go at it. But a man to a different woman—Whup! Hold it. They back up. Whoadie! Wait a minute! Hold it!

Unless they're really drunk or on drugs . . . that's something different. But if he's just up against a woman, unless he really hates women out and out or he had a bad relationship or something, they generally want to see where a woman's from; they want to talk. You know, how many guys have I made a deputy; they want to talk to you.

* * *

Sometimes brawn is an advantage, but sometimes guys will just challenge a big cop. They want to get in a fight with the big guy. But with a woman, where's the sport?

You'd think big officers would have no problems, but they've got it rough. One officer I worked with was a bodybuilder and a weight lifter. He was just a very large man. We were called to a domestic with another large man. This guy was *not* going to go to jail; there was a confrontation between my partner and him. My partner got handcuffs on the guy on the way to the car. Later, the arrestee complained of undue use of force.

It was probably his ego. This guy had never been manhandled because of his size. So my partner's size worked against him. If an officer is really big, he's got to be really careful because he's running up against all the other male egos out there. Everybody wants to take the big man on.

The worst ones—I would take on a 250-pound guy any day rather than a 100-pound woman. They will call you every dirty, filthy name in the book that you can conceive of. I've been called unimaginable names by these women. And they're dirty fighters.

Women will give you the worst time. Even drunk women. Women change so quickly, more than a man will. They get real strange. Give me a guy any day.

To be honest, I've had very, very few physical contacts. And I'll tell you what—I think the ones that will hurt you the most are the little ones. Little guys. I've never had physical contact, I mean, one-on-one, with *big* men. Never. Never.

It's the little guys . . . I was in a situation two years ago where I literally had to fight for my life with a 130-pound guy. He was shorter than I was. He weighed less than I did. It was down to the wire.

I stopped him for speeding. He had no driver's license. It turned out he was using aliases. The truck he was driving was not his own. The identification he gave me was a bunch of papers like a marriage certificate; you name it, just odds and ends of paperwork. I ran his name through the computer; came back with a warrant.

I got him out of his truck, patted him down, he had like seven dollars in his pocket, nothing more. Got him back to the patrol car. I had just stopped a guy on I-94 and taken a hundred-dollar bond from him. I have a clip on my clipboard where I slip my bond money—it's a real strong clip—and I had that sitting on the front seat. When I started asking him a little bit more about himself, his date of birth, he couldn't tell me when he was born. I knew, of course, then, that he wasn't who he said he was. But he was smooth. This guy was a professional con man.

Suddenly, he runs back to his truck. Unbeknownst to me, he had taken the hundred dollars off of my clipboard and stuffed it into his pocket. Then he runs back to his truck. I had one handcuff on him and then, the next thing I know, we're fighting, we're rolling around on the ground, he's trying to get back to his truck, I couldn't figure out why, and he's telling me, "I haven't done anything wrong, I haven't done anything wrong, *I* haven't done anything wrong—you don't have to arrest me, I haven't done anything wrong." He's talking fast and trying desperately to get back to his truck.

He tries to get back there, and we're fighting, literally fighting, all the way up to the truck, you know, wrassling around. He manages to get the door open to his truck and I thought, "Okay. He's got a gun. He's got the gun in there. And whoever he is, whatever he's done, he doesn't want me to know about it." So I blocked him and I threw myself into the truck so whatever he was after, he couldn't reach because he kept trying to reach in there and get something.

So he was laying on top of me. I bit through his ear—because he was literally laying on top of me. I couldn't get to anything; I couldn't get into my gun pocket, I couldn't get my gun because then we still had our cross-draw holsters. I couldn't get my gun. So all I could do was bite him and . . . I ran my hands down his pants and grabbed his testicles and pulled as hard as I could. I didn't do that because of my training. That's the way I used to fight with my brother.

Then I literally tore his ear in two—his earlobe—I just clamped on until it ripped—and he screamed, and then he tried to reach his leather jacket on the seat and he started to pull on it. I thought, "He's got the gun in there." And I pulled it out of the truck and I threw it underneath the truck so he couldn't get to it.

And we kept fighting still. He ran across all three lanes of I-94 and I thought, "This guy's *nuts.*" He started running . . . then he stopped right in the middle. He turned around and looked at me, very calmly, and said, "I'm not gonna do anything. I'm not gonna do anything." And then he ran back to his truck and I drew down on him. I thought, "There's something in that truck he wants desperately and something's gonna happen." So I drew down on him and I'm running, trying to keep him away from his truck, and he grabs for me because I'm trying to head him off, and he goes for my gun.

So we're fighting against the truck. This is eleven o'clock in the morning on I-94. This guy is nuts. And the gun is up in the air and it's coming down and I'm looking at the barrel and it's going back up . . . And he's screaming at me: "Don't shoot me! Don't shoot me!" He's trying to get my hand off the trigger because I've got my hand over the trigger *and* cylinder, so the cylinder won't move and he can't get his finger in there. And he keeps trying to pull it down and pull it away.

And, finally, two guys happened to stop. I don't know where they came from. They were driving by, as I found out later on. Citizens. And they were standing there looking at me, and I thought they were football players. They were huge men. It turned out they were realtors. And I said, "Don't just stand there. Help me!" Because we are literally all *over* his truck and wrassling.

One of them managed to get the guy's hand off of my arm and then . . . I didn't know who these guys were, but I couldn't reach around in front of me to put my gun back in my holster, so I *handed* my gun over to this guy, not knowing who they were. And I'm still fighting with this man. And we're fighting into I-94. And then, these guys—one of them finally helped me get this guy down to the ground. He was strung out on something; I mean,

130 pounds. These guys went over 250 themselves, and it was all we could do to keep him down. They had to stand on his back while I clamped his hands with the handcuffs.

Then we got him into the patrol car. He starts kicking at us, he starts kicking over the seat because we don't have those guards. Unbeknownst to me, somebody had called the post and said, "Hey, I think one of your troopers is in trouble out there."

It turns out, he's a professional con man. He had about twelve aliases. In his truck, we later found his driver's license with his name on it. And it had been suspended. That's all there was. There was no gun, no drugs, nothing. We tore that truck apart.

A week later, we got a call from the jail saying, "Hey, this guy of yours has been ordering VCRs, flowers, and everything else on stolen credit card numbers." So they started running his fingerprints, found out who he really was, and that he had done this all over the Midwest.

That's the closest I've ever come to . . . I really, I really knew that something was going to happen. I thought, "Nobody knows that I've got this truck stopped other than—I ran his name. They know where I am, but they don't know what's going on. I'm gonna get shot and—we don't know who this guy is."

That's the only time I had to fight. And the only time I had to fight a big guy, I was with a partner. The guy was a mental; I kicked him in the nuts. But—I don't think it's the big guys. And I've even heard male police officers say, "It's not the big guys that you have to watch out for. It's the little ones."

So this nonsense about being in an alley with a 250-pound guy—most of the big guys are "Yes, ma'am. Yes, ma'am." They don't have anything to prove.

It's a survival instinct. It just kicks in. It was real weird, it was just a sensation I have never . . . I have never had to fight for my life before. Now I know I can.

Women are dirty fighters. Men can probably box and wrestle but, you know—I'll do what I've gotta do.

My husband lifts weights every day. He's got the strength

that I will probably never have. Just sheer bulk. I'll never have that.

That's why you reach for the nuts.

Everyone has their limitations, given certain situations. I wouldn't think to try to take on some guy who's 6'5" and 250 unless I had to. If it was a life and death—well, hey, we're in it, we're goin' for it. But there are other ways of dealing with it. At the same time, I don't know too many of the guys that would want to take on that guy either.

When I started on the job, my friends and relatives always said, "People are gonna take advantage of you." I didn't have that problem because my demeanor was such that I always came on low-key. Now, they always told you, you can always start low and get high. I was always low-key anyway. So I came on low-key. When I made a traffic stop and I'd have to make an arrest, I'd make a joke out of getting them into the car. I'd say, "Well, listen. I've got to pat you down, make sure you ain't got no tanks, bazookas, hand grenades." I'd make them comfortable because they figured, "Who's *this* dumb broad?" I'd say, "I gotta put you in my backseat. It's procedure, you know."

So I'd get them in there. And the guys that work with me, to this day, say, "Boy, you sweet-talk *more* guys into that backseat of your squad car to get them down to headquarters." I said, "Well, shoot. Most of them were bigger than I was. I wasn't gonna take no whippin'." I was just real low-key, you know.

You can start at a low level and say "please" and if they don't respond to that, then you have somewhere to go. But if your first response to them is "Listen, motherfucker, I told you not to *do* blah blah blah," then what do you do?

It's like giving yourself no options. They'll do something like take their gun out and stick it in somebody's ear and say, "You do this or I'll blow your brains out." And then when the guy turns around to you and says, "Go ahead," what are you gonna do? You *could* do it years ago. Now you have to back down.

* * *

You have guys that go around—*"I* can handle this. *I* know what to do." And next thing—you know—they're rollin' down the steps. So you have to go in there—*"Okay* . . . let's try . . . let's . . ."

My friend and I had to beg to work together. Two women. A Hispanic and a black woman. The bosses didn't think it was a good idea . . . but finally said yeah, go ahead. We worked West Dallas and to get there you have to go cross the river bottoms and it takes a while. It's not like, if you need help right away, someone's gonna get there in a minute or two. Guys were always cruising by, checking up on us, seeing if we were okay.

What happened was, my partner and I got a call one time of a drunk on the street. Well, that is no big novelty in West Dallas. We get there and there's this drunk. We're trying to get him in and he starts to get very belligerent. Well, this guy and his partner come by—and he decides he's going to take over the situation and he's gonna put a restraint on him, you know, choke him out and make him pass out so we can handcuff him.

This cop is telling us, "Step aside. *I'll* take care of him." So I said, "Okay, big man, go ahead." I'm as small as him and he's gonna choke him out, which is—you go from behind and put your arm around his neck and try to make him pass out.

Okay, he does that. He had him down. But the drunk stands up. He stands up with the officer hanging behind him. The guy's hanging onto his neck, and the drunk is walking around with this officer hanging behind him. His two feet are hanging off the ground. And we're all laughing. None of us are helping him. We just were all laughing.

And, of course, being late at night, everybody else comes and they're looking at him. We had about three police cars there. And this guy's walking around with this police officer hanging on him.

I mean, we finally helped him. We went in there and helped him. He was so funny. Here's this guy that's saying, "Step aside, girls. I'm gonna be the man and I'm gonna put him out for you."

We never let him live it down.

* * *

There's different ways of having a person comply. It's being able to use verbal skills—talking to him, or tricking him into something, or just stand back and if they don't comply—"Sir, will you put your hands behind your back?" "No." You take the approach of talking and if they don't comply, you say, "Okay, no problem," and you jump on the radio: "Request an RA [Rescue Ambulance] Unit and a backup." The guy says, "Why an RA Unit?" "Because once my backup arrives, you're gonna need it." The bottom line is, they're not gonna win.

We do it a little different, but we get the job done. There's not just one way, the man's way. There's not. There's different ways to handle different situations.

This is the classic example.

There's a call at a 7–Eleven, a confrontation. I'm by myself, I'm close, so I swing by. I get there first.

Here are two Hispanic males, brothers—one is drunk. A Hispanic male, especially drunk—they don't like a female police officer telling them what to do. It's their culture. They will go up on you faster than anyone else. They are the *worst* from a female standpoint.

I say to the drunk: "Give your car keys to your brother. He will drive." Meanwhile, two male officers arrive. They stand back; I'm handling it. I say, "If you don't give your brother your car keys, I'm taking you to jail." The drunk says to me, "Say 'Please.'" So I say, "Sir, would you *please* give the car keys to your brother." He hands the keys over and walks around to the passenger side. They drive off.

One of the two officers who have been watching this says to me, "I wouldn't have said please. No way in hell I would say it." And I said, "Yeah. And it would have ended up in a confrontation and we'd have to take him to jail."

It's hard for a man to back down. A woman doesn't have that problem. It doesn't bother us. What women can do— we can *talk* people into jail. The skills are there to de-escalate, defuse situations.

* * *

Policing is like a chess game. The whole goal is to outsmart people. Sadly, there are rules we must follow that our opponents *don't* have to. It's very intriguing—you have to outsmart your opponent. It's a game of finesse, of skill, of luck. It's not a game of brute force.

Sometimes, it takes acting stupid. I don't mind acting stupid as long as I win the game.

It doesn't mean we can't also be physical. But our first choice is verbal. Second choice is hold the gun in your hand and put a little quiver in your hand and say, "Gee, you know, this is my first night out on the street and I've never done this before. Don't make it happen." Third choice is knock 'em cold.

Heaven forbid a female officer, you ever have to take your weapon out. Immediately, the male public, for some reason, thinks that at the Academy we're trained to shoot testicles off. And it's the only thing they can ever see a female officer with a weapon hitting.

But it works to our advantage because once they see that weapon out—I remember making an arrest for robbery. That man stayed *perfectly still*. He said, "Lady—oh, mother of God!—lady! Don't be—careful with that gun!—watch where you're putting it! I'm not gonna move!"

It's the only target they think we can hit.

My philosophy is you talk them into jail—no need to get my uniform dirty. And that is, that *is* the only way to do police work. I mean, why would you—anybody—I don't care if you're a 6'4", 240-pound man, why would you want to get in a fight?

If you *do,* then you've got *paperwork* to do, it goes in your package, which is a big no-no, especially anymore; you get your uniform dirty; you can perhaps get hurt yourself; you can get your partner hurt—I mean, there's a whole gamut of reasons why you *wouldn't*. If I can say to somebody, "Sir, would you put your hands behind your back? You have an outstanding warrant." Hey, no problem—versus "Hey, idiot!" You know, you do those types of things, then you just escalate it. And there's no reason for it.

I haven't had any down-and-dirties that weren't started by my male partners. Really. Nothing ticks me off more than to go back to the patrol car, run a license or something, turn around—I mean, two seconds—and there they are, rolling around in the ditch. It's like . . . everything was fine when I left. What went on in that two seconds?

So naturally, then you have to jump on the pile. You have to. Well, you have to help your partner. It's that male thing, that macho thing that we don't understand. It's just that instant hatred.

One time, when I was a sergeant, I had this patrolman with me and him and this drunk were there just . . . back and forth, this and that, all the way in the car. So we get down to the station, I tell him, "I can't stand it another minute. This bicker, bicker, bicker." These one-liners, back and forth. It went all the way from the Breathalyzer at the post to the jail, which is fifteen miles.

Standing there in booking, all of a sudden, I hear, "Aaaaggh!" Here's my partner making the guy do the chicken. So I had to *pry* my partner's fingers from this guy's throat. Literally. It's this thing that I just don't understand. This male thing.

That's one of the differences in the personality traits between males and females. One of the *many* differences. One is machismo and we're more like, "Whew! Boy! I *did* it!" Honest to God.

We get a suspicious vehicle call. The deputy working midnights and myself were the only two deputies working this whole area, and the roadway stretches probably twenty-five miles till you get to the next county line. So we start looking for this vehicle.

We got a description of the vehicle. There's only one route through the whole area; I head west toward the ferry landing and the other deputy heads east, and he finds the vehicle. And he calls it in. So I do a U-turn and I'm heading back.

We're talking six-thirty in the morning; it's dark, about half-foggy.

So I'm hurrying up to get there. Next thing I know he comes on the air and he's hollering, "Shots fired! The guy's fleeing the scene." Now I don't know who shot at who. He's saying the guy's heading westbound. So I do a U-turn and get on the shoulder and wait for this guy to come by because there's no other place for him to go.

He comes by me. I pull in behind him and I've got my lights and sirens on. He's got a flat tire. He pulls over. I'm doing a felony stop. I reach over; I turn my siren off and I'm trying to talk to him through the intercom system on the car. I really honestly believed at the time that I couldn't get my siren to turn off. But this guy is still listening to me and doing what I'm telling him to do: he's got his hands stuck out the window and he turned off the car; the keys are out on the ground.

Next thing I know, this deputy that was working with me comes racing by me, cuts into my line of fire, yanks this guy out of the car, and the fight's on.

It was his siren. It wasn't my siren. It was his siren behind me. My lights were going; I didn't see him pull up behind me because my overheads were going and everything. And I pretty well was concentrating on the car. So the fight's on. I move up on him cautiously to make sure this guy still ain't gonna pull a gun and I end up holstering my gun and we end up having to tussle this guy. And we finally get him cuffed, get in the car—the guy I was working with had his handcuffs in his hand and he was beating on this guy, or trying to beat on this guy; the guy's rolling all over the ground, trying to get away from him. And I hollered at him and I said, "Don't!" And he left off and that's when we actually started to get in the wrestling match.

We get him in the car and everything and I ended up doing the hospital detail with this guy; the deputy had hit him in the ankles pretty good and busted him up pretty good. And we find out later this guy's an LSD addict and had just got out of a mental hospital—wasn't high or anything but was still—his brain was fried.

So I end up doing this hospital detail and after we get through with the hospital, the doctors release him and he acts like he's gonna pass out on the bench. And I looked at him and I said, "I'm gonna tell you something. I've had about all this I can stand. Now you're either gonna get up and walk out with us or we're gonna take you by your hair and your heels and we're gonna carry you and throw you in the back of my patrol car. Those are your choices." And that sucker popped up and walked right out to that patrol car with me.

Come to find out, what had happened—the other deputy had him stopped, had him on the patrol car, had turned his back on him to go back to the patrol car, to the driver's side of the patrol car—guy jumps off the patrol car, back in his car, speeds off, almost running over the deputy. The deputy thought he was trying to hit him deliberately, or at least that's what he said, so he pops a couple caps at him.

I was basically very infuriated. I had the situation under control until he decided that he was gonna whip ass. That's the only knockdown, drag-out fight that I have ever been in. Other than that, I have been able to talk my way out of them. Or I'll buffalo—whatever you want to call it.

I let them know I'm not gonna play games and usually . . . In most cases I've been able to look them in the eye, tell them to cut the shit, and have been able to control the situation. In this case, though, the deputy basically got us into a knockdown, drag-out, and there was no call for it. The guy was doing what I was telling him to do. The deputy lost it, lost his cool.

This deputy went back and was telling two of my sergeants that he didn't appreciate having to work with a lightweight because I wouldn't let him beat the shit out of this guy.

I wrote a little note to him. Actually, I wrote two. Basically, it said, "From One Lightweight to Another: If you ever need assistance again, give me a call." I put one on his locker, and I put one on the bulletin board for him.

I was pissed, to say the least. Because we didn't have to fight that man. I didn't *have* to sit in the hospital all day long. It was uncalled for.

* * *

Another thing that women have brought to policing is different ways besides fighting of getting people to do what you want. They might be more apt to listen to a compassionate . . . Women are known for compassion, usually, and they have more of a maternal instinct.

Another thing is—I'm not proud. If I can get someone to do what I want them to do by being polite and charming and saying, "You knooooow, if you don't do it, I'm gonna hafta call for help. I can have lots of people coming. I've got lots of brothers." Instead of just going, "Listen, asshole!"

I was told to go pick up a prisoner and transfer him to the Sheriff's Office. I got there and the officer working the sublock area was basically harassing this man. This man was handcuffed behind his back. And this officer was mouthing at him and starting him up and basically cussing him and calling him names and just . . . harassing him.

This prisoner was fired up. Now, we're talking a man who was approximately 5'10", black male, weighed maybe 190 pounds and was not fat. He was all muscle.

I was trying to get all my paperwork together so I could transport him and I told him to sit down. And he looked at me and basically told me to fuck off. And I looked at him and I said, "Sit down." And he still just stood there and he was mouthing with the officer, so I walked around and took him by the upper arm and I applied pressure on his arm as I was telling him to sit down. And he started to blow up on me. He said, "You don't have to put your hands on me." I said, "I will take my hands off when you sit down." And he sat down. I got my paperwork together and I transported him.

Basically, though, if I hadn't been looking him dead in the eye and letting him know that I wasn't going to back down, we would have had a fight on our hands. Because somebody else had been irritating and agitating the situation. For no good reason. The man's in cuffs, he's in custody, he's not going anywhere; there's no point in talking to him that way.

* * *

Textbook is all the same: How do you handcuff a prisoner? Fine. How do you fill out a report? Fine. But when it comes down to those split-second decisions, very often a female will resort to her verbal skills, whereas a male will resort to his physical skills.

And why is this? When a boy is growing up, he's playing football, he's playing baseball, he's playing hockey, he's playing soccer—physical contact sports. He's wrestling with his dad on the front lawn. When a girl is growing up, she's taught to go inside and help her sister or her brother—can you soothe the baby? When she starts dating, she talks herself in and out of precarious situations. Verbal skills—always negotiating. And so you take that with you into policing.

Most of the women I knew who worked out here talked a lot more and could talk people out of confrontations. And the men, some of them, didn't seem to have the patience or—they wanted to hurry up and get whatever was happening over with and go on to the next thing.

It's not to say that all women follow these patterns, or practice these things. I was working last year with a woman who was not my steady partner. My steady partner was a woman, but I was working one day with this other woman who was Hispanic and gay.

There was a dispute. A man had called us because there was one of those "Women Against Pornography" tables set up at Eighth Street and Sixth Avenue and two women at the table, manning the table, "womaning" the table. And this man—now when we pulled up, I kind of got the impression that the man was a little bit loony, but we didn't have enough time yet to make a determination like that.

The man told us that the women, when he passed by— that the women were threatening him with their signs— they were waving the signs close to him and he thought he was gonna get hit by these signs . . . And my partner started cursing at him. And I said, "Wait a minute, what's wrong with you?" And at one point, she called him "an ignorant Jew bastard." That's what she called him. And I was . . . furious.

So I took her and I pulled her aside: "You haven't heard his story. You're always complaining about how straight white society treats women who are Hispanic and gay—what about the way you treat this man?"

So I don't want to give the impression that all women bring all these wonderful qualities to the job. It's not like all women are wonderful and all men are bad, which is largely true. I'm kidding, I'm kidding. Incompetence isn't gender-colored.

Women can be just as short-tempered as men. Women can have just as much lack of communication as men. I can also be as big of a jerk as a man.

Make no mistake about it. There is a significant proportion of women who have the ego thing—and it's not that they fail, but they're not as good as they could be because they're trying to be something that they're not. They want to be one of the boys. And no matter how hard you try, you're not gonna be one of the boys. You're not a boy. So you have to bring your own strengths to the job.

Some of the more sensitive men understand it. And almost all of the women understand it—that there's a *time* for confrontation and most of us are astute enough to know that sometimes you're not gonna back down. It's important that you not back down. There are other times where it's a little less important. So why risk getting yourself hurt—you get into a fight, then you gotta call an 85—you gotta call for help, they're gonna come, lights and sirens, they might get into a car accident—why jeopardize all these people simply for the sake of ego? Why not just try to find some other . . . if you can. And you can't always. Sometimes the bottom line is you've gotta roll around on the ground and do whatever you gotta do to make the collar. But very, very often there are other alternatives.

There was an incident, and I remember this so well because I thought it was pretty funny, there was this woman cop, who's gotta be all macho and prove herself to all these guys, and every time you get somewhere, she escalates it. And I just want to grab her head. And one time she's going

21

on and on and on and on and we've got seven or eight guys up against a wall somewhere and there's only three of us— it was a drug thing—and she's going on and on and on and these guys are gettin' nuts.

So the male police officer stopped and told these seven or eight guys, "Listen. When you're done kicking her ass," he goes, "I just want to let you know because I know you're gonna"—the way he said it, it was almost like he was allowing them to—he says, "I know that when you're done kicking her butt, and I want to let you know it's okay when you do it, but I'm gonna have to kill all of you, okay?" Then they lightened up and laughed. He handled it the right way.

In my experience, the women that *try* to do the job as men do are not successful. Obviously, they're not successful as men, and they're not really successful as women, either because they're not approaching things the way that a woman would and in the way that they probably would if they just let themselves be themselves.

But sometimes I think they feel the pressure that—"I have to prove myself to the men on the job, I have to prove myself to the other women on the job, I have to prove myself to the public"—and they might see some men that have been there before them and so they try to emulate them instead of really relying on their own strengths. So they fail on both counts.

My philosophy is, no matter how big you are, no matter how tough you are, no matter how bad you are, there's always gonna be someone bigger, tougher, and badder than you. Always.

So my theory is, you have to go in with your brain. I talk to people. And I talk to big guys and I talk to little guys and I talk to big women and I talk to little women. I talk to everybody. I think it comes in with this basic amount of respect for others as human beings. I don't take things personally. You can't. But see, a lot of police take things personally. As far as I'm concerned, the uniform walks into a situation all by itself. But it's not me.

Unfortunately, every now and then you run into someone too drunk or too high to talk to you. But even then, if I take an extra five minutes talking, instead of just fighting right away, I take that extra five, ten minutes de-escalating the situation, just talking to people—I talk big guys who wanted to fight into handcuffs all the time. By myself.

My partner is smaller than I am. She's a lot smaller. And we get people into handcuffs all the time. We're two women on the West Side of the city of Chicago and we have no problems.

Here's the logical thing. You say, "Look. There's always somebody that can take somebody. I mean, there isn't an officer walking the street that can take on his own, or even with his partner, everyone he runs up against."

And while, yes, women are smaller, that doesn't mean that they're not gonna be able to take control of the situation.

That used to be a big rumor before women went on the street: "Women are so small and so physically not strong that we're gonna have all these women shooting to death all these people because it's the only way they'll be able to control the situation. That's the only thing they're gonna be able to do—they're gonna have to shoot and kill."

It didn't happen. We don't shoot any more than male officers, and we probably shoot less because women try to de-escalate the situation through conversation rather than escalate it into a confrontation.

I was working with a guy once, and we arrested a guy who wouldn't leave a bar. We did all the stuff right, but the guy, when asked even by us—we were real polite; we walk up, "Sir, you know, the bar has asked you to leave and this is our first time, we'll ask you to leave, too, and if you leave, nothing will happen, and if you don't leave, we'll be forced to place you under arrest for criminal trespassing." "Fuck you!" "Okay, fine, sir, we'll place you under arrest."

This was two of us, we were both kind of rookies, so we didn't handcuff the guy right then and there and we should have. So we're walking him out of the place because we were being too polite and nice and he starts acting up, getting a little hinky, so I just grabbed him, reached his arm behind his back, and kind of slammed him down and he hit the pavement. It was pretty funny because then we're walking him into jail and he turns to the male officer and says, "Wow! You must know karate!" because he didn't know I did it or he didn't want to believe I did it. I'm like, "Whatever. You're in jail now and everything's okay."

I used to help teach Field Training Officer seminars for other departments. And we used to have this little panel: There was a black officer, a Latino officer, and me, and we used to travel around the state. And I used to always get that kind of question about size and how I would deal with it. These are police officers from other agencies. They would ask that same question and the guys on the panel with me were really supportive. They'd say, "Hey, we've seen this woman in fights and, you know, she's just whackin' away at the guys just like everybody else."

The size issue is not a good analogy anymore. On the LAPD, there are no longer any height requirements. I think it's five feet tall. We have got a lot of men who are under 5'5"; we are hiring a lot of Asian officers who are traditionally not very tall; a lot of Hispanic officers, and, unfortunately, a lot of 5'3" ex-Marines, skinny little guys, who happen to think they can do anything.

I just tell them it's not a good analogy because all of us know very, very short male officers. And, of course, there's some big galoots that cannot handle themselves well in the field.

I've worked with small men, and a lot of times I'll go, "Oh, I hate to work with him 'cause I know we're gonna get in a fight." And I'll work with really big guys and I'll go, "Oh, great!" Because I know that these . . . bigger guys have nothing to prove, and they go in and ninety-nine times out of a hundred, people will go along with the program. But these little guys go, "I've got to prove I'm a man!" I've worked with some small men that are great, but a lot of them . . . trying to prove something.

A lot of these small men are with women partners. They think that they have to come off tough because they are the male. They're short and they know it, and then they have a woman with them, so they're thinking, "Jesus Christ. Everything's against me." So they right away think they have to go in tough. And they go in tough.

Small cops are the worst. I'm 5'6". And I've always found that the guys who are most resistant to women being cops are my size or smaller.

I don't care how much the men want to hold on to the old "You gotta be a big guy," I'll run circles around them any old day. I'm five feet tall and a hundred pounds. And I *can* do the job.

Defensive tactics is a learnable skill. Anybody can do it. It's not dependent upon size. If you have the right mind-set, you can get the skill level. Anybody can.

I just finished doing my second term of teaching take-down tactics at the Academy. We know everything that they know. When it comes to taking it down, I may only be 5'1", but I've taken down 6'2" guys. We can carry our own weight. We may do it in a little different style, but we do it.

I think that the violent aspect of this job is overblown. It happens. And it happens very suddenly and it can happen and you can be dead. Or you have to kill someone.

But routinely, your job is dealing with people in trouble, dealing with people suffering trauma, dealing with people *suffering.*

And women are very good at that. So are some men. I've seen men so skilled at this job that I'm just in awe of them—and their empathy and their concern and their care. But I think that women bring a particular balance to this and women fulfill that role, I think, of caring and concern and helping and defusing. I think women bring a lot to that. And that's probably at least, *at least,* sixty to seventy percent of police work. So it doesn't make any sense to exclude women from sixty to seventy percent of police work based on the supposition that they can't do the other fifteen or twenty percent—which they seem to be able to do because they're doing it: They're shooting people and getting beat up and beating them up and doing all the other stuff, too.

We're out here to do a job together. Whoever gets it done? Once it's done—yay for us. And that's what it's all about. That's the bottom line.

I've always been treated fine. I've never, ever . . . well, actually, the only thing I've ever gotten . . . I was working with this new guy who says right off the bat, "I don't like working with women." I said, "Why? Okay, that's fine. But why?" "You're no good in fights, You're no good in fights." I said, "Well, you know, I find that I'm very able to minimize them, you know, even the possibility of fights, through my brain . . ." And that obviously had never occurred to him.

But later—we're working the wagon—later that day, we go into a hospital; we have a call for a removal of a body to the morgue. This was an eighteen-month-old baby who had died during the night.

And I walk into the room, and the mom's there, cradling the baby, crying. It was a beautiful baby boy, a little boy. There wasn't going to be a crime there; this baby had had a history of medical problems, respiratory problems. It was a Hispanic family, the type of hardworking—Mom, Dad probably both worked about a zillion hours a week, you know, *labor,* and they had two other sons, six and eight years old. And the mom's sitting there, cradling her baby.

I went back out, and I said to the nurse, "Look. I'm not going to tell the mother to put down that baby. When she's done saying goodbye, I'll go in."

Finally, the mother was done. She put the baby down. And I went in there . . . my partner had been with me— well, he *disappeared.* He disappeared completely.

And I wrapped the baby up. I wrapped it in one of the hospital sheets. I waited for them to go. I didn't want them to see me carrying the baby out. I left the baby in the room. I checked the waiting area, and then I checked outside. And I could see the family walking away. They were all together. What really got me was their heads were bowed and they were all holding hands.

I carried the baby outside. And I took it and put it in the

wagon. I strapped it onto the little stretcher in the back of the wagon.

Then I went to find my partner—now he's disappeared, this complete son of a bitch! The macho man has disappeared. Finally, I find him, I can't remember where.

Then we go to the morgue—Boom!—he's out of the way; he's got to get his fucking paperwork in. I carried the baby in and turned the baby over to the morgue workers.

Well, it turns out, he had an eighteen-month-old—he couldn't deal with it. Couldn't deal with it.

Yeah. I may not be able to bust some guy in the head in a fight, but I'll carry a little dead baby for you.

He didn't give me much crap about working with women after that.

CHAPTER 2

THE
UNIFORM

Something isn't right. Whether it's the big-city woman cop who looks like a kid in a snowsuit in her uniform or the Texas Ranger who has to search through hundreds of Debra Wingeresque cowboy shirts with spangles and fringe before she can find a suitable uniform shirt, something isn't right.

Women's uniforms *are* much better than they used to be. Women used to wear high heels and skirts and carry their guns in shoulder bags equipped with built-in holsters. Some state police had women troopers wear badges that identified them as "Trooperettes." The first patrol uniforms were absolutely uncompromising in waist and hip measurements and arm lengths. Women were faced with the choice (and some still are) of living with outsized clothes, paying for alterations themselves, or taking the long route of lobbying for changes. The basic approach is still to take a man's uniform and assume it should fit a woman.

The uniform isn't just about fit. It's about your fit in the organization and the many strange ways the public sizes you up . . .

I had the funniest experience right out of the Academy. I was smaller then. I was in uniform, doing some Christmas shopping at Foley's.

Two older women came up to me. "Oh! You're just the cutest thing!—Are you a real policeman? Or are you like a toy policeman?" "I'm a real policeman." "Oh—aren't you so cute!" I was shocked and upset. I thought, "Oh my, this is gonna work out great. I'm real intimidating. I'm a regular Betty Badass."

* * *

30

The typical thing is, you pull somebody over for a traffic stop, get out of your squad car, and go up to their car. I don't know how many times this has happened to me—the men say, "Honey, is that a real gun?" I always think, "Why don't I just put it next to your temple and we'll find out?"

There's nothing that pisses me off more than having some civilian call me "honey" or "sweetheart." They'd never call a male in uniform anything but "officer." But we're honeys. It makes my skin crawl.

You get a radio call, and this could be anytime in a twenty-four-hour period, but this would strike me more often in the middle of the night. They open a door and say, "What do you want?"
I'm a police officer, I'm in uniform, here's my squad car, here's my backup—get a call, this address, and they're "What do you want?" "How about a cup of coffee?"

When I came on the LAPD in 1957, we carried our guns in our purses. It was just ridiculous. You couldn't get to it. You had to fumble through everything to get to it.
Their big thing at the time was that it wouldn't look ladylike to wear a gun around the waist. They didn't want us going around looking like a bunch of gun molls. Safety was secondary to appearance as far as women were concerned.
It drove me crazy.

In the Chicago Police, we went into uniform in 1955. Policewomen wore powder blue blouses. We wore navy blue shoes that weren't attractive unless you had a three-inch heel. We always wore three-inch heels. The only way you could wear a midheel or flats was if you had a note from your foot doctor. There were some fat old ladies that had to wear flats.
Policewomen used to work either as matrons in the jail or in Youth. If you worked in Youth, you had your own office and telephone and you were like the little queen in the station because you could change diapers and you knew exactly what to do with these abandoned kids and you knew

how to wash bottles and fill bottles and send the men out to get milk and food for the children. You were just sort of welcomed. And nobody swore in front of you—oh, never.

When they would be interrogating a prisoner, you could hear them swearing and screaming and, you know, "Tell me the truth!" You know, the usual. And then the fellows used to get real quiet. I said one time, "Boy, everything quiets down when I come in." They said, "Well, we hear your heels clicking and then we know to shut up." Because if they swore in front of you, the captain would hear about that. You were just a . . . you were just a baby doll.

When we first went into patrol in Chicago, in the seventies, they neglected to change our uniform, so here we were now, driving around in squad cars, still in skirts and high heels. It was insane. And we wore these disgusting little beanies like stewardesses had—people used to call us "Sister" when we'd arrest them; they thought we were nuns.

We had big, square cardboard policewomen purses which had a holster built right in. There was a flap on the front with one of those turn buckles. Inside, there was a holster with like a restraining strap on the holster. So you had to open your purse and unrestrain your gun to get it out. They were semilogical, but how can you run with a purse hanging on your shoulder? And how can you run in high heels and a skirt?

When women first came on the job as state troopers, everyone was just baffled. They didn't know what to do, how to treat us. We were state troopers and we were issued culottes—and pumps. I never wore my culottes and pumps; it was ridiculous. And we had handbags. And little teeny-weeny meter-maid caps. They went through stages where they dressed us as stewardesses and then meter maids and then finally we got uniforms that were identical to the men's.

Before I came on, they used to have badges that said "Trooperette"! I never had one, but they were "trooperettes," not troopers. In '77, a couple guys called me a trooperette and I looked real puzzled. They said, "Well, that's what they used to be called. Trooperettes." They really didn't know what to do with women.

Right at the beginning there, there were some terrible, terrible nasty things. I had put in a report to Research and Development because—they were trying to come up with uniforms for women on patrol, okay? They said we had to have side zippers on our pants. There's no such thing as a uniform with a side zipper, so all our uniforms had to be custom-made. Men could walk into a uniform store and buy a pair of pants off the rack. We had to order them three weeks ahead of time at twice the price.

So I put in a report suggesting changes: Why can't women have a front zipper? And why can't women wear the same hat the men do, because the checkered band is identifiable as the police? This is a major psychological necessity—if I intend to confront you, you better know I'm the police. I took up some other things—pants, no high heels, that kind of thing.

A report to R and D is supposed to be confidential. This one was copied and sent all over the place and considered so outrageous and so scandalous at the time, things that now just seem common-sensical. I started getting anonymous notes through the police mail, one from a policewoman: "Maybe *you* want to be a man, but *I* don't." Another one said, "If you want these uniform changes, why don't you just ask them to put a little revolving blue light on top of your hat?" You know, just real hostile.

They just didn't know how to deal with us. They just didn't know how to deal with us.

Nobody would volunteer to work with us. So they would assign people to work with us. They assigned me to a tall black man, wonderful human being. Twenty years ago there were no blacks in this district. It was so odd because we'd pull up on a call, a black man and a white woman in uniform, and somebody would come running out and they'd stare at my partner, "Uh-oh, he's black," and then they'd stare at me, "Uh-oh, this is a woman. Where's the real police?"

We used to take bets with each other when we pulled up—which one is he going to talk to? Because people would be going back and forth between the two of us—they didn't want to talk to him and they *sure* didn't want to talk to me because I'm a woman.

I was one of the first five women on the Seattle Police Department to hire on as women patrol officers. That's not to say that the policewomen hired under the old Women's Bureau didn't do a lot of incredible things, they were the pioneers in doing police work, but we were the first on patrol.

We got a lot of reactions. There were instances where citizens would call back and say, "I want a male officer." The Seattle Police Department responded with—"You called for an officer. You got an officer. What is the problem?" And that was not widespread, and it was very quickly quelled.

What was funny—you'd make a traffic stop on a woman. You'd go up to the car and the voice would be low and the skirt would be up and the blouse would be down. And then they'd look over and they'd see you and it was like, "Oh shit!" It was like a classic movie double take.

And they'd sit up straight in the car and the skirt would come down and they'd be rebuttoning the blouse. It was really funny because they'd be all set up to sweet-talk some male officer out of a traffic ticket.

When we first went out, that happened a lot. They had *never* been pulled over by a woman. Nobody had.

I went to a call with a guy. It was a call of somebody being in this woman's yard or something. And she answered the door and she had on this jumpsuit with a big zipper down the front. This zipper was undone to her navel. I'm the first one to the door and she was like—"Aaagh."

There was a guy behind me. And she just didn't know how to act. She didn't know whether to keep it up for him, or to turn it off for me, you know. She saw me and I was like, "What did he look like? Where did he go?" And she was making it up—it was so obvious. There was nobody in her yard. She probably wanted to get laid by an LAPD cop. Fantasy time.

A lot of offenders prey on your modesty. A lot of times, when you're stopping a woman, the main thing that I have learned, especially if you get a big-breasted woman, for instance, she'll throw her jacket or something open and go, "Yeah, baby, I see you ain't got no titties up there. Go on and look at these because this is a great pair! You know you want these; you want them—" Yeah. They'll say that to you.

And most women, the first thing you'll do is kind of—withdraw. You'll kind of withdraw and you'll get timid and your femininity will come out and you'll go, "Well, no, I don't really swing that way—" Anything of that nature is a little repulsive to most women. *But*—it's a throw-off. A lot of times you'll find that. It *is* to get to you and make you embarrassed.

Because a lot of times, they're hiding narcotics. You'll find—you take one of those big boulder holders and throw it over their shoulder, that they've got hypodermic needles taped underneath their breasts, or they've got packets of cocaine or heroin and stuff taped up under them. And guns. Guns as well. But that's the whole idea, to throw you off and embarrass you—"No, I don't want to see your boobs, lady."

Or one time, we chased a lady into a basement. What she did, this big fat woman, she spread her legs: "Go ahead, honey, I know you want to see mine. Go on, this is the best stuff in town! But you're gonna have the surprise of your life—I'm bleeding *all over the place.* I'm on my period. So, baby, if you want to look between these legs and see all this blood . . ." What would you do? Oh, God, nothing's worse than an old nasty bloody . . . thingamajig down there. The last thing in the world you want to see is a big, fat, funky lady with her legs spread open.

But if you grab yourself—and I had to have this happen, I had to be ordered one time by my FTO (Field Training Officer), "Search that woman!" "But she's on her period." "Search that woman." And I just had to do it, to find out exactly what I'm talking about. She had like sixty packets of cocaine in a Zip-loc bag stuffed up her crotch.

I fell into the same trap that most women would have fallen into: It was the "I don't want to feel your breasts! I don't want to go in your crotch when you're bleeding all over the place! God, that's the *last* thing I want to do." That's a normal reaction. And that's just exactly what they play on. They *count* on you to do that. They *count* on you to do that.

It's like—God!—nothing's sacred anymore. It isn't. I wouldn't *dream* of putting a loaded pistol in my newborn's diaper. But they do it. It's come to that. I've recovered a .22 automatic, fully loaded, off a two-week-old baby's diaper. I've recovered narcotics, money, hypodermic needles—*you* wouldn't do this. But these people—it's a business, it's a way of life to them. *Nothing* is sacred.

But people don't look at *them* like "God, is there nothing sacred?" They look at you. Because *you* searched the baby. You're in the public eye. Here you are ripping the Pampers off this kid and they're, "Oh my God, look at her. That police officer ripped the diaper off that poor child." They don't realize that's what these people do. They're heavy into drugs. Nothing is sacred. Nothing is.

You have to think like that. You start thinking like that, that's when you start coming up with a lot of stuff.

I was the first woman on patrol in St. Paul, in 1975. They put me into the uniform—having been the first woman, when I went down to Uniforms Unlimited to get fitted, it was all men's stuff. They didn't have anything for women. I weighed 127 pounds when I came on this job. So when I came in to get fitted, I got these really small men's pants and they had to take them in because women's bodies are different than men's and I had some hips, and most men don't have an ass, and I had a little butt on me.

At first, they just measured me and put me in these pants. They just didn't fit me like they should because they did it like they'd do a man. So I complained and I went back down there—I said, "You know, I've got a butt. You've gotta give me some more room in here. My hips and thighs are a little different."

The uniform shirt. The smallest men's uniform shirt was

a size fourteen—at that time, the average cop on the St. Paul Police Department was six feet tall. The smallest shirt, size fourteen on *me,* the neck was about three inches out from my neck; they had to cut the sleeves because the sleeves were too long. So here I am, I've got the shirt, and they're cutting my sleeves so they'll fit me.

The kicker was the tie, this clip-on tie. Remember now, this tie is for a guy that stands six feet tall. So when I put this tie on, when I sat down to go to the bathroom, it was like a health hazard because my tie is hanging in the toilet. I mean, I could have been condemned for being a health hazard with this tie that's hanging down there in the can, you know. So they ended up fixing my tie so it hit me in an appropriate position, other than the toilet.

I had to wear this hat. My hair was short. When I put this hat on, I looked like a guy. So people were always calling me "sir." I'd get real pissed. I'm the mother of four kids; I ain't no "sir," you know.

I decide I'm going to wear this wig. It makes my hair a little longer, so when I've got the hat on, at least some people can tell that I'm a woman.

The men complained that I was wearing a wig. A friend of mine who was going to the FBI Academy for training researched it. And the FBI had determined that a wig was not a hazard because if they grabbed it, it was going to come off your head. So there wasn't an issue.

Then the men said, "Well, if *she* can have a wig, then we can have them, too." And that's when the men got okayed to wear toupees. It worked out good for them.

The trials and tribulations of getting a uniform to fit were hysterical. In 1974, we had to go to this formal-wear place for men. And there was this wonderful weirdo guy there who *loved* to measure us women in uniform. So we got measured, oh, two to three dozen *times,* we had to be darted here and fitted there; our pockets came together in the back because our waists were so small then.

And it only took them about fifteen more years before they decided, "Shoot! We got enough women now—let's make uniforms for *women!*"

* * *

I learned early, and you know, I'm one of the only women that does it, but I learned how to go to the bathroom with my gun belt on. Most women take the whole gun belt off and everything; it's just terrible. But I figured out a system where I didn't have to.

I was just scared to death . . . I think one of my biggest fears when I became a policewoman—I knew I was one of the first women—this is probably going to sound really dumb, but women will understand it—I was so afraid that I was going to do something just really stupid. So that all the guys could point at me and say, "Oh, look at that stupid woman. She can't do the job."

And one of my greatest fears was, if I ever did take my gun belt off to go to the bathroom, that somebody would grab my gun belt under the stall and run with it. And then what do you do? Walk out of the stall and say, "Oh, gee, I was going to the bathroom and somebody stole my gun belt"?

Those type of things were always at the back of my mind. I'm real careful about that kind of stuff. Some would call it paranoid—just always walking around being afraid that you are gonna really do something just really dumb. And have everybody point at you and say, "Yeah. See? Those stupid women, they can't handle this."

Another problem we had was the gun belt; we're still having a problem with it. Something to do with the pelvic bone—I don't know the exact term for it, but I do know when I was out on patrol I had the same problem a lot of the women still complain about. The uniforms are fashioned for men. Something with the construction of the gun belt causes a great deal of pressure and a great deal of pain around the pelvic bone. They keep saying it's not the gun belt. But I as a female know in fact that, yes, that gun belt hurts! I would sling it all the way down past my bones, almost riding on my butt, to relieve some of the pressure because it *was* painful.

They won't even acknowledge that it even exists, even though so many women have complained about that gun belt. That's something they don't take into consideration with unisex equipment. Men are straight, and we've got all these curves and lumps and bumps.

In 1980, when I came out of the Academy, the city of Philadelphia was so strapped for cash that we didn't have patrol jackets. So unless the city bought us coats, or you went into your own pocket and bought a coat, you couldn't go out on the street. You had to work in the Administration Building. You deal with a strapped-for-cash department like Philadelphia always is, these things happen.

I did that for three weeks and I couldn't stand it. And so, my cousin's brother-in-law had an extra coat. I said, "Let me have it." And I wore it and I said, "I'm out of here! There's no sense me going to work wearing a gun under my hip under a long dress coat."

But then our uniforms—they were made for men. It wasn't till maybe about 1983, 1984, they started putting darts in the women's blouses and tapering the blouses for women, to account for them having breasts and waistlines. The pants—they're still not fitting the pants as well as they could. Women do have hips and stuff and they're still not making accommodation for women.

Why do you think people want to get out of uniform? Besides the danger factor because you're wearing that target—that's right, that uniform *is* a target; you're a walking target—it's not comfortable. It's definitely not comfortable.

The men—oh please. They always get so mad. "What do you want them to make for you? Evening gowns? So you can run after the criminals?" "Why do you take this job if you don't want to wear the uniform?"

I say, "Well, I can understand that you're not crazy about us. But I still think that they could make the pants a little more wide in the hips. They accommodate the men, why can't they accommodate the women? If the man wants a little more room, they're gonna give it to him. So how come they give the women such a hard way to go?"

I became a Texas Ranger in 1993. My biggest challenge is having to prove myself. There are no role models for go after because even though there have been many Texas Rangers before me, there have been no women before me.

There are all types of little obstacles that get in there like—How am I supposed to dress? That's been a big issue. And how I handle it is going to affect everyone that comes after me.

We don't have a uniform. It's more like plainclothes, but it's a certain type of clothes that you need to wear. We dress Western. Texas Rangers wear Wranglers, they wear suit jackets, they wear boots, and they wear a hat and they wear a badge pinned to their shirt. They wear a shirt with a collar and a tie.

Well, you know, that's not typical everyday dress for a woman going to work. For me, it was difficult because I felt that I looked silly. They have made a few modifications for me and the other female Ranger. They will let us wear colored jeans and blouses to go with it. But women's pants aren't made to be worn with boots unless you get a jean. Some of the pants I have found have a little pleat in them. Up until this year, no Ranger has ever worn a pleat.

The hat—it's been difficult for me. It looks great on the men, or on Debra Winger, but I feel I look silly in them.

Pockets. You need pockets. But if you find a nice woman's blouse, it's not gonna have pockets on it. And I need pockets. I need something for a tape recorder, a pen, pieces of paper. These little things—gosh! What am I gonna wear around my neck? I'm not gonna wear a man's tie; that would look stupid. I found a little short tie, probably like stewardesses wear. Little alterations on things to try to look as much like the men do as possible. It's a real challenge.

The men say, "I can't believe you can't find clothes just like ours." I've taken a couple of them to the stores. "See? Look at these women's Western shirts. They have all these spangles and glitter all over them." When I show them what is available, they're like, "We had no idea."

Most cop shows, when they show women—they look like Heather Locklear, it's like let me toss my shoulder-length hair around. I don't know too many agencies that allow women to have long hair in uniform. It's dangerous. You don't want to give anybody anything to grab ahold of.

One night, my partner and I get in a car chase. A guy beat up his wife, he jumps in the car and goes. We get him. He puts the car in drive and *drags* me; I'm holding on to the door for dear life. Luckily, it was all muddy, so the car wasn't going too fast.

My 6′3″ Irish partner cuts the car off. The guy gets out, and he makes the fatal mistake of pulling my hair. At the time I had long hair and I have a very tender head. I lost my mind. I tried to rip his face off. I'm banging his head against the car window. My male partner, who always thought I was this overly nice Catholic girl, said, "I didn't know you had it in you!" I told him, "He pulled my hair!"

Hair. That is my pet peeve as a supervisor. If you're in uniform, your hair has to conform to guidelines. You have long hair—that's fine. Put it up. As long as it conforms to guidelines.

Now, male sergeants. I think they felt a little funny about being too strict to female officers. Up until the point I got there, females' hair was whichever way they wanted. I got there—when I got promoted, I had very long hair. I chopped it all off because I just didn't want to deal with having to put it up every day. But I'm not asking anybody else to chop it all off.

I see a female officer, and her hair is like . . . Cher. And there is a reason why you have to conform to guidelines. Number one, it makes you look professional. And the way you dress and the way you treat yourself is the way people perceive you and treat you back. But the biggest thing is safety. If your hair is long, somebody's gonna grab hold of you and that's the end of that.

I see this lady and I say, "Officer, put your hair up." "Oh, it's not that long, and the sergeants, they never said anything to me before." "Well, *this* sergeant is telling you. I'm giving you half an hour to get that hair up and it better be the way it says in the department guidelines because I will discipline you." Sure enough—every time she saw me after that—oh God, get the hair up. Here she comes!

One thing I strongly believe in is keeping my femininity. So many women on the force think they have to be men. They stop taking care of themselves. They get overweight, they act like the men, they talk like the men. With me, my appearance has always been very important to me.

I'd have a fit if somebody broke my nail. Once we were locking up a guy, I had just had my nails done the night before; they had rhinestones on them, they were beautiful! This offender broke three of them. My partner said to him, "You're gonna wish you hadn't done that." I gave him a lashing like he hasn't had since his mama. I was hitting on him. I told him, "You better watch out. Because I'll *never* forget you."

But you know, our hair and nails are the only feminine things we got left in that uniform. When I'm in the cruiser, I'm always checking the mirror, combing my hair, checking my lipstick. A friend of mine says he thinks I've got a blow dryer instead of a gun in my holster.

We have to wear our hat. At first, they tell us you can wear your hair however you want to, as long as you can wear the hat. Well, then, here's some Susie-Q with the hair piled up in a beehive and she's got it shellacked with a can and a half of hair spray—she couldn't get her hat on if she used a *power drill* to get it on; she can't do it. So what does that do? That reflects—all policewomen again. Now we're back to— we have to wear our hat and now we have a restriction on how we can wear our hat.

Again, it keeps continually making you masculine. *It makes you masculine.* It forces you into that masculine role. That's what I don't like about what the job is gearing up toward. Not at all. They're not allowing us any femininity at all, not at all. You've got to take great care in doing other things in a roundabout way to preserve that femininity.

The one that I fought really hard personally was the fact that we could not wear jewelry when we came on this job.

Before I came on the job, you could wear jewelry and you could wear your hair any way you wanted to. And just as I was coming on the job, we had a bunch of incidents where women police got hurt because they would get into fights in the lockup—they wore the big loop earrings; they start fighting—What's the first thing a woman does? She grabs for another woman's face. Their fingers would loop in the ears, they'd snatch the earrings out, the lobe would split, it would rip, it would tear, it would do whatever. So now we've got a bunch of detention policewomen with no earlobes.

And these big, beautiful hairdos—those have been snatched out by the roots; the hair is stiff as a board, I mean, they're just pulling, and policewomen are losing all their hair—well, they stopped it. They said, you can't do any of that anymore. You have to be just nothing. We couldn't wear makeup. We could not have any jewelry on whatsoever, and our hair couldn't be any longer than our collar.

I didn't mind the hair so much. What bothered me was the earrings. Everything about this job is so male-oriented. We have to wear these big, ugly black shoes. We have to wear black socks. We have to wear the pants. We have to have the shirts. We wear the guns. And we look just like the men.

To me myself, I thought there should be a little leeway to allow us to experience some sort of femininity in this job. So when I came out of the Academy, I rebelled. I started wearing these little tiny gold balls. My boss would catch me, and he'd chew me out. So, I'd wear them again and he'd chew me out. And he'd catch me again and he'd chew me out. Finally, he said, if you're so bent on doing this, why don't you do this in a constructive manner? He got me a special form to go before the Police Board. I filled it out, saying I didn't think there was any reason women couldn't wear the tiny gold balls—for one thing, we've got the little breakaways in the back of them; if you pull, it snaps right off. There's nothing to snatch through the earlobe, there's nothing easily accessible. It's kind of hard to grab this little-bitty ball and pull it out. I said, "Give us a break. We have nothing of our own that's semifeminine. We look like the guys, for God's sake."

It wound up getting passed. We could wear the little tiny gold balls. Well, that opened—here we go into phase two. They took it and they ran with it. If you can wear *these*, then you can wear these. So we started in with the jewelry again and the problems started again and again and again. So now, we're back to, we can't wear any jewelry. Can't wear a bracelet, can't wear earrings, can't wear nothing.

I think it's a shame, in a sense, because we should be allowed—I don't think a little gold ball should cause any problem. We lost out on that. It's not allowed. So we're down to nothingness again.

Now there's no thought even to something different for the women as for the men. We even wear the same ties as the men. Very few of the women will wear the cross tie, like a stewardess. We wear the regular clip-on tie like the guys do.

They found out that there was money in it. They didn't do it just to be nice. Let's face it—the companies figured out that there were more and more women; there's a demand now.

I still don't like the way they make the uniforms. They still think that they should be made for men. They take a man's uniform and they say, "This fits you." The sizings are way off. The way they fit is terrible, the jackets especially. I still think they're terrible. I don't think they're any better.

The way the uniform is, you look like a pear because you've got all this stuff around your hips. You look like shit.

In fact, with my leather jacket, my first one that I had, when I'd sit in the squad car, it would always like be up around my ears. I'd be sitting there—"What is *wrong* with this jacket?" There was something about that goddamned jacket where I looked like a little kid in a snowsuit. And I hated it.

I went out and I paid to have another one made, custom-made. You know what? I never regretted it because it fit right.

Attitudes toward women. You know what's funny? It was really funny sometimes to be the one on the scene or to be the case deputy, the one that rolled up first and took control of the scene. With some of the people in this county, it just threw them into such shock to have a woman standing out there in uniform, telling them what to do.

I had another deputy riding with me one day. And we had a burglary call, already occurred, on a motor vehicle. And we went over—the male deputy did a good job of not taking control because the victim, the guy that owned the car—I'm standing there trying to take this report and he keeps looking at the male deputy and answering *him.* I'd ask a question and he'd talk to Mac. And then he'd ask Mac something and Mac would turn around and say, "You have to ask her." Eventually, he got around to answering my questions and looking at me, but it took a good fifteen minutes of Mac telling him, "You need to talk to her. I'm just her backup. Go ahead. Talk to her."

It just comes from conditioning. That's the frustrating part. It's that they don't all do it deliberately; it's just ingrained; they just don't know how to deal with it. They are not used to having women police officers working their district. It just really threw this guy for a loop that this *woman* had a gun on and a badge.

What happens on the street—it goes on with both genders and with different ethnicities as well—people tend to address the person that they think is in charge, or the person that they think they're gonna get the most satisfaction from. This is true of men *and* women.

Very often, if a female cop and a male cop show up on the same job, even if the female police officer is handling the situation and asking the questions, the answer will be directed towards the male officer. Absolutely. The eye contact will be with the male, they will turn away, and then they will proceed to ignore the female. If I were to jump in again and ask another question, they'll just pretend they didn't hear me. This happens *all the time.*

And see, women civilians are among the worst for the way women cops are treated. Women civilians are—"You're a woman and I'm not talkin' to *you.* I'm talkin' to a *man."*

Women's issues demonstrations. I've had it when I'm on line where they yell at me, "Why are you a cop? Why are you on *that* side and not over here with us?" They're like,

"Put down your baton and come over here with us." And I'm like, "Hey, this is my job. I'm just here to keep the peace. My opinions don't matter." I guess if I said, "Okay," and took off my helmet and joined them, they'd be happy. I don't know. They always call me names and things.

It's still such a perception problem. This happened this year. Not *ten* years ago—*this* year. I'm in a car by myself. A civilian says, "I didn't know they let women work by themselves." Or I'm working with another female—"I didn't know they let women work together." This is still what we're encountering from the general public. It's always "You're so *small*. How can you handle this job?"

The real dirtballs give us a hard time. And certain people. Certain decent people. They kind of still expect a big 6′4″ man to show up. A blond-haired, blue-eyed big guy. And there aren't any 6′4″ men in the department anymore. There just *aren't*.

A few years ago, my husband and I were both highway patrolmen. We went to lunch with two other highway patrolmen one day. We were *all* dressed exactly alike, in uniform.

When I got to the cash register, they said, "Well—who do *you* work for?" Here I am with three highway patrolmen. "I'm a highway patrolman." "Oh, I thought you worked for the bus company." I had to laugh because we were all dressed exactly alike. Then it was "Do you do the same thing they do?" No, I just hang out with them. I'm just here to prove the department hires women. I'm the face girl.

Or people will see you in uniform and say, "What are *you?*" "I'm a human being." That's mostly how I answer people. But everybody always does that. "What are *you?*" You feel like saying, "I'm a female. Ever seen one?"

We went on a husband-wife dispute. It came over as being violent, so they assigned two radio cars. Myself and my partner are the backup. We show up, and this man is going berserk on his wife. Not physically, but he's calling her every name under the sun, I mean, things I never even heard

46

of and things that you will not find in *Webster's Dictionary*. He's going berserk. And with that, he turns around; he spots me. He goes, "Oh! Oh, my God! I'm so sorry. I didn't know there was a lady present."

What was his wife?

The public likes women cops better than male cops. I don't know why. It's an offensive job. Maybe women come off as less offensive.

On the other hand, of course, a lot of them just don't like women in authority positions and they'll attack you because of your gender. There are people who get really riled up if a woman officer encounters them because they do *not* like to see us in authority and they will not take orders—they get agitated, *real* agitated, just by the mere suggestion that we can tell them what to do.

We're still tested by people on the street. Civilians. Oh, yes. They test you. They continually test you. They still smirk and they still laugh when they see a female coming up on the scene.

I go to a family fight—I go to a fight because I work by myself. So I go to a fight; it's like—*"You?"* "Yeah, that's all you get." "I want a *man.*" "This is all you get. It's either this or nothin'."

This one woman—I'm called to a domestic. She says, "Honey, if I couldn't do it, *you* ain't gonna." And she was a *big* woman. And I said, "Give me a chance. You might be mildly surprised." I was saying it with a smile, but I was seething.

I'm African-American. When you're an African-American woman cop, they call you names. I've arrested people and they're saying things like, "Just wait—*your* son is not ever gonna be the president. I don't why you're working for *them*"—you know.

African-Americans. Other African-Americans. It bothers them. Not so much that you are a woman, but that you're African-American. I've been called "handkerchief head" and "Uncle Tom" and whatever they thought would hurt at the moment. This is from African-American victims and suspects when things aren't going their way.

Or you're driving in the black and white [squad car]. You'll get a shout every now and then from somebody, sure. They see it as you're going over to The Man. I think the African-American women officers get it worse from the men—I run into more male suspects, mind you.

In bigger situations, where I'm on the street, say, in a crowd-control situation, there's always someone, when you're standing in the front of a line with a baton and a helmet on, there's *always* someone or two that will ask you why you're on that side. And that has become a way of trying to make you move off the line, trying to make you swing, trying to make you mad.

When you're a black officer, the public—it's "Hey! Officer Bitch! You ain't *shit*. Now you're just working for The Man." They act like you're a traitor. Or else it's "Give me a break, sister. Help me out." Help yourself out. I've always had a job. I've always had my self-respect. Help yourself out.

I get a harder time from black suspects than a white officer would. If you're a black officer and you go to a situation involving blacks and you tell somebody something, they look at you like you have seventeen heads. Along comes a white officer, tells these same people the exact same thing you just said—"Oh. Yes, sir." *I hate that.*

If I'm by myself, I won't have any problems with an arrest. The confrontations come in when I'm with a male partner. A male being arrested *cannot* be put down by a male in front of a woman. So he'll verbally attack me and say nothing to the male. A female officer is a figure of authority. This is their retaliation against a woman being a figure of authority.

Or you're by yourself, you take some man prisoner, there's absolutely no problem, but as soon as you get to the jail, he's gotta put on a show. I've seen this time and time again.

* * *

It seems to be so in vogue to bash police. I always say this to people I know when they start in with the police-bashing. I always tell them, "Give me another line of work where you have to put on a bulletproof vest and put a gun on and put all these things on that protect you. And think about it. Think about going out to a job where every day you have to put a bulletproof vest on." And yet, if you say that to people, "Yeah, *you* do it"—"Oh, I wouldn't have your job for a million bucks."

When you put on that uniform, you do not represent yourself, you represent *everyone* in a uniform. None of the citizens remember your name. All they know is that you're the police. And your name has nothing to do with it. They don't know that you may be married and have two young kids and your mother's sick and your dad died a year ago— they don't have a clue to that and they don't give a shit. So don't bring that to work and take all this personal. Because it isn't. This job has nothing to do with us personally.

The uniform is entirely separate from you. As far as I'm concerned, the uniform could walk through my house all by itself. I just have to wear it. That's the way you have to see it. I just happen to be in that uniform.

You know, people say vicious, vile stuff to you all the time. But it's just words, you know. Because this person is *angry*—Who knows why that person is angry? You happen to be the one there.

In the ghetto? I refuse to believe that people live there by choice. No one says, "I like being a strung-out junkie. I have no desire to do anything else."

No. I don't believe that. I believe we as a society have failed them. Every day I go to work, every day I'm in the ghetto, I know. I know we as a society are failing. And I'm as big a part of that failure, but I'm trying to be more part of the solution.

People get angry and they need to vent and they get angry and they want to say things to you. If they want to call me a white cunt bitch, they can call me a white cunt bitch. I'm not gonna hit somebody because they call me a white cunt bitch.

You can't take things personally. Some police officers do. They're arresting somebody and that person upsets them. Why be upset? You're going home at the end of the day; that person's gonna be in an icky little cell—Why are *you* mad? You know?

But a lot of police are—"Don't disrespect us." Hey, we've already lost respect. They can't disrespect us any more.

I hate the uniform. I hate it because it's polyester. But it fits okay. The shirt's okay. I guess I mostly hate it because . . . I feel sometimes like I look like a Nazi. It's very fascist. I have trouble just with the fact that I'm in uniform and I feel like a fascist.

It's hard sometimes to be one of "them," especially when your friends are radical feminists and you're more radical than any of them. I grapple with the issue of how can I be part of the oppressor, you know, the strong arm of the oppressor.

I take two different approaches: One's the big picture and the other's the little picture. In the big picture, police are there to protect the haves from the have-nots. And I find that repulsive.

I identify with the little picture. That's what I do for people on an individual basis, the support I can give a woman victim, say a domestic battery victim, a woman unable to lock up a bad guy, help her through the legal system so she can be safe. With rape victims, I can give as much power back to them as possible in that moment and as much control back as possible. That's what they need.

My mom joined the NYPD in 1973. I became an NYPD officer in 1992. I wear my mom's shield number. After my mom became a detective, her shield number as an officer was never reassigned. That left it open for a family member to get her shield. That's really nice—a lot of the guys, they have a great-grandfather, a grandfather, a father who was on the job and they can apply—on the NYPD, it's Form 49, you write a 49—and if the shield is available, they get it.

I work in the same precinct my mom did. I see her awards in the house and everything, and it's great to know that you know the shield number—now it's my shield number that I'm walking around with.

It's a good feeling. It's like—although I have her shield number, I don't feel that I'm following in her shadow. I just feel that a torch has been handed over. And I can take it and run with it.

CHAPTER 3

THE ACADEMY

We were among the first twelve women to volunteer to be patrol officers in Chicago, in 1974. They gave us women a special class at the Academy. An older policewoman addressed us on the good grooming of policewomen: "Use deodorant." They also had a woman come out from this charm school, she was a woman from the old Patricia Stevens Modeling Agency. She came out and gave us instructions on how to enter and exit a squad car gracefully.

—Chicago Police Department officer

I taught Physical Training and Defense Tactics at the Police Academy. You always have some guy in your class—when you walk in and say, "Hello. I'm here teaching Physical Training and Defense Tactics," you have one guy that just looks at you like "Oh, God. Who does this woman think she is? And how can she teach me anything, because I'm this big macho man?"

So usually, you kind of, you know, not hard, but you kind of get ahold of that guy right there at the beginning and dump him on his ass right in front of everybody. That's always kind of a beginning thing.

—Seattle Police Department sergeant

Time was, women police trained separately from the men, even taking separate breaks so as not to distract the male recruits. Police science for women consisted largely of learning report writing and listening to their instructors, mostly old-timers, gas on about their adventures on the streets, adventures they kept reminding the women they would never have. Physical training? A joke. Weapons training? "You ladies won't need to learn this" was the refrain. Women practiced filing or typing while male recruits filed out to the rifle range.

Then came same-sex police academies in the seventies. A level playing field. Women were given the same opportunities, the same training, and in this intensely paramilitary structure, the same hazing male recruits had always undergone.

But with a difference. While male recruits were broken down and built up as part of an initiation into a force that welcomed those deemed worthy and excluded wimps, women, many times, were broken down and broken down and broken down as a way of weeding out *all* of them. The stories that came out of police academies in the seventies and early eighties are stories of harassment and discrimination with the explicit purpose of driving women away.

They weren't driven away. These stories also reveal heroism on the part of the male recruits and instructors who supported (and support) women, and the women who bucked the system and won through. Women today receive equal instruction at police academies and often are highly prized instructors in the macho arts of Physical (Defensive) Tactics. Yet there are enough stories to indicate that equality in the Academy is still a hard-won field . . .

* * *

Most training is a mind game. They play mind games on you. Can you make it through the mind games? I've been through the DEA Academy, the ATF Academy, and the military. We did everything the guys had to do. But just the typical, the male-dominated things. What you tell everybody is, most of it's a mind game. If you make it through that, you can make it through anything.

In the early days, they just had it in for us. Even in the physical, when we went the day of the physical, which was before we were told to report to the Academy—you're there all day in the basement of this old Police Academy. It's hot. You're waiting for all these tests. Finally, towards the end, after a whole day of being there, one of the instructors— "Okay, now it's time for the urine test. How many of you are having your period?" So a bunch of us raised our hands. "All right. You're kicked out." They actually kicked us out, on that, saying we couldn't take the urinalysis.

So immediately everyone called the director of personnel and, of course, we were back in school on Monday.

But that's what they tried—it was all this mental, to try and get you not to take the job.

In 1964, I was in the Women's Division of the Portland Police. The Training Academy—we went to the same classes; we did all the same things. But, like when we got on the range to shoot the guns—I'd never shot a gun in my life; I'd shot a BB gun, but that was it; I didn't know anything about guns; I was lucky I knew which end the bullet came out of. But most of the men were from the military or had some kind of knowledge.

There happened to be four of us women. I remember so clearly, the first day they decided they were going to have us shoot shotguns. They called me to the front of the group and they handed me this shotgun and they told me to, you know, "Just kind of put it up on your shoulder here"—they were shooting at clay pigeons—"and when we let the pigeon go, you just go ahead and shoot the shotgun."

Well, unbeknownst to me, the instructor then walks around behind me and stands behind me with his arms out. And I shoot the shotgun and it knocks me right off my feet.

And I fall right back into his arms. And, of course, I am *bruised;* you know how they kick! The whole class of two hundred recruits—they were all laughing. They thought this was really, really funny.

The instructors set me up. They knew what would happen. It was pretty cruel. Then they tried to show me the right way to shoot, but by that time, I was scared of the shotgun. And I'm still scared of a shotgun. I still won't shoot one. I'd hit somebody over the head with it, but I wouldn't shoot him with it.

It just was those kinds of things. We had self-defense training. I had a brown belt in jujitsu that I had earned in college, so I was probably more highly trained than most of the men in the room. They always used me as the guinea pig, sort of. They'd say, "Now we're gonna show you how to get away from somebody grabbing you. Okay, Mary, come up here. Let so-and-so grab you." That was fine and I thought I was being of some help since I had had some training.

One day, I was supposed to throw this guy. And we were wearing jeans and sweatshirts. This guy grabs me and I throw him and as he goes over, he grabs the back of my sweatshirt and pulls it off over my head. And it was all ha-ha, isn't that funny. Everybody thought that was great fun.

I didn't identify it for what it was at the time. I hadn't been exposed to sexual harassment and discrimination in my life, and this is the first time I'd ever faced it. And I just wanted to be one of the guys. Of course, I didn't say or do anything about it, either. Because I didn't want to make them mad.

In the PD Training Academy in '74, they assembled the twenty-five of us, the first women who were "allowed" and who wanted to work the street. They called us all together, and they had all the political bigwigs on the podium. The superintendent at the time got up there and he says, "I want each of you to look at the girl sitting next to you and behind you because a year from now they may not be sitting there. Because we're gonna send you to the worst, most dangerous districts, and some of you aren't gonna come out alive."

After this meeting, there were only eight of us left that

still wanted to go. So the superintendent was able to go to Washington and say, "I've got seventy women. We gave them the opportunity. Less than ten percent want to be patrol officers." That's a true story. That's exactly what he said.

I went to the Academy in 1981. There were four females in our class. Originally, our class had about sixty-five or seventy recruits. After the first day, a good portion of them decided they didn't want to stick around and find out what the rest was like. A lot of the guys dropped. There were only four women to begin with, and we stuck it out.

What I found were real good true friends with the women and some of the men that were in the class, something that I had never really experienced before. What do you call it? *Camaraderie.* It was something new to me.

There were problems, though, with the young men's egos. A lot of them had ego problems. That's true even today. Men just don't think women should be police officers. I don't know what ground they still have their heads buried in. A lot of them don't want to face the fact that we have the same capabilities that they have to get the job done.

A lot of the guys got away with a lot of stuff. Comments and—there was a lot of what I considered sexual harassment. Their reasons for doing what they did, they'd tell us, "Well, you gotta experience it here so that you're not shocked to experience it out there on the street." This was just bull, but I played the game and did what I had to do.

There were just sly little games that they'd play. Here is one incident, in baton training. One of the females wasn't well liked by the guys in her group. So they all got together as a class, we're talking fifty-something individuals, got together as a group and developed this skit, where they'd take their batons, and after they'd go through their little routines, they'd eventually position their batons above their mouths as if they were giving oral sex. And this is—they'd get on their knees, and then they'd do this all together, all at one time. They were trying to embarrass this woman. And what they were saying basically by doing this skit was that she was getting by because of what she used. And that's what they were signifying by doing the skit.

They performed this skit in front of her and all of us females one afternoon and in front of a couple of the instructors. At that time, you really couldn't say much without getting yourself in trouble. I came back at them after they did the skit. They thought it was real cute and funny and I just told them, "You know, I didn't know all you guys knew how to do that sort of stuff. God! Where'd you learn that? Have you been practicing on each other or what?" And that just shut them up. They never did it again.

They were kids being kids, boys being boys, you know. But we held. We held our own.

I'd probably have a better time in a funeral parlor in the freezer section where the bodies are than I had with some of the men in my class in the Academy. Basically, the women—if you came on bubbly, or if you had other family members on the force when you came on, and some of these family members were supervisors—that made a difference in how you were treated.

The black women just had to deal on their own. They had to be especially careful; they had to toe the mark even more than everybody else because they were looking for them to stumble. They really were. It wasn't the instructors—but with our classmates. It was a racial thing. It was racial and sexist. They were really cold.

I was really disappointed because there were two other classes at the Academy and they had such cohesiveness, they were warm, they were having a good time, they were having parties, they were having their own study groups. Our class—we had the pits. I think we had the most polarized class in the history of the Academy. We had men who were telling the women, "Our worst man here is better than any of these broads." These are our classmates. And *they're* rookies, too.

Then, too, some of the instructors weren't very helpful unless you came across as a bimbo. Then they would fall all over you. But if you came across as intelligent and you had a head on your shoulders and you weren't particularly good-looking, you were more or less on your own.

The tension was so tight in our classroom that the

instructors had to tell some of those men, "Come on. Come off of that. Because you're gonna need each other on this job and you can't be walking around with these biases. You can't be taking this crap with you on the street because you don't know who's gonna have to put that dime in the telephone to call for assistance if you need it."

What killed me about the instructors was they never had a second thought about—in the course of their lecture—they'd throw on a transparency of some woman half-naked or some kind of a sexual joke and, and the women, we'd sit, and we'd go, "Oh, yeah. Hahaha"—because we wanted to be one of the guys.

I've even seen this happen in in-service training. Guys are *still* doing this stuff.

In 1947, when I started working for the LAPD, there were about six black women on the Los Angeles Police Department. All together. The class that I came along in had the largest number of women that the LAPD had ever hired at one time. There were eighteen women in my class in September of 1947. In that class, they hired three black women. One of them was so fair that the two of us, who were discernible as black, didn't know who she was.

Such an interesting thing happened during the time we were in the Academy. The press was interested in this class because it was the largest group of women the LAPD had ever hired and it had some minorities. And this was the first class of women who were in uniform and who they had ever put out on a street patrol—this is walking a beat downtown, not in cars. Walking a beat, downtown Los Angeles, out of the Juvenile Division.

So the press was very interested in this group. When they took photographs of the group doing various things, they would have one group of people and then change and have another group of people. What we began to notice—they never used either one of us. But there was this one woman, who was not discernible as black, who was in *all* of the pictures. Even though they changed the other participants, this *one* was there. We began to question who she was. She was very fair and had blue-gray eyes and had soft, dark curly hair. She could have been . . . anything. She never denied— but she never made a point of saying anything about it either. When we were transferred out to go to work, she and the other black woman went to work together. That validated that she was black. Because they would not assign black women to work with white women on the street. We could work together in the jail. But outside . . .

Discriminatory practices were *unconsciously* done. It was sexism *and* racism. It was just a way of life in those days. Let's face it. It was done almost without thinking because there was a general attitude of leaving black people out.

Part of what was emphasized in the LAPD Academy when I went there in 1957 was this thing about being a lady. Remember *A League of Their Own?* Remember how they had those people dolled up in hats that were making the ballplayers into models? That's what they did to us. You had to fit into this model of a perfect woman in their eyes. You had to wear a hat, gloves, and three-inch high heels to the Academy.

We had a Sergeant Daisy Storms. Her job was to take the women's classes in the Academy, she was the Academy coordinator, and she was your god. She set the example by the way she dressed and the way she acted, and she made sure you followed the example. There was a class or two, not a whole bunch, but a class or two on deportment, how you should conduct yourself as a lady.

It was very, very much like *A League of Their Own*. They were very, very careful about you. You were kind of like a Women's Auxiliary to the police. You were a *lady*.

In Seattle in the sixties, we did a completely different job than the men. We worked in the Policewomen's Bureau, which had a woman captain and two sergeants, but those were the only exams we could compete for. But if the women who had those positions didn't retire, there was no place to go. And we were not allowed to take the other promotional exams.

We handled juvenile runaways, child abuse cases, and

assisted the men detectives when a woman was a suspect, which, of course, was really rare in those days, and assisted detectives in what was called "Morals," involving child molestation, and assisted Narcotics in search warrants when they needed someone to go along and do strip searches.

They waited till there were two or three of us at a time and then they'd send us through the regular Police Academy. But we were not allowed to do pursuit driving. The day the men went out to do it, we stayed at the Academy and did filing. I'll never forget it, we did clerical support jobs. And we did not have to pass the physical fitness part of it. I did because I figured I wanted to compete equally. I did all of it, but the other two women did not pass the exam. Same thing with shooting—you didn't have to qualify. Two of us did, though. We qualified.

It was a different world. It doesn't seem possible now.

When I went to the NYPD Academy in 1968, the class consisted of 950 recruits. There were ten women, and we were put into one company with fifteen men. We trained academically together, our firearms instruction was together, but when the men went to phys ed, women were scheduled to go to typing.

We didn't know that we were being discriminated against. That was not a word that was in our vocabulary. Yet I *knew* that when the men went to gym and the women went to typing, there was something wrong with that, you know? I put my first grievance in the Police Department my first week in the Academy when they told me to go to typing.

I had an idea of what I wanted to do as an officer and I'd already been interviewed to go to undercover. I thought, "Well, typing isn't going to do me any good if I'm rolling around the streets with some junkies. I might be called upon to defend myself against some kids—where you can't resort to a gun—or I just might be trying to avoid a rip-off or some other type of encounter." So there had to be an alternative to typing. I mean, was I supposed to say, "Hold on, let me get my Correcto-type"? I mean, it doesn't fly. It really doesn't.

We women got phys ed after my grievance. We were segregated for physical tactics and training. They taught us separately, in the garage, with a male instructor who was about 6'3", and it was like, see what you can do against him.

There were some guys in my Dallas Police Academy class that weren't real keen on the idea. There was a guy in my class that stood up in front of the whole class; he said, "I better not have a woman trainer when I get out there because my wife will not allow it." And I thought, "Well, why don't you just take your little happy ass home and let your wife whip it like she does obviously on a daily basis?" I mean, what a weenie.

There were a lot of guys that felt like that. They didn't want to work with us at all.

We were in this pilot program, the first women to go on patrol in Houston. When I think of what they put us through . . .We were on the street for about three days, and there was so much complaining about us that we had to go back to the Academy. We had to shoot in front of the guys at the Academy so we could prove to them—they couldn't even find their guns in their waistbands—that we could shoot okay.

We were the first class in Chicago to train with the men, P.E. and everything. There were about thirty-five women out of two hundred men.

The men we came on with were great. Definitely the teachers, some of the teachers, went out of their way to make it tough for us and to discourage us from continuing on. Their comments, yelling in your face, the military stuff.

The Academy then was in an old Civil War hospital. We had to run around the basement, work out on Universal, run outside, all that stuff. On rainy days, you'd run in the basement, and I'll never forget, one day, we're running and one male teacher, every time I would go by, went, "did*it,* did*it,* did*it,* did*it,* did*it,*" with his hand going up and down, implying that my boobs were bouncing. Everybody noticed this, men and women. He only did it when I went by. So I immediately went over to the head of P.E. and I told him I didn't like the way they were watching my boobs bounce. From then on, the guy just looked straight ahead and didn't bother me anymore.

We didn't even know what sexual harassment *was* then, know what I mean? They didn't even have running shoes then. We ran in gym shoes. Times were so different then. And I grew up with six brothers, so it wasn't like everything offended me.

In the NYPD Academy in 1973, the training was totally equal, except that instead of chin-ups, we had to do broad jumps and we didn't have to do the man's push-ups. But everything else was equal.

The instructors. There was resentment that the women came on. Back then, no one had any qualms about saying it, including the instructors. We had one instructor who was outspoken. I remember one time in the gym, he came out with a pink baton, you know, the nightsticks? He said, "This is the ladies'." And then he kept remarking how small they are. "You put one woman on top of another, she'll make a full-grown person." Stuff like that. They would make remarks. It was definitely . . . there were problems. A lot of problems. But it passed, and we went on.

I always wanted to be a cop until I became one. You know what happens? You have this view. You put certain people on a pedestal. You see the cop on the beat and you think, "My God. Look at him. He really must be somebody special to be a cop. They let him be a cop, and he's gonna take care of us." You have a childlike view of what a police officer should be and what he is.

Until you actually sit side by side with an individual just like yourself, and you begin to see that *this guy* is a goddamn idiot! And this is who I'm competing with? When the mask is unveiled and you see the type of people that they allow to become police officers, you think, "Don't they see what this guy is about? What this woman's about? How can they send this idiot here out on the street?" And it becomes a situation where your mind is going, "These are the people I held in such *high* esteem—these idiots?" And you find that out, then you're like, "Give me a break; get me outta here!"

And that's really what happens. It's sort of like an unveiling. As the people become human, they're not some cop on the beat in this police uniform you think is so great, superhero. And you're sitting next to these people, just like *you;* you know, they might come from different backgrounds, but you really begin to see that this profession is not what you thought it would be. You know what I'm saying? We're human. We have the same problems as society, we're just a microcosm of the outside world, so we have the same druggies, the same alcoholics, the wife beaters . . . you name it, we have it.

Just being in the NYPD Police Academy. Sitting next to people and seeing the types of people that they're hiring. The blatant racism that was there, the statements that were made—these are the people that I used to look up to as an African-American because they were gonna protect *me;* now I'm sitting there, thinking, "Yeah, they're gonna protect *me,* all right." That's when it begins, that process of the unveiling, I think, happens right in the Academy when you're sitting next to individuals and they're being *somewhat* honest. Then you begin to see that, hey, you know, something is wrong here.

I'd notice when we'd come back from the weekend. And this is not to point the finger at anybody, but when you sit there and you smell alcohol reeking from various parts of the room and you think, "Are they *all* drunks?" You would sit there, it was like aaaggh!

But they say it's the job that does it—it's the job that causes divorce . . . everything is the job. And I just don't buy it. I don't buy it.

I remember in the Academy that we had these classes on ethnic awareness and different backgrounds and all that good stuff. And it just doesn't happen. So you talk about it and everybody loves everybody for six months and then it's a whole other story when you leave.

The guys really acted like the women were wasting their time. You got that attitude a lot, even from the instructors. It does not change. The same people that they're hiring with their attitude as cops become bosses and carry the same attitude all the way to the top. It's unfortunate, but that's the way the New York City Police Department has always been.

After a while, you begin to see that you're certainly not the worst candidate there. I'd look at some of the men that they hired at the same time they hired me—one guy, his other past job was, he worked in a noodle factory. I mean, give me a break. The guy had zip for brains. So I wasn't anywhere *near* either the dumbest person there or— although I may have been close to the smallest person there, I'm only 5'4" and about 115 pounds when I went through the Academy—I never had a problem with my size.

In the Dallas Police Academy in '76, we had the same requirements and there was absolutely nothing different for the women. The only difference was that there were three of us—one black and two Hispanics—versus thirty men.

The guys were *great.* We had to work very hard. We were older. I had no idea what a push-up *looked* like, much less do one. It was very difficult. I remember going home the first week and thinking, I never knew hair could hurt. I mean, the hair on my head hurt. My *nails* hurt.

We came in at six A.M. every day and would run or do weight lifting; at eight we were ready for class; we went to school from eight to five and then at five, if we had done weights in the morning, then we would run to improve our timing in the mile.

And the guys were great. They all took turns in helping us, timing us, pushing us—they were really good. And so, we *did* pass.

Most of my class is still here. Some of them have trained women and been supportive of women. I think out of my class there's only one that has not been supportive. But the rest have remained the same, not only with me, but with the other women.

The first time that I was exposed, well, to sexual harassment, if you will, was in the Training Academy in 1979. I didn't understand—one guy wouldn't talk to me; I thought,

"I didn't do anything to this guy." I was pretty young, I was twenty-one at the time, a bit naive, a *lot* naive. Sometimes guys would make comments, they would make jokes, and not just my fellow students, the instructors would.

To this day, I remember, there's now a lieutenant in my department, he was a sergeant at the time, and he came in—I don't even remember what his lecture was about, but one of the first things he did, he put up on the overhead screen a real sexist cartoon. I can't remember what the cartoon was, but I remember thinking, "I don't like this man." This was the time, too, when there was no such term as "sexual harassment"; it hadn't been coined yet. To this day, I still don't like him. I still think he's a dickhead.

But I have to say this—we had two sergeants that were in charge of the Academy at the time. Right at the halfway point, right before Christmas, they took me aside. I hadn't said anything to anybody. And they said, "You know, we've been watching you in class and we notice you really seem kind of down. Your grades haven't suffered or anything, but we're concerned. What's going on?"

Another thing they noticed was I hadn't gone to the Christmas party. There had been one or two parties before, I had taken my boyfriend, and people got real drunk and started making very hurtful comments about me, very sexist jokes and teasing. I just didn't enjoy myself. I thought why should I subject myself to these things?

I said, "I'm getting really sick and tired of all these things that have been happening." I even mentioned some of the guys that I rode in this car pool with, that are very good friends now, but at that time they made comments. It just got to be too much.

These sergeants were very supportive of me. They said, "We think you're doing a great job. We think you've got a great future here. We don't want to see anything happen to you that will jeopardize your chances here." So what they did without my knowledge was they took the recruits aside and said, "Look, you know"—it was kind of a left-handed compliment—"she could be a lot worse." But they were trying to say give her a break, give her a chance. Later, a couple of them came up to me and said, "Look, we're sorry. We didn't know this was getting to you this way."

Not too long after that, we were in the classroom. The orders were that if the instructor asked you to respond, you had to respond to a question. There was a woman instructor there, she was a guest. I don't know what she asked me, but she wanted to know what my opinion as a woman was. And here I am, you know, in this class, all guys. I also know that no matter *what* I say, these guys are gonna get me later. I'm gonna be attacked. I say, "No. I'm sorry, I'm not going to respond to your question." She says, "Why?" And I say, "Well . . ." She says, "Don't you feel comfortable?" I said, "Yes. You're correct. I do not feel comfortable responding to that."

I have to give one guy credit. He stood up—and I didn't know him real well—he's a short guy, he's my height, 5'7", he stands up and he says, "I don't know about you guys. But I'm sick and tired of you instructors picking on Sally just because she's the only woman in this class." And then another guy stood up and he said, "I don't care about any of this, but I know that if I'm in a bar fight, Sally will back me up and I know that she may not be able to knock somebody down with one punch, but she'll do all she can. And that's all I ask."

It moved me a great deal. To be supported like that. Then—suddenly—it got better. Once somebody was able to get up and say hey, she's okay, then everybody said, okay, we'll give her a chance. From then on, things got a lot easier.

It was the hardest thing I have ever done in my life. I was twenty-two years old, this is 1977, and two months before, I started working out and running and all that. Well—I wasn't even *prepared* for it. It was very physically demanding.

The guy that taught Physical Training when I went through the Academy was a sadist. I was warned about him by a lot of people—"Hey, not only is this guy a sadist, he thinks women are the last people who should be police officers." What he did was he made me mad. I was determined to do it just to spite him.

On the first day that we had a physical workout, they had a uniform they wanted us to wear: PD shorts, PD T-shirt. But they weren't in yet. So he told us that we could wear anything we wanted to. Well, I had on a pair of green socks, they weren't a pair of loud green socks, they were just green socks. My last name at the time was Hayes. What he did, we got out there and started doing push-ups and sit-ups. And he'd say, "Let's do five more sit-ups because Hayes has on green socks."

And then what we had to do, we had to do what we called "running the lake." At that time, the Police Academy sat on a very small lake. You had to run the lake, and the distance around the lake was three and a half miles. Every half a mile we had to stop and fall down and do push-ups and sit-ups, do like fifty of them, and then get up and run another half mile. Well, I was throwing my guts up about halfway through. But every time we fell down to do our push-ups and sit-ups, if I missed one, this guy would point it out. And he'd say, "Hayes missed a push-up. Everybody do five more." It's almost like he tried to turn the class against me. It worked just the opposite. They were very angry with him before it was all over.

Me and a guy named Harrison were the slowest guys in the class. The truth is, running was just then becoming popular at that time. I wanted to learn how to run. But the instructor didn't want to teach me how to run. What he wanted to do was abuse me. He wanted to make an example out of me as far as "See? I told you that women couldn't do it." And he didn't teach me anything. When I couldn't do it, all he did was use me as a whipping post.

Like I said, me and this Harrison guy were the slowest ones in the class. And so one day, he told the class, "The rest of you all can leave early for lunch. Hayes and Harrison have to stay after and do wind sprints during lunch." I wasn't by myself, so I didn't feel like I was being completely slighted. So we did. And then, he said, "Okay, now I want you to write a letter to the sergeant over in Basic Training, and I want you to tell him what your time is now and what you're doing to improve your running." So we wrote these letters, and after class we had to stay after and meet with the sergeant.

Me and the P.T. instructor walked in the sergeant's office. He said he'd read my letter. It was very short and sweet: I run this time now; I work out every night after I get home, and this is what I hope to do. And he said, "Is there anything else you'd like to say?" I looked at him and I thought, "Well. You know. This is it." And I said, "Yeah. You know, I'd really like to learn how to run, but this guy sitting here hasn't taught me anything. All he does is abuse me and tries to humiliate me in front of the class. I wish somebody would teach me. I want to learn. And I want to pass this. And I want to be a cop and I'm *gonna* be a cop in spite of this. But I'd really appreciate it if somebody would teach me how to run."

Boy, his lips disappeared. He said, "Thank you very much. You can leave." And I got up and left.

I left, and nobody ever got back with me. Nothing really changed. That was probably about halfway through the Academy. Nothing changed.

There was a class ahead of me; they were two months ahead of us. And there was a girl in that class called Liz. She called me one day and said, "I want to know if this P.T. instructor is treating you badly." I said, "Hell *yes*, he is." I started telling her, and she says, "They're flunking me out and I'm gonna **file** a discrimination suit against him. Do you want to participate?" And I said, "Hell, no. I gotta make it through this. I'm not ready to do that yet. They're not flunking *me* yet. I've still got a chance." She said, "Yeah, but look at all the things he's done." "You're absolutely right, but I'm not geared that way. I've gotta make this. I've gotta keep my mouth shut and put up with it to make it."

Obviously, she went ahead with her plans because they transferred him out two weeks before I graduated. So it wasn't just me. This had been going on for a while. And the guys that came in after him helped me. They truly did. They were very encouraging and very helpful.

And I *passed*.

When I came on, I was not in good shape. I'd been running, but I didn't have a lot of strength in my upper body. They would do things like—I'd get paired up in defensive tactics with a smaller guy. But, you see, the two smaller guys in my class both had martial arts experience.

And this one guy—I had to hold the mat right up against my body. I'd go home and I'd have bruises on my hips because this guy hurt. It hurt. He was trying to hurt me— you'd have this mat that you'd hold right tight against your body and then they'd kick out at the mat. He was quite powerful. He was really giving it to me. It was just abuse.

A lot of things, I think, happened back then that would not happen in the Academy today—things that happened to the women that would not be stood for today. I think there's a lot more support for women now.

In a class which followed mine in '77, which you'd think would be better, you'd think they'd be better as they go along, a situation was set up where the tac [undercover tactical unit] officer who was teaching the wrestling control techniques set up a situation where he had the two women in the class fighting each other. They may as well have had mud there because that's exactly the type of situation that was created: You know, these guys sittin' around, hootin' and hollerin' about the women, the two girls, fighting each other. They were yelling out, "Cat fight!" It was really silly. That just wouldn't happen now.

I went to the Police Academy in 1979. Probably the very first worst experience was the medical exam. They called us women in. The worst part was, when we had to face this doctor—we were there in our bras and gowns because they had asked us to remove our panties—we had a nurse there, and she tells us to bend over and spread our cheeks. And we're all looking at each other like, "You've got to be kidding!" And the nurse is going, "Now, now. If you're going to be a police officer, you better be professional about this." Then suddenly it starts to dawn on you. My God, men have been going through this all their lives. This is a terrible feeling. We were all blushing. It was like, "Oh my God, this is horrible." But we had to do it.

It gave me so much sympathy for what the poor men go through because it was like you were stripped of all dignity. I mean, here you are with other people, being asked to drop your pants and spread your cheeks—it was like the worst invasion of privacy.

The LAPD set the hiring goals for women at twenty-five percent in the early eighties. They jumped from three to five percent women coming on to twenty-five percent. That's a major change.

But at the same time, they still did not want—they honestly believed that they were still somehow gonna stop women from going out on patrol. To the point where, in the Academy, up until the time they graduated, they said, "You know, you're never going to go on the street." Because they were so sure that they were somehow going to stop them from going on patrol.

At some point, you can become extremely paranoid. I think that happens to some women at the lower levels. They just become totally stressed out, and they never become effective police officers because when they come to the job, they are not prepared for all the harassment they will receive just because of the fact that they're a woman.

It starts in the Academy. Don't fall out of a run in P.E. because they'll say, "See, we knew women couldn't do it anyway."

Women who are very self-confident, who carry themselves in that way, suffer in that department because men start trying to tear you down. They cannot stand a woman who feels too comfortable about herself. They *want* you to be timid, they *want* you to have low self-esteem. There are a couple of women around here that I have seen the guys really come at just because of the way they carry themselves.

One woman was a trainer at the Academy. Evaluations came. They called her a bitch in the evaluations, and, you know, who does she think she is? Don't send her back to the classroom because she thinks she's better than anybody.

The other woman—the lieutenant she was working for gave her a negative evaluation, said she didn't work well with others. But then she checked with her immediate boss, found out that this woman carried herself in a certain way, she didn't sit around and joke—she didn't talk to these guys. So they said she wasn't a team player. That's another thing. They'll write you up and say you're not a team player if you don't sit around and laugh at some of these jokes they have.

When I was an instructor at the Academy, I noticed there were two types of women: the ones that came here looking for a career and the ones that came looking for a husband. And you knew who they were. They were the ones that their pants were so *tight* you couldn't squeeze a finger through them. Or if we were running, you could see both cheeks in the shorts because they were so short. You knew the deal— they were trying to get a husband.

There's different reasons for women coming on this job. Some genuinely want to work, get good pay, and the others are looking for husbands, the easy way out, and they do well. They do quite well.

The old concept of what a female police officer looks like is just not true. There are some very beautiful women on the job. And you see some of the cops' wives—God—blugh! blugh! Some of the wives are unbelievable. You meet them and you think, "My God! That's the *wife?*"

So you've got these young women coming on the job, energetic, gorgeous. And then you've got the hag at home with all the kids. Some of them take advantage, and the women know that. The man doesn't have a chance. Some of the women in this job—the things that they do to get a man in bed are *unbelievable*—the poor guy doesn't have a chance. And if it's a bigwig, forget about it. Because they really will do anything for someone if he has a little bit of power. And I mean anything.

A friend of mine who heads a team, and this isn't even a glitzy team, told me this one recruit, she came right up to him and said, "You take care of me. I'll take care of you. Right here." You have women that will do that. But see, the men aren't filing any complaints. They're loving it! With AIDS, yeah, some of it has calmed down, but the stories we get in this job are unbelievable.

Sometimes, when you hear these women talking about the sexual harassment, and you know their backgrounds and know what some of the women will do just for a little spot—unbelievable. Just unbelievable.

The thing that was kind of funny about the Academy—people I was in the Academy with in 1988, we all say the same thing—that building was so full of sexual relationships. It was. It was a revolving door. We were laughing because as we were watching new classes come in, and they were getting so many that they had to keep hiring new instructors or bring more policemen in to teach, it was like a revolving door. If we'd have parties and we'd be drinking with some of the new instructors, they were all getting divorced, they were all starting to live together because they all got kicked out of the house because they got caught fooling around. So then they'd have to get in a whole other crew because these guys already got kicked out; we've gotta get some new ones in. A revolving door. It was. That's all it was. Every day, another new scandal, another new scoop.

I remember one girl that was a recruit. She was married to a cop. And she was jogging with one of the gym instructors every day, so they were having a little thing.

Her husband came into our class on Physical Training one day and grabs the gym instructor and tells him to step outside. They had a fight out in the hallway. This instructor was really muscular, really built. We're all sort of off to the side going, "Who do you think's gonna win?" We're betting money and everything. The fight got broken up, so nobody collected.

One of the girls got pregnant. And this instructor left his wife to marry her. And then she supposedly had a miscarriage. He left his wife and then she didn't want him and then she quit the job. There's just always something.

The instructors don't get kicked out of the Academy for this. They'd have to close the whole Academy down. What happens, some of the instructors' wives ask them to please change assignments.

What was funny, there were a few female instructors—a few of the male recruits in the class were sleeping around with them. Kind of a reverse thing because the male instructors were sleeping with a lot of the female recruits,

73

you know. Of course, everything's denied. Nobody does this. And nobody thinks they're being open and blatant about it. You know, one of those—they think that they're hiding it, but everybody knows? It was just constant, constant.

Even the commander of the Academy was doing a female recruit—we used to call her "The Bicycle Queen" because they'd always ride bikes together. That's the excuse in the front: "We just ride bikes together." You know. Whatever.

What was funny to me was, when we would have parties and talk—as usual, the double standard—the guys would talk about the girls sleeping with these instructors. But yet, certain female instructors I know had these guys . . . And I thought it was kind of funny. It was like, fine for the male instructors, that was allowed, but a woman instructor is not allowed to sleep with a male recruit. I personally thought, "It's about time! Good for them! Let them get under *your* desk for a while now and ask for a favor."

To me I guess I thought you'd have to be on the job for a while to get into that. Here it was from the very beginning, this was all going on. I thought it was kind of funny that nobody wastes any time—it's like we're just gonna jump right in there.

And there was always this certain girl who we all hated and was a bitch, but I kind of admired her in my own way because she didn't waste her time with any p.o.'s—she went right to the top. You know, if she was gonna fool around, she took something with some brass on it. So I kind of cracked up. I thought, "This girl knows what she wants and where she's gonna go."

And how has she done? *Fantastic.* She's a detective. She's doing fine. She'll be a boss someday.

We had one girl at the DEA Academy, she had been sleeping with a highly placed agent from where she came from. In the history of the DEA Academy, no one had scored lower points than she did, and yet she was allowed to graduate. She was an insult to women, but as a whole, most people are afraid to get rid of the ones they need to get rid of.

Nobody documents anything. If anybody had documentation—she was terrible. She pointed a loaded gun at her partner's back a week before graduation. We were going through an obstacle course where you have to pop up and it's a safety thing to keep the gun down. She was crawling through an obstacle and put the gun up. That's a safety violation. And she's still doing that a week before we're graduating.

Just horrendous that she was allowed to graduate. At the end of the class, you have critiques. Everyone in the class wrote about her. I wrote, "We're trained that we're the elite of the elite, that we're the best, that we're *trained,* and yet this woman is allowed to graduate. I'm embarrassed."

I heard a few months after she got back, they were trying to fire her. If they had done the job in the Academy, in my eyes, they wouldn't be going through this.

When we were going through the Academy in the eighties, we encountered sexual harassment all the time. There was a lot back then. What people are bringing up now? It's *nothing* compared to what I know a lot of women have gone through, and even a lot of men, depending on what type of environment they work in. When we were going through the Academy, it was around all the time.

Sexual comments were always being made. Instructors were always hitting on the women and then telling you that your attitude is bad and if you don't shape up, you're gonna be terminated.

There wasn't really anybody you could go to either, back then, to talk to. Not even the counselors. The counselors either didn't understand or they didn't want to understand. They wanted to just go with the flow instead of making waves.

At one point, I was disciplined because I spoke up for myself as a female. They were threatening to suspend me. I came back at them and I told them, "If you come to me and tell me I can't handle this physically, I'm gonna call you a liar. If you come to me and tell me I can't handle this academically, I'm gonna call you a liar. But if you come and tell me that sometimes I realize I'm a female—I'm gonna have to agree with you. I *am* a female. But I can do the same job any of these guys can do. But bottom line is, we go home at night, we are females and they are males. So that's something you're just gonna have to adjust to and get used to."

The Academy when I went through was six months. Six months of hell. I'm 5′4″, the smallest one in my Academy class, very few women in '82, and we weren't accepted. They just put us through the wringer. And on a daily basis, they told us to quit: "You're not wanted here. You don't belong." So when you got through *that,* boy, you thought, "Wow. If I can do that, I can do anything."

The training in our Academy was very vigorous. It's changed quite a bit. In fact, it changed right there in '82. They had a big upheaval where they couldn't be so mean to recruits. My class was one of the last classes before the big upheaval.

I was one of those people that fought and worked hard. I remember going through and I didn't cheat on the sit-ups because I knew I *had* to do every sit-up because I had to be strong because I *was* small. When we did the six-mile runs, I ran the six miles and I ran it as hard as I could run. Never lagged behind. That's because I was fighting for myself and for my partners.

My peers were very supportive—in the Academy you get lumped together and you feed off each other. The instructors were still not used to seeing the women yet. And of course, being a small little redhead with a small voice, I just didn't fit in. Let's face it.

I got hurt in the Academy. I tore a ligament in my knee, and I finished the Academy with a torn ligament. They wanted me to quit. They put me into the next class because I couldn't do the P.T. for a couple weeks. But come five years later, I had knee surgery and they discovered that I had hurt it and I had split my ligament in half. They didn't know how I had gone through that Academy. It was just pure *"I'm gonna get through this."*

That experience, the day that I fell and hurt my knee, is something that's torn into my mind because they sat there—I was going over a hurdle in the obstacle course and my knee went out when I was in the air. I landed and the instructor—my knee was on the side of my leg, I could see it, and he sat there for five minutes yelling, "Get up, you baby! You don't belong here, you baby! Get up!" And my knee was out on the side of my leg.

Finally, when they looked at it, they pulled up the sweat . . . I couldn't get up. They lifted up my sweatpants and I could see their eyes thinking, "Oh. Well. Whoops." What they said was "Let's get her down to the hospital." And then their doctors said it was just a strain, no big deal. I went for five years before finding out that that day I had actually torn it in half.

They never apologized. My goodness, no. Never apologized. These guys were horrid—horrid! To this day, I see them and I go, "Yuck!" These guys had not a sympathy bone in their body. They're very macho, very "We are the best."

I was sent to the West Coast FBI school for marksmen when I became a sniper on a SWAT Team a few years ago. So here I am, I walk into—there were probably thirty-five, forty guys from all over the West Coast and this is an FBI school—and they're all dressed up in their macho camouflage things with their pins and badges and all this, and I walk in and about thirty-five guys look at me like, "Who the hell brought the woman?"

The instructor gets up and the very first half-hour of his dissertation—"All right, you guys, we're gonna do this and we're gonna do that; what the fuck do you think about that?" And then he kind of steps back and looks straight at me and says, "I'm sorry, little lady. I didn't mean to say that." The whole week of that class I was "the little lady"— "I'm sorry, little lady this; I'm sorry, little lady that; I didn't mean to say that, little lady." I just kind of sat there and oh, God.

For a good part of this, I was so, so fortunate to have a guy that went through that school with me. He basically was my partner through that school. He was so supportive, you know: "You can do this better than anybody." Every time

I'd do a good shot, it was "God, that's great." I ended up coming out number three out of a class of about thirty-five, forty men. They didn't like that, either.

I was the very first female bomb technician on the LAPD. When I went to Redstone, they were very upset. This is the military training unit run by the FBI down in Alabama; they are responsible for training all the bomb technicians in the U.S. and Canada. And they had only seventeen women come through there in over twenty years.

The people at Redstone were very upset. I said, "Look, I'm not gonna take bombs apart. The only reason I'm doing this is for safety so we don't kill ourselves in the course of doing search warrants and so that when we question bomb suspects, we will know what they're talking about. Strictly safety issues." And then they calmed down—"She's not gonna be in charge of anybody, I guess it's okay; she's not gonna take bombs apart, I guess it's okay."

The DEA Academy is run like the military. You wear combat boots, fatigue pants, and T-shirts. Most classes aren't allowed to use the elevator. By the end of the first week, you run four miles. You're on the mat at seven-fifteen. Fifteen minutes of stretching. For the next hour, you do calisthenics, weights—no stops—push-ups, sit-ups, any kind of exercise you can imagine for an hour. Then you go straight into defensive tactics, which is punching, wrestling, handcuffing, takedown holds. You then change into your running shoes and then you go run.

The second week, you start out at five miles. At any one time in a DEA class, we had one third of our people injured. DEA Academy—if you're injured or anything, they send you home. They don't let you come back and start out where you were. You start all over again. We had one girl on one of the cross-country runs, she fell and badly damaged her knee. She was in her seventh week of training, yet she had to go back and do everything again. So we had people with injuries who just kept going. You don't quit.

The physical part was horrendous to me. The first few weeks, I didn't know if I could do it. Then you get to a point where you know you're gonna do it, it's just, it hurts so bad, when is it going to end?

When I was there, my roommate and I were the only prior law enforcement among the women. There were six of us. The FBI, out of their class of twenty-four, they have to have at least six women. DEA, it's usually two to three women in each class, out of a group of about forty-five.

My roommate was a black female. You have four instructors assigned as counselors to go through the whole class with you. They're supposed to be our mentors, our counselors, to help us when anything goes wrong. My friend's counselor, a black male, started putting pressure on her to the point where he was calling her down to his room. In DEA, if we do anything wrong, we have to write memos: "I walked up the stairs the wrong way." My roommate started getting those; he would hold her back in class and talk to her. Everyone in class was noticing, and we were trying to protect her.

It started out as just harassment, then it got to the point where he showed up in our room one night when I was gone. Our counselors were so conscious of women that they never came to our rooms, and if we came to theirs, they always left their doors open. But here we have a counselor coming to one of the women's rooms, especially when the other female isn't there. She said he didn't put any physical moves on her; however, he said he was aware she was friends with white male agents and he wanted to know what was wrong with black males. He used mainly mind games with her; she told me things he had said to her about not getting along and not giving the proper respect.

It got to such a point where she was handing in her resignation to leave the Academy. She almost quit several times; he had her in tears. He basically threatened her that she wasn't going to make it through. The class was called in one by one and had to give written statements. He was finally sent back home. That had never been done before.

Here we had a *counselor* and he is harassing one of the very students he was supposed to protect. And we're talking—this is about our *Training* Academy.

She didn't quit the Academy. We found out later that he

had physically assaulted a secretary in the office, had grabbed her and pushed her against a desk.

We had to fight. We had a two-minute fight at the end of our Academy, after we did our final physical tests because they didn't want us injured before we did our final P.T. test. And they split us up—and they made sure the girls fought with guys, which was fine. And the way they paired us up was they made us line up according to height and then they split us off.

And I ended up fighting with this guy, who was probably two inches taller than me, but he was like a bodybuilder. And his arms were longer than my legs. Actually, I got the shit beat out of me. He knocked me down once and I saw stars. And I'm trying to shake it off.

Now, one of our P.T. instructors—really hard-nosed, but I appreciate that—I mean, he was like a Marine Corps drill sergeant; at one point during our P.T. he got in my face: "I'm comin' after you." I couldn't hold up in the push-up position—we were supposed to hold the push-up position for thirty seconds. I couldn't do it. About halfway through, he came to me and said, "I'm comin' after you." And I thought, "What the *hell* have you been doing for the last three months?"

So, in the middle of this fight, I'm out of breath, I've just had my bell rung, he says, "If you want this star as bad as I think you do, you get back in there." That's all it took. I got back in there and we're punching away.

I came home with a black eye. I graduated the Academy with a black eye.

I look back now and I think that was probably one of the best times of my life, but it sure didn't feel like it at the time.

The only thing that upset me in the Academy was I was never in a fight with anybody. In Defensive Tactics, they pair you up. The day we did that I thought, "Great! Now I'll see what I can do." Before we went in, the instructor whispered to me, "Tell him you're pregnant and see if that stops him."

The idea is you shouldn't see who you're gonna fight ahead of time. They put mats on the floor, you close your eyes, they walk you in, you sit back to back, and then you turn and face your opponent. When the guy I was supposed to fight turned around to see who he was gonna fight, I could see he was really disappointed. His face fell, it was—"Oh, God." That made me feel awful.

I taught at the Academy a few years ago. Women are very interesting. Women cops, I suppose, more than any profession. It's like they either want to be very supportive of their fellow women—although I have to honestly say that I have not seen *that* till recently, *or,* like when I first became a cop, there seemed to be this real competition among women. It was almost like some of the women liked it if the other women on the department screwed up. I think it was nothing but a lack of self-esteem.

The women I taught at the Academy—it seemed they were either real happy to have a woman there or they were ticked because they couldn't get away with the stuff that they can get away with with men. I know the guy that was there before me was there for quite a long time, and God, these women would run up and: "I'm having my period. I can't do it." He would get so embarrassed. They could do anything with him. "It's a woman thing, you know." They kind of blinked their eyes at him. And a lot of women *did* get through that way.

With me, it worked for about one second. It did not work at all. Don't tell me your problems.

I remember when I first went out there. I trained with this male instructor for a while before he left and, oh yeah, I saw women do that to him all the time. And watching them with him and watching them with me was just hilarious because some of them would have a whole different personality with him—blinking their eyes, getting all wriggly: "I can't do that. I can't do that." I ended that real quick.

Some women—in the Academy I could see it start when I taught there—they just feel that they have to be a man or act like a man to be accepted by men. You see it start in the Academy. These women come in and they start taking on these personalities, basically, just to be accepted. Their mouths would get kind of dirty . . .They try so hard, and they just so badly want to be accepted.

I always wanted to take them aside and say, "Look. Be what you *are*. Be a *good* what you are."

Some women don't belong in the profession. They're upset all the time. Everything upsets them. I remember in the Academy, one girl started crying on the line. And it just infuriated me. You know, they think we don't belong here anyway and you're *crying?* Thanks a lot. That's just what we need.

They were extremely hard both physically and mentally on the women. I don't think it was personal. They really were preparing us for real life, what we were gonna get. Nobody's gonna walk up to you and call you "Miss Lady." They tell you to get "your f——ing hands off me, bitch." Nobody's nice to you that you're getting ready to arrest. You get called those names.

Our instructor would say things like, "All right, fat ass. Get down and give us those push-ups!" And some of the women I could see were absolutely "Humph! We're shocked and appalled!" I remember one girl in my class, she was a teacher: "Is it absolutely necessary to call us bitches? Is it absolutely necessary to use such profanity?"

Bottom-line answer: No. It probably wasn't necessary. But in the long run effective? I think what they were seeing was down the road. Because if we got out there, and some of them hadn't prepared us that way, I think this lady would have done the same thing on the street. She'd have been "shocked and appalled!"

This one particular girl that I have in mind that was utterly "shocked and appalled" is one of the ones that quit because she couldn't cut it. This was after completion, after graduation, and after going out into the district. She just got a dose of reality out there as to what it was really all about and not what you think in your mind is such a pretty, professional job. She quit. She couldn't do it. She couldn't deal with it.

So down the line I think it did pay off.

* * *

When you're training to be a Texas Ranger, you go to the Austin Academy. You live there night and day. At five-forty-five you get up and do one hour of exercise. Classes are from eight A.M. to eight P.M. Lights out are at ten, *but* anytime between ten P.M. and six A.M. they can blow the whistle and have you get up. It might be, oh, a spelling test of the small towns of Texas—like Aspermont, Catullah, Nacogdoches. I remember one night, we had to get up in the middle of the night and spell Falfurrias.

Of course, at the time, we thought they were just sadistic. But there was a reason for everything they did: If you get called out in the middle of the night, how will you handle it?

Like boxing—it's how much can you take? Are you gonna lay down and cry? Or are you gonna live or die?

By the time you get out, you're proud to wear the uniform.

Going to the FBI Academy in Quantico was the first experience in my whole life of being truly equal. They required thirty-five push-ups to graduate. These puppies had to be done from the toes. I lifted weights and by the time the test came, I *did* thirty-five. By the time I graduated, when I dialed the phone, the muscles in my back rippled. It was wonderful—exhilarating to be in such good shape. Conditioning is the great equalizer. You find out you can do what you never thought you could do.

Training is incredibly important. They teach you that in the crucial moments of your life you revert to training.

Officer Survival Training. A few years ago, a California Highway patrolman got killed in a shootout. They found his spent brass [bullets] placed neatly in his pocket. They train you that way so you don't mess up the range. Unconsciously, he had done the same thing.

And that's why he was killed. The fact that he dumped his spent brass in his hand and then put it in his pocket cost him valuable time. So whatever level of training officers have, that's what they'll resort to in a crisis.

If you have no training, you're at ground zero. You're in a mental stall. With many, many civilian women, this is what happens. They freeze.

With women in law enforcement, it's a bigger problem for us than for the men because we're not brought up to fight. You think you can get by with a kick in the nuts, but I'll tell you what—that doesn't always work. Men expect that from a woman.

All this represents a bigger obstacle for women. But an obstacle is something you can overcome.

I teach Defensive Tactics, Spontaneous Knife Defense, and Collapsible Baton. By the time the recruits walk out of my class, there's no doubt they don't want to mess with me. I always take the biggest one and take him down just by empty-handed defense. I do it to demonstrate to small-frame people, and now this includes a lot of men, too, more and more—what they're capable of doing. It makes a believer out of the women *and* the men, let me tell you.

The more techniques you know for handling an individual, the more things you have in your bag of tricks, the better. You can think, "I'll try this little old trick," and you reach in and pull it out. If that doesn't work, you've got a whole mess of other ones. You've got to build that bag of tricks.

Say you're in a crowded apartment. There's a fight between Mom and Pop. Pop pulls a knife. Do you go for your gun? If you do, you're dead. You need twenty-one feet between you and an attacker for you to use your gun.

In that knife situation, I'll go to a blocking blow with my arm in front of my face. I'll see blood, but it'll be from my arm, it won't be from my jugular vein. I won't die from it.

I know from teaching these classes—women can do these things. They can handle themselves in a confrontation. There's no reason why a woman cannot do the job of police work on the street. There's physically nothing to preclude a woman from doing the job. I don't care how small she is. It's a matter of mind-set and training. And those are *learnable* skills.

Unfortunately, what's happened in the whole state of Washington is they've gotten rid of any type of physical requirement at all. And you don't have to pass the physical now. The majority of it is because a lot of women couldn't, and they're looking out for women, as an affirmative action thing. What they originally did was lower their standards to accommodate women. Even then, a lot of women couldn't pass it. So now, they just lowered the standards to a point where there really are none. I think it's totally ridiculous.

It was very rigorous when I went through in 1977. You had to do so many push-ups, sit-ups, squat thrusts. You had to pick up a 160-pound dummy, you had to run up, pick it up, put it up on your chest, and drag it along about a quarter to a half a football field.

When I first wanted to be a cop, I knew that I would have to do that. So I'd go drag my ex-husband around a football field. I knew even *then* he was a dead weight.

It was very hard when I went through, but then when I taught at the State of Washington Police Academy, it wasn't hard at all. Very, very minimal requirements for men *and* women. While I was there, they were looking at completely getting rid of it, and I fought that tooth and nail. Right after I left, they just completely got rid of requirements.

It's a terrible thing. It's a complete liability. It's one of those things where what they've done to help women actually hurts them.

What they've done to accommodate women, to me, is utterly patronizing. In the fifteen years I've been here, they've lowered their physical standards; as far as promotional standards, they have a white males' list, a women's list, a black persons' list. In my mind, what they're saying to women is you're not capable of competing fairly. We have to make exceptions for you. It's patronizing. It's really a put-down.

Now that the Academy has gotten rid of any type of a physical requirement, I think some women are happy about that, it makes things easier. But by the same token, they aren't competing fairly. They've lowered the standards, everyone knows that. And how can you expect men to respect you or feel you can do an equal job if basically you aren't even physically capable and nobody's expecting you to be?

We have a great controversy going on in Dallas. For some reason, the police administration put out a survey that asked, "Do you think women would like to have more practice in Defensive Tactics and if so, why? How would you like to have this class?"

A lot of women, apparently, responded that maybe they were not as comfortable with it as a behavior that they would automatically do and that they really would like to have a temporary class, maybe one or two classes, only women, and then disband it so that the women, especially the veterans, would be able to participate in a mixed class because they don't want to be embarrassed.

All of a sudden, the controversy is that it's illegal to have an all-women's class and that they're going to get themselves in a liability problem. They see it as discriminatory to males.

I thought it was funny. Why did they put out the survey if they didn't want to hear the response? And secondly, they do everything for everybody else; why not take the tack that hey, the women are willing to do this, they're even willing to say that it be temporary—let's do it and get it over with? To me, that's just common sense.

I was teaching Verbal Judo to rookies in the Academy a couple years ago. Basically, what this course is is how to talk to people without losing your cool and without getting real pissed off. Teaching rookies is a lot of fun because you can tell them to light their hair on fire and they think you're right, you know?

They're so eager. They don't know the real world yet. They don't know how bad it is. They still think they're going to go out and solve the world's problems. And as funny as that is . . . it's still kind of refreshing.

I taught Defensive Tactics at the Academy in 1991. The way I taught, not everything is for everybody. This involved the males as well. I would teach that you have to understand your limitations and work with those limitations. If you get someone who's 220 pounds and solid muscle, you're not gonna walk up to him and try to put some type of hold on him when all he's gotta do is flick you off; you know, you're gonna go and apply something *else* that will take him down a little quicker where you can *then* get him under your control. You have to know your limitations.

The males also. There are some males out there—they think because they are men that they can walk up to someone—even if they're 5'10" or 145 pounds—they think they can walk up to someone that's 220 pounds and make them conform physically. And you can't, unless you have this extreme background in martial arts. If you look at people who have a martial arts background, they do things that are—smart. That's how they get over on people. They don't go for the obvious; they go for the things that people don't even think about, the weak spots.

We all have a lot of weak spots. That's what I would teach the cadets: You're only as strong as your weakest point. If somebody catches you in that weak spot, you're down and out, I don't care how big you are. So understand that and know your limitations.

When I initially went to the Academy, the plan for me was to solely deal with the female cadets. That didn't bother me so much as the attitude behind it. They were creating the impression that females only deal with females, males deal with males, and that we cannot work together. My biggest battle was that we're not there to teach separate ideas like that; we were there to teach them all together, and teach them that they could work with one another. I went around in circles with the heads of the Academy on that one.

It's all a matter of conditioning. Women are conditioned to believe you can only do so much and that you cannot possibly lift yourself up—the thing that I've always heard is that women are weak in their upper body. Well, *anyone's* gonna be weak in their upper body if they don't use it. Period. If you use it, you train, you work out, you exercise, you're gonna build muscle.

When I first went to the Academy, they would have females do certain exercises that were quite different from the males'. I was against that. They were setting an attitude. They were telling the females: "You're *only* expected to do this" and telling the males: "See, this is *all* they're expected to do, this is *all* they're capable of doing, so when they hit the street there's *also* gonna be a difference there."

My attitude was they're all police officers and we're gonna train them all as police officers. If they can't hack it, they can't hack it, but in six months, if you've got the capability of physically training people, you're gonna train even the worst person to be physically fit, to handle the requirements of the job. If the student wants to do it, they're gonna do it.

We went around and around over that—one of the other excuses was for males and their sit-ups: Males can't do as many sit-ups as females because their center of gravity makes it more difficult. That's asinine. Prove it to me. Women have been conditioned to do sit-ups ever since they were little girls, whereas boys have not been conditioned to do that. It's not that they *can't* do it, it's just a little difficult.

I always pull my students to the side, the weaker ones, the ones who were not able to pass the physical standards we had set, and there were just as many males as females. But what they were doing, they were overlooking the males and their inadequacies because they were so focused on the females. By the end of the six months of their training, some of the men were having difficulty passing the physical requirements. Their inadequacies were being ignored, and then four months into the Academy, when they were being graded and their job was on the line, then it was too late. I told them, just because they're males you can't say they're capable of doing everything. They're not. You should look at them as individuals instead of by sex. If you train, *anybody* can pass the requirements in six months.

I realized this when I started weight training. I wanted to be able to handle myself and be able to do normal, everyday things without having to rely on someone else, to be able to pick up a twenty-pound bag without having to rely on someone else. I started weight training long before it was popular. Then I realized that what was always said about females was not true. It was not true. I had always been told you can't do this and you can't do that and it's not true. You have your limitations, and some of that has to do with your size, but that's not a hindrance—you can develop yourself where you can handle your own body and help yourself.

They had a lot of problems with my approach. I didn't have problems training the cadets, the people at the Academy just had problems with my ideas simply because they didn't *want* me to speak up that way. I was supposed to be there just to serve the female cadets and just for the minor little things, whenever they had menstrual problems or something like that.

They did *not* want me to train; they did not want me out there as a trainer when in fact that's what I was out there to do; I was there to train. Because I was so defiant, they kind of left me out on a limb to work by myself.

They didn't like my training and my ideas because it went against theirs. They wanted to create that perception that women were second-rate officers. Within a year, I was no longer teaching at the Academy.

I come from a very athletic background. For me, going to the LAPD Academy a few years ago, I would drive there every morning so excited and a big smile on my face, thinking, "I cannot believe they are paying me to study and to work out." I felt like I was in college again on my athletic scholarship.

It was just a wonderful, wonderful experience. I never saw any type of discrimination, any type of derogatory comment up there, from my classmates to the instructors. Never.

In our Crisis Intervention Unit, they talk about domestic violence, cultural diversity, sexual harassment, and sexual orientation. We have a whole Behavioral Science Unit that comes in, these people have doctorates, they come in and basically, over and over and over again, it's pounded into you—this is how you talk to different cultures. Those of you that have been raised in a white middle-class culture, coming to L.A. is a culture shock—where Asians might do this, Hispanics might do something else, blacks might do something else—"Women, don't be offended if the Hispanics or the Asians talk only to your male partner." We have to adapt to their culture.

Takedown tactics. If you're a 280-pound male, or you're a 120-pound female, it doesn't matter because these particular techniques they teach you can work really on anybody, excluding a few of them. Wristlocks and twist locks I cannot perform on a 6′4″ male since I'm 5′4″. You have to be of equal height or taller to use those particular techniques.

But you've got a whole grab bag of techniques. They

move you through and they teach men and women the exact same thing, anything from various moves and locks that can work on *anybody*. It doesn't matter. It's all technique.

I was in the NYPD Academy in 1993. From the beginning, the instructors were very strict, and they have to be just to give people a feel for the kind of stuff they'll have to deal with. The first month, about a hundred people dropped out. You know, it was somewhat tough. It was like boot camp.

I thought it was fantastic. Three courses and you work out. I couldn't believe I was getting paid to take classes and work out.

The women were treated no different from the men when it came to working out and the Physical Training part: You had to do the runs, push-ups, sit-ups, whatever; when it got to the point where we were working with the tactics with the handcuffs, women were expected to be able to pull a guy down to the ground just like our male counterparts were—you're a female, that's no excuse, you're a cop. We're all people in blue here.

While I was in the Academy, I was thinking, "When I get a partner, I'm gonna want him to be just as physically fit as me." Whoever can do the better job, that's who I want to work with—that's the general attitude.

I was hired by the San Jose Police Department in '76. By the time I got through, I was probably about the sixth woman that had gone through the Academy. We were constantly being questioned by the other recruits about "Well, what are you gonna do when a fight starts?" And we were very young; I was twenty-six, you know, you're not all that . . . So I'd say, "Well, you know, I'd just fight as hard as I *could*," you know.

Now I know what I'd say: "Same thing as you, asshole."

I get thunderstruck when I look back. I live so much day to day and week to week, just, you know, taking care of the job and the kids and the household and the dogs and the cats that when I stop and think how much time has actually passed and how far I've come . . .

How far *we've* come. I mean, the kids were there with me when I was so sore from doing push-ups and running that I couldn't lift my arms over my head. And one would take one arm and the other would take the other—I'd be laying flat on the floor—and they'd be stretching my arms over my head just so I could—function.

It was traumatic. I had a lot of pressure as far as knowing, if I don't make this, what am I going to do? I gave up my security at my old job so I've got to make it through this one.

The academic part wasn't that hard for me. The physical part was. I had guys encouraging me and taking me aside during breaks in class and watching me do my push-ups to make sure I was doing them right. I had guys who would finish their run and come back to me and run *with* me, encouraging me to run a little faster, dig a little deeper.

One of the guys—he would actually get down on the floor with me, doing push-ups. In between breaks and at lunch and whenever the thought occurred to him, he'd say, "Rickie! Hit it!"

And the guys were always . . . we had a situation where we would run through the woods. And they had routes, trails and stuff, and they would run a certain distance and then get down and do push-ups and jumping jacks, until everybody caught up that was behind. And I was always behind. My first goal was to be able to run the whole distance. My second goal was to stay in position, stay with the group the whole run.

The guys . . . we had a lot of people who were sprinters, runners, and could do this and stay in the group and no problem. None of them ever gave us a hard time because we fell behind. None of them. None of them. Nobody gave you a hard time. They encouraged you: "Come on! Run harder! Run faster!" But nobody ever got on your ass about falling behind.

My husband came on the job when it was all men. I came on the job with men and women. So with my class there was more unity, there was more a college atmosphere, there was more of a "We'll help you with the run."

As we were running our timed laps on the outside of the

track, the men would be on the inner circle, and they would run with us, encouraging us, running right along with us, saying, "Come on. You can do it. Keep doing it." And you need that encouragement. And at that last burst they'd say, "Now you gotta *sprint* the rest of the way! You gotta really kick it in!" And we would. And we made it.

CHAPTER 4

THE HOUSE

In police parlance, your "house," many times, is the police facility—precinct house, station house—you work out of. If you're with the NYPD, "house" has a broader sweep: NYPD cops call their entire precincts, everything and everybody in them, their "houses" and judge other cops by whether or not they work in an "A" (high-crime) house. To some extent, you own your house, whether it's the station house or the area you patrol. But the house also owns you.

You cannot escape who you are and how you're accepted in the house. Everything in the house marks your place. Where do you sit at roll call? Who sits with you? What's in your mailbox? Do you appear in a glorious, shameful, or scatological light in drawings, poems, and doctored news clippings posted on the bulletin board? What happens when you approach a group? What happens when you tell a war story?

Station-house culture shows who's in, who's out, who doesn't stand a chance. Rewards and punishments are meted out physically—who sits where with whom, who's included/excluded from groups, who's listened to and who's ignored. Of all the indicators of how you're doing in the house, the most devastating punishment is to be ostracized. Silence in the station house. You're no longer there. That's death to any cop.

The house is a mirror of police culture. This chapter shows how women cops have coped with a house that can be riotous fun or turn into the loneliest place around . . .

I remember the first whore I ever saw on the job—I was walking into the Twentieth District for processing; I looked over behind the desk, and the desk is one of those elevated kinds, the old-fashioned kind; and maybe a half-dozen policemen there, writing reports, bonding people out, a desk sergeant, people answering phones. And there's this whore running around, with no top on, with her boobs hanging out—running around behind the desk, screaming and yelling. And everyone else is minding their own business; they're on the phone; they're writing bonds, taking reports; they're talking—and she's running around screaming, "Hey, how do you like these, coppers?"—you know— and I looked over and I said, "Oh, man!" You know, I thought that was the norm. What did I know? What did I know?

One thing you learn as a cop. Every desk crew on every watch has its own personality. It's like one single personality. You can have a desk crew that's a lot of fun, you can have a desk crew of dogs, and you can have a desk run by total assholes. It's really weird.

If you ever go to a police facility in New York City, never take the coffee unless you want to have the runs for three days. That's one thing the show "Barney Miller" got right— remember that guy who made horrible coffee? That's absolutely true in every station house in the NYPD, the coffee is always *terrible*.

Every NYPD facility has rats. A while ago, they discovered the holding cells were rat-infested. They shut them down. The police officers' locker rooms are also rat-infested. Those were *not* shut down.

It's asbestos city around here. You go into a police department lounge—there are always mice in there. It's horrible.

Other police departments have beautiful facilities; they're incredible. The NYPD has seventy-five precincts, we're the sixth largest standing army in the world, and the conditions in our station houses are *horrible*. But you sort of like it, you know? It gives a certain *character*.

In 1957, there were just about one hundred women on the LAPD. When I went to the Seventy-seventh, I was told: "You don't have to go to roll call. The guys play around in there. They talk dirty. You don't want to be offended." But that's where the information is exchanged. I sat in the office while the men went to roll call.

Very soon after I came in, the Watts car would come in. Two black officers. They didn't go to roll call, either.

I used to talk to them, try to be nice, offer them coffee. My partner, seeing me bringing them coffee one night, took me aside and said, "This is not good. Don't be so cozy." I learned the truth about life fast.

I want people to know this was the LAPD because we've come so far. When I came on, there was this open prejudice against blacks, there was segregation in the department and brutality on the streets. When I look back on what it was like when I came on, I realize how far we've come.

I can remember when I was working as a juvenile investigator in the Watts Substation in the fifties. Some young white officers, uniformed officers, brought a black man in, a suspect in something.

They brought him in there. That station is sort of isolated over there on 103rd Street. They brought him in and took him into a backroom at the station. And I was concerned about that because I'm wondering—patrol officers weren't actually assigned out of that station. There was a desk man and the Juvenile Unit in there. And that was *it*. And these uniform officers came in and brought this man in and went into a backroom.

So anyway, they were back there awhile and I heard some loud talking. So I decided to go back there and see what was going on. They were sort of browbeating this guy. When I walked in, they were a little startled—they had his identification laying out on a desk, and he was sitting there handcuffed, sitting there in a chair handcuffed. And they're kind of walking around. And when I walked in, one of them grabbed a card off the desk and said, "Look at this! He belongs to the NAACP!"

And I looked at him and I said, "And I do also. So?"

And I think they got the message because they left with him. But I—I'm saying that there are some practices that had gone on *for years* that were accepted that were not right.

I'm not saying this was confined to the fifties; it went on for years. It still *does* go on. That's the whole point.

What I was trying to convey to them was you don't come *here* and beat up a prisoner. *I'm* here. I hear what's going on. You don't do it here.

Women can keep men from doing stupid things, you know—as in *real* stupid? Prior to women getting on the job, I guess they had their locker-room pranks, you know, their dumb pranks they'd play on each other. Seemed like, all those dumb kind of pranks diminished somewhat with women coming on; it changed their focus. They were like, oh, well, we don't want to look like *complete* assholes. So we won't be doing *this* much longer.

Men love to play pranks and jokes on each other. They could open up their locker to anything: It could be filled up with condoms or sex toys. They could give a phone number out to some poor, unsuspecting female on the street who's a cop groupie and next thing, this woman is trying to tail him and he has no interest. They sort of calmed down their pranks. A lot of that crap calmed down.

You know, like the old bucket-of-water-over-the-door routine. Because we asked them like, "Is that really necessary? What does that prove?" And they're like, "Well . . . I guess . . . it's . . . stupid." Or the men would get into the "dozens," the put-downs and all that. And I'm like, "What does that prove?" "Oh, you're no fun." "Yeah. But why? What is the meaning behind this?" And they're like, "Yeah. I guess you're right."

Before, maybe they would rough-handle a prisoner. Well, they may or may not, depending on how the prisoner behaves. They may or may not rough-handle the prisoner. Or play a joke. See, a lot of cops say, "Oh, yeah. He tripped down the steps." But with a woman present—nah, they're not gonna do that. They're not gonna be apt to be that crazy.

Or men like to gun-play and do all kinds of stupid things when the supervisor's not looking. Well, if they got a woman partner around, they're not gonna do that, either.

As long as it's a boy's club, they can do anything they

want. But as soon as girls get into the club, they're like, "Well, wait a minute, I'm gonna see how she's gonna react." Yeah. So women do have an effect on them. But it's still a boys' club.

When I was on light duty for a little bit and I had to work the desk and it was Christmastime, buying stuff for the bosses' girlfriends—that was my only job. Every day, they'd give me a couple hundred dollars and I'd go down to Water Tower Place and I'd have to buy perfume, maybe jewelry, and a sexy nightie. "What size does she wear?" "Well, she's about as big as that girl over there."

And some of the guys that I hated, I'd buy the most atrocious, ugly nightgown and the worst cologne I ever smelled in my life. Just to piss them off.

When I become superintendent, things are gonna be different! I'm gonna have a cute male driver. He's gonna take me to get my manicures—somebody to do all that bullshit—my lunch. Yeah. "Get some clothes for my boy-friend!" "Christmas is coming—here's a hundred bucks. Go buy my boyfriend a nice pair of silk boxer shorts for him, will you? Something tasteful and silk. And here—buy yourself a pair while you're at it."

The new guys come in. They're talked to and they're shown where the coffee machine is and where their new desk is. I walked in my first day and nobody looked up. It's just automatic.

You know, I guess it stings a little bit. I wish I couldn't read faces like I can, I wish I was a little dizzier—and that would go a long way because I do not have a poker face. I wear everything on my face. And I get hurt. I'm much better now, though; my skin is about ten feet deep.

But when you first come on and you watch your male counterparts just get accepted so easily and you walk in and you're just chastised and ostracized, it hurts. It's a lot of hurt.

You watch the eye contact in a circle when you've been introduced. And the conversation is between the men. Because their eyes are speaking to each other. Very, very seldom do you get the eye contact. You may be in the circle with the guys, but very seldom do you get the eye contact.

I can't believe the atmosphere is still like this—I'm talking to a coworker in Homicide and he pulls out a centerfold. Right in front of me. Doesn't bat an eye. In our station house, there are pictures pasted up all over. One is a poster of a frog with a hard-on. These are your coworkers.

There used to be a poster; it shows the back side of a car with some women bent over it in string bikinis. They bring people in here for interviews! We have to bring people in here. They're not doing it to be malicious; it's just stupid.

When you work Sex Crimes, you have to be real careful not to take the victims through the Homicide offices that are loaded with porn. That's a real challenge.

There's the insanity of the role-playing that a lot of females have to get into. I think I should speak for myself. Maybe not all the females in the department feel like I do, but it doesn't come natural to me to just start saying, "Hey, you! Come here." I mean, I was brought up in Catholic schools—it'd be easier to say, "Excuse me, I hope I'm not bothering you, but . . ."

When I was a recruit in the Mission Station, I had a sergeant that made me go downstairs and go "Hey, you! Get over here!" in the full-length mirror. "Lower your voice. Speak from the diaphragm." Voice command. Your presence should command—which is a joke, there is no respect for the police out there anymore—"Hey, you! Stop!"

I mean it. I had to go downstairs to talk to this full-length mirror. I forget if it was in a gym or whatever, but they used to have a full-length mirror. And my sergeant used to make me go down and he would like say, "Okay! You! Stop!" And I would have to repeat him and look in the mirror and say, "Okay! You! Stop!" I used to feel so stupid. It made me feel stupid. Then I'd be down there by myself going, "All right, you!" Who was that guy? Jimmy Cagney? I felt so *stupid* down there.

Whenever it worked, I thought, "Phew! Jeez, they listened

to me." And if they didn't, then I jumped on them immediately. You just go get them; you go for the throat.

1980. My first day in the precinct. My first roll call. Oh, Christ. Here we have the police union delegate—you have no choice; you belong to the union. This is a person that's supposed to be representing me. So what does he do? He gets flowers, and he acts like a flower girl as I'm coming to my very first roll call. Strewing rose petals in my path.

And when I get into the roll-call room, lo and behold, the podium, where the sergeant is supposed to be addressing us from, is decorated with sanitary napkins and tampons. And they all stood there watching what my reaction was going to be. And the sergeant, I felt so sorry for him, he was an older man, when he walked in and he saw that, the man wanted to die. He was like, "Get this stuff outta here!" Not that he knew what it was, but he knew it couldn't be anything too flattering.

I sat there and smiled. I said, "I might need those in the near future. Don't throw them away." That was a good answer, but no one would work with me. None of the other officers would work with me.

I think it's a rite of passage. I don't think it's especially PD. I think any job you go to, you have certain rites of passage. I really never felt I was being tested all the time, just certain times, like when you're brand-new. I really didn't feel that way throughout my career.

There were other things. There were other little incidents, I mean really awful stuff.

One thing—what happened was, the sergeants—they have a locker room and they eat in their locker room. And the officers eat in like a kitchen. There's kind of an unofficial thing that bosses don't eat in the kitchen, you know what I mean? They eat where they got to eat, and officers eat in the kitchen.

But I was a boss, I was a sergeant, and I had no place to eat. I had no locker room. So I think, "Well, the kitchen really *is* open to everybody, in the main areas."

So I go in the kitchen this day and I eat my lunch. And— there was nothing on the walls.

The next day, I go in again. And I swear to God, you're not gonna believe this, but I did not notice this until I was getting ready to leave. On the wall across from me were pictures of vaginas—not women, just the vagina, cut out. And there was about—I guess there must have been about at least fifty of them. Can you *imagine,* you couldn't even tell what that *was* in pictures all posted together.

So anyway, I look up, and suddenly it dawns on me what it is, and I was—shocked. And I didn't know how to handle it. So I go outside and I get my driver and I say, "Let's take . . ." and I go—"Just keep going around the block." I'm trying to figure out what the hell am I gonna do here? We were gone five minutes.

I go back and I say, "That's it. I'm taking it down." I go back in the station house, I walk into the kitchen, you know—*angry*—and there's guys sitting there eating, and I look up—the pictures are gone.

That fast. They did it specifically for me. As soon as I left, the pictures came down. Because they knew. They knew. And I don't know what they expected—I couldn't blame it on anybody, I don't know who did it.

But I'll tell you, it was really shocking. I said to myself, "They hate me. They *hate* me to do this."

As time went on, they began to see that I was a person that would take on responsibility and do my job and the relationship became quite good there. But it takes time.

We kept our briefcases in a public rack, a public rack in the Write-Up Room. And I went and got my briefcase one time and opened it up and there's this huge dildo in there.

I mean, they had their fun. They had their fun. I hate to say it wasn't malicious because some of it really was. There were some people that were just really malicious. And I think there were some people that were just sitting back waiting to see if women could do it. I guess I feel two ways about it. One, it is kind of malicious. Two, on the other hand, they do things to males, too, that are pretty tacky.

You know the mailboxes in a police station, right?—little boxes that have your name? After I came on, in 1976, constantly, they would take my name strip off and move the others next to it. Every day I'd come in and have no mailbox again. I'd have to go to the front office—"Can I have a mailbox?"—and they'd have to move them all apart again. They went to a lot of effort.

I came in one day and found a used sanitary napkin in my mailbox. My friend found one in hers, too.

I walked into a man's domain when I got transferred into the SWAT Unit. There had never been a woman there at all.

The first thing I find when I walk in is "The Boner of the Month" award. This thing is a plaque that says "Boner" on the top, and it has this huge rubber dildo thing hanging off of it. You know, like the male penis. The thing's got to be six to seven to eight inches long, obviously not made in their own image.

It was a joke among them. It was given every month for the biggest screw-up, whoever did the funniest screw-up, then they got the Boner of the Month award. And they'd leave this thing in their mailbox, this huge rubber hanging dildo thing.

So that was a little disgusting, you know. I laughed it off.

A couple years ago, I got a real tasteless comic in my mailbox. It involved something about the male anatomy being an ALCO-SENSOR, okay? It said, "Blow on this."

And I was just shocked that I got it. And we tracked down the guy that did it. And he said, "Gee, we just figured 'cuz you're so into drunks you would have just thought that would have been really funny. You're one of the guys. What's wrong with you?" Like don't be so sensitive— where's your sense of humor?

Because you know—if you don't laugh along? We had a woman, she's not with us anymore—she *didn't* laugh along. And, boy, she really got ostracized because of that. The worst thing you can do, especially when you're a rookie, is be ostracized. You wonder if you're gonna get backup.

I've never felt mistreated. This is definitely a man's world. You're coming into a man's world here.

A couple years ago, I was the only woman in the Homicide Unit, a team with six to seven guys on it. We had these pigeonhole mailboxes in our office. One day, I go into my box and here are two silicone gel breast implants. The guys probably got them from an autopsy.

Now, I know some women who would go ballistic over something like this. I could have taken something like this and really made a case out of it. But I thought it was hysterical. It was meant as a joke, and I took it as a joke. It's all in how it's meant. If it's meant to be disrespectful, you know it. And some things *are* done that are harassing and disgusting. But this was a joke.

You ignore it. You ignore it. It's no big deal. Like every day. It's very important not to let other policemen know that they're getting to you.

I made this mistake. I read a funny little column by Dave Barry about when you have a song stuck in your head, how you can't get it out. So he said the only way to get rid of it is to give it to somebody else and then it's stuck in *their* head. So I just thought that column was hysterical.

I was sitting up at the desk talking about it and I said, "For me, it's that rotten whistling from *Bridge on the River Kwai*. It makes me nuts. It just makes me nuts." Well, wrong thing to say. Wrong thing. The intercom rings—it's *Bridge on the River Kwai*. The PAX rings. It's *Bridge on the River Kwai*. I walk up to the desk with a prisoner and the whole desk breaks into whistling. I mean, never let them see a chink. Never let them see a chink.

Now the big thing is to learn my "word." A friend of mine can't stand the word "boogers." This is a policewoman. She will just get up and run out of the room. So, we're all sitting around the desk discussing words, you know—most women don't like the "c——" word, you know. So then everybody's going, "What's your word?" I said, "No. I learned with *Bridge on the River Kwai*. I'm not telling you my word."

What do they call it when you go to a place and you're different? This was a place where I was the most unhappy. I was unhappy because a few years ago they sent me to a watch and I was the only black and more than that, I was the only female.

I think being a rookie sometimes you might need a little reassuring and when I got to that district it was like "Do it yourself." In the district I was in the year before, it was like a family. When I got here, it was like nobody wanted to be bothered.

They *don't* talk to you *because* you're a female, and they put you with the derelict cops to work with. You're gonna work with the drunk, you're gonna work with the person nobody wants to work with, you know what I'm saying? But I got this drunk, Tommy, he was so sweet. I really loved him. He was so sweet. He didn't talk down to you. He just talked real nice, and he'd talk to you all night long, slurring all the while.

I was so unhappy I kept putting in a P.A.R. (Personal Action Request) form to get out of the district, and the captain told me, "You're gonna mess up my racial quota." And for three periods I could not get out of that district. I finally got it on my fourth or fifth try; then he told me, "You won't be able to get back." I was like, "If I didn't want to get out, I would've stayed here, you know." But by that time, I *did* want to stay because I had finally gotten a partner I liked, another black woman.

All the suspects we brought in, the supervisors used to tell us that it was usually a white person. It wasn't on purpose, either. They'd say, "Well, can't you find somebody black to arrest?" This is what they would tell us!

We made an arrest one day. A white guy. The guy had robbed somebody. When we brought him in, they would not sign the complaint for him to go in the lockup. We went to the sergeant, we went to the lieutenant, we went to the commander, and it was like three hours later, and they still hadn't signed the paperwork. And they said, "Do better— go get some black person to arrest. We're not gonna put him in our lockup." We went to call downtown; *then* they signed the papers.

They wanted us to go and get the black people. One night they said to us, "Why is everybody you're bringing in here white?" And we looked at each other—we didn't think everybody we were bringing in *was* white. We just shook our heads, kept on doing our work. "Can't you find some blacks to arrest?" People don't believe me when I tell them this. I'm telling the truth.

This one district I was in, they didn't treat me bad. A lot of times, they just acted like I wasn't there. I don't care if people speak to me. I can *work*. It's just—when I *needed* something they weren't helping me. I didn't know where things *were*. I don't care if you speak to me, but if I need to do my job, I can't do it if I can't find the proper paperwork to do it on.

And then if I went to look for it, they'd say, "You're not supposed to be back here."

In 1971, I was promoted to detective. They put me in the Fraud Detail, which I knew absolutely nothing about. Now, I'm really paranoid because I was on probation. And I thought they're gonna try to dump me on my probation, I just know they are, because the animosity, you could cut it with a knife.

They didn't talk to me. They wouldn't teach me anything. One of the first cases I had, I had to do a throw-down of different pictures to see if the victim could identify them. They wouldn't tell me where to get the pictures, they wouldn't show me how to put it together . . . After about the first week, I was just on the verge of tears. I thought, these assholes—they've got me. How am I gonna do this? And, of course, I was reading everything I could about investigations, but it was the procedures that I didn't know anything about.

One day I was in the women's restroom. I was just on the verge of tears. I was in there and I was so upset. And one of the secretaries walked in and she saw me and she turned around and she walked back out. Pretty soon she came back in with four other secretaries. And she said, "We think that what they're doing to you is terrible. We're going to help you. We're going to teach you everything you need to know."

And they *did*. We had meetings in the restroom. They would teach me what the procedures were. And we had a little code where I could walk by and kind of scratch the side of my nose and they'd know that I needed to talk to one of them. And they'd meet me in the restroom and I'd say, "How do you do a Teletype?" So they told me how to do a Teletype. I knew that if *they* got caught telling me, then *they'd* be in trouble. They were wonderful. I tell you, I have a soft spot in my heart for secretaries. I'm always good to secretaries because they saved my bacon.

I really could have failed miserably if it weren't for them. Especially when the men are hiding the ball game from you; they're holding all the cards, and you can't even see what the game plan is. But these women knew it; I mean, they'd been working there for years. And they just weren't going to put up with it. And they really were putting themselves in a dangerous position by helping me. But I never told, and they never got into any trouble.

The matrons in the precincts back in the fifties and sixties—the men treated us like dirt. They'd bring a woman suspect in—"Search her! Hurry up!—I gotta get *outta* here!" You were made to feel like an attendant. We were just a little above the horses.

I worked the lockup a lot, a real lot in 1977. We had a district commander that did not believe in women being at the front desk. We had to be out of sight, back in the lockup. I mean it. If you walked up to the front desk—"What is she doing up here?"

I went up to the front desk with paperwork from the lockup one day, and one of the girls had a new squad car, it was with split seats, first time. So the guys—"Oh! Let's go look!" So I started out the door to go look, too. And the commander is saying, "Sarge! Stop that woman! She's leaving the district!"

The sergeant came back to me, and he put his arm around my shoulder: "Just go back to the lockup. We'll have a drink a little later. *Don't say anything.*" And he walked me back there, and I was furious. I felt like *I* was a prisoner.

Another time, I had been at the front desk bringing up paperwork and the phone was ringing. The commander said, "Officer, when you're up here, answer the phone." The next time I brought up paperwork, a call came, everyone was in roll call. So I went over the loudspeaker: "Tony, call on -93." The commander stopped the whole roll call, one of the sergeants told me later. He said, "She's away from her post again. *What* is she doing at the front desk?" He made a big production that I was not in the lockup.

He got a brain tumor later, and people say maybe that's why he acted like that. But that's not . . . he was just very antiwoman.

It's really hard to explain. There are some people—and it *was* hostile. There are some guys—and it was very hostile. But I would have to honestly say for me the majority of the people—when you first came in, you were like—different, and everybody looked at you and I'm sure they talked about you and everything. But once you were there, if you really tried hard and did your job and really didn't ask for any favors, they kept an open enough mind to accept you. I look back now. It was hard, but I don't think it was everybody. And we have a tendency sometimes to blame *everybody*. It wasn't everybody. It was a few people. The majority of them were actually after a while pretty supportive.

And I have to say, on the other hand, there are a lot of women that *do* dog it. They walk in there and, "Hey, I'm a woman. I want this; I want that." I mean, I've had a long career. I've taught at the Police Academy. I've dealt with women. And they *do*—"Oh, I have female problems; I have this, I have that." And they expect men to understand that. Why should they?

We *do* have some—there are so many women now that some are . . . an embarrassment. Just like some males are. Some are nitwit airhead dipshits. Cutesy.

Most of the guys I receive the most resistance from on this job are my size or smaller. It's funny to go to a call now and a lot of times, the male cops are smaller than I am.

I remember when this one guy got hired, he was the first Asian hired, I remember some of the comments—he's like 5'4", 130 pounds, he's real wiry, very strong. When he first came on, one of the comments I heard one of the guys making down the hallway was "I'd rather work with a woman than him." And, of course, that's supposed to be a compliment for us in the same breath. You're supposed to say, "Well, gosh! Thanks!"

I'm not a particularly tall female, I'm just under 5'7". I worked Internal Affairs for a time, and at that time, three-to-four-inch heels were popular, *the* thing to wear. So, three to four inches on top of my 5'7" put me up there.

The captain who was in charge of Internal Affairs at the time was a very small man with a nervous twitch. He called me "Sergeant Sweetie." It was not really as offensive as it might sound. It was a little bit of—she probably doesn't like this; let's see how long she can keep from showing this bothers her. In not a real malicious way. I don't think he realized how demeaning it could sound to somebody else to call me this.

But . . . I took to doing things that I knew would bother *him*. Like, he had a habit of walking in and walking up to your desk and standing over you so he could talk down to you—that was the only way he could do it.

I'd see him coming in the door and I'd stand up. So now I'm six inches taller than he is. And now he's standing and talking up to me, which would make him very nervous. And for every "Sergeant Sweetie," I would give him a "Captain Dear."

The guys would get hysterical. Our work area was just a large kind of squad-room thing. He would walk up to my desk, and the other guys that were in the unit would see this and behind his back, somebody would then start dancing because he would—twitch. Because he would get nervous at the fact that he had to look up at me. And the guys would be imitating him behind his back, and they'd all twitch around.

In 1974, I had a Trans-Am, I bought a brand-new Trans-Am, black Trans-Am, and in the Sixteenth District, you'd park at an angle, up against the side of the building. So I'd park the car there, not realizing or even thinking that it's directly under the men's bathroom window.

I came out after work and it was a summer day; there were wads of soaking-wet toilet paper that had been thrown out of the window and were *baked* onto the hood of my car. I mean it just literally faded the paint right off. Big blotches, all over, a brand-new car. Wrecked it. I had to have the hood repainted. Oh, I wept. This was my baby.

So then I started parking in the bank lot across the street so they wouldn't mess with my car. So I came out one night, all four tires were cut. The car was flat on the ground. And a Trans-Am, those tires even then were $100-plus apiece.

And then, another time I came out and somebody had taken a toothpick and put it in my driver's lock and snapped it off. So I couldn't get in the car, I had to take it in, they had to pull all the locks out, all this kind of stuff. This was just constant. It was constant.

And then I started parking a block and a half away. And I came out one night, my windshield and both side windows were Crazy-Glued with pornography of a white woman and a black man—my partner was a black man. Totally destroyed it. I had to have those windows replaced.

The pornography they put on the window . . . it was all carefully pieced together. Cut a naked black man out of something . . . they made it; I mean, sat there and *worked* at it. It was created, a created thing. A pornographic collage.

I contacted Internal Affairs then. I had already gone to the watch commander over and over. So I contacted Internal Affairs and went down there and made a statement and told them all the shit that was going on and they said that they would do surveillance.

But what clowns they are! They have a van that looks like People's Gas, kind of gray with a dull yellow stripe. I came into work one day—one of the guys that was friendly said, "I don't know what you're up to, but you better watch your step because Internal Affairs is watching you." I said, "What!" He's like warning me because he thinks I'm like moving out of the city or doing something nasty. I said, "How do you know?" This is at roll call. He says, "I saw that van. They have this stupid truck. So I took the plate down and I called the garage and I asked them who signed out that vehicle." And they gave him the unit number—

Internal Affairs. That's real secret. So that ended the surveillance; there was no point; everybody knew it.

Nasty times.

At roll call! The roll-call room was a very large area; you had two long tables with two long benches at each table, and on the four-to-twelve shift, quite a few officers were there to attend roll call. And there the room would be with my female partner and me sitting at one table by ourselves—we had our own table—and the rest of the watch sat across the room at the other table. A fifteen-foot-long table. It was ours.

Whoever got there first—if one of us got to one table, all the men would sit at the other table. If the next day, I sat at that one, they'd all sit at the other one. Even my male partner. Because he had to get along with the guys, too. They all kind of felt sorry for our partners, as though they were the sacrificial lambs, so our partners had an image to keep up, too. Not going over to the other side.

In 1984, I was assigned to a watch, six to about three in the morning—the machos of the machos worked that watch. They *hated* women. And I was a woman. There was another woman on the watch, but she was like a guy, had that truck driver's mouth? I never played one of the guys.

My first day in roll call, they asked me, "Well, what do we call you?" And I said, "Well, gee, a lot of people call me Mac. I was raised with that nickname." And one of the guys said, "We ain't callin' you that because we already have a Mac and he's been here twenty years." "Well, then, just don't call me anything—well, then, Jones is fine." You try to pick yourself up.

They did things that were just horrifying. I don't even like to think about it. You have to understand I'm very proud and I knew that I was good at what I did, so this was all horrifying.

Roll call one night. My regular partner was off, so they assigned me to some guy. He stood up and he said, "I ain't workin' with her. I'm sick." And this is in front of roll call, in front of everybody. Talk about public humiliation. And I stood up and I said, "He doesn't have to be sick. *I* just got sick." And I stood up, and I walked out.

That's how they were: cold, callous. And, basically, they won that day because I went home. I should have stuck it out. But I turned them around. I only stayed eight months, but I vowed, "I am not leaving until I've won them over." And I did.

In our department, when you first come out of the Academy, you have to sit in the front row at roll call. And then as you gain time on the job, you get to move back further. So most of the older guys sit in the back. And everybody else, who's kind of in the middle of their careers, sits in the middle.

So there's this division right away. The newer people, who are primarily women, only sit in the front. You are constantly reminded by these various things that you have less time on, you have less respect.

When I first went to patrol, in 1984, at least on the watch that I worked, there was only one other woman on, and she had been on about fifteen years. But she only worked the desk. She didn't work the field. So once my probation was over, I started sitting in the back. The men couldn't handle it. They felt a loss of control. I got so many comments from them on an individual basis—"Oh, it's because you have a *college degree* you think you can sit in the back," that kind of thing.

It's not unusual—you'd be assigned to work with somebody at roll call. You wouldn't know who this person is because you're new. Well, they wouldn't come up and introduce themselves to you. They'd walk out of the roll call and go downstairs and you'd have to ask these people, "Who's so-and-so?" Their usual comment is, "Go get the equipment." So you'd have to go in, you'd have to carry your kit bag, which has your helmet and all your books and everything, the shotgun, a Taser [stun gun], two Rovers [Remote Out-of-Vehicle Emergency Radios], and the car keys. So here you are walking out, loaded down with about a hundred pounds of stuff, and here's this guy just strolling ahead of you.

But they treat *both* the new men and women that way.

When I went to another station, in 1991—I think there

are still problems, but you don't see nearly as much of it as I saw when I first came on the job. And if there *was,* I was in a position to do something about it. Because now I'm a sergeant.

We had a representative from our district's gay community at roll call one morning. When he was done speaking, he asked if there were any questions. One of the old-timers, this old-time wagon guy, said, "Don't you think it would be a better idea if someone from the PD was a liaison to the gay community? You know, like one of the broads on the job because they're all dykes anyhow." I was the only female officer in the room. I'm sure I turned red. I just couldn't believe it. I had no one to look to for support or someone just to make a face at. I *didn't* have anyone.

People that have experienced some form of harassment—the unspoken is that you're supposed to tolerate it, it goes with the territory. And those that don't, lines are drawn; those who have had an alliance with you may not after you've spoken out.

I speak of this from personal experience from being in a squad where I had experienced comments being made concerning gays and blacks. There was this one male officer who continually made comments about gays, called them faggots and "I don't know why these fruitcakes should be treated any different" and "I don't know why we have to do special things for queers."

One day at roll call, a few years ago, they had a memorandum come out that if somebody was deaf, they needed to have an interpreter there for him. And this man made the comment back: "Do we have to have that for queers, too?" It pushed my button. I admit it.

The supervisor, the lieutenant at the time, had been in different roll calls and had heard this person make different comments, would kind of roll his eyes, but he never did anything about it. I talked with him, and I talked with the officer twice. Then I filed a complaint. The attitude was if somebody does something just buck up, take it, suck it up, live with it.

The people that were responsible and should have changed things didn't take responsibility. Males that previously thought you were just one of the guys and tolerable, the tables were turned, they no longer wanted to talk with you—you were now nothing but the bitch. They wanted to push it back on you that you had a problem with yourself.

The department's stand is, if you have a problem being called a nigger, that's *your* problem. You should be able to accept that. They make *you* the problem. It's not the problem that the person is saying that to you, it's the problem that you have with it being said. That's what happens.

With me, being a woman on the department has been an ongoing struggle. My saturation point, I guess, has been met and I'm not gonna take any more. Though I do draw the line at being gay and being out. Too much pressure. Too much flak.

I mean, they really do not care for women on the department. And then to be outwardly gay—I mean, they may suspect it, and as long as it's not talked about, there's no problem with it.

It's my feeling that if I were to let it be known that I am gay, that I would be ostracized. So, even though I say I don't buy into the system and the old-time mentality, I guess I do to a certain extent. I cannot leave this profession and make as good money as I do now. So I have to buy into a certain amount of what's going on.

But my biggest fear is that if someone were ever to ask me, "Are you gay?" I would have to say, "Yes, I am gay," and then I'd be ostracized.

They refer to the women who have been pretty much out—I just remember when I was on first watch, they're bastards, bottom line, but they were making a reference to one of the gay women and one of them was about to say "dyke." And I just cupped my hands and said, "Go ahead. Speak into my microphone because I'm gonna retire on what you're about to say." He didn't say shit.

If I came out, or someone yelled the fact that I was gay over the PA system or something like that, I would have people that would continue talking with me. But they might not want to be seen with me outside the workplace for fear they'd be associated with me.

It's so subtle. Some of the gay men have been *trashed* through the years. There's women, there's quite a few women on our department who are gay, but they don't come right out and say, "I'm gay" because there's no point. But those who have said, "I *am* gay. I take offense at what you have to say about gay people"—they take a big risk. I was in a sensitivity training about a year ago and I was in, unfortunately, a group of *turds* and the issue of homosexuality on the department came up—oh, my God.

Although I don't live in fear of it . . . I signed up my partner on our domestic partnership plan, which allows me and anybody else who has a lifelong companion to sign them up for medical and dental benefits. Not that many people have taken advantage of this plan because they're fearful. They're fearful because it takes a certain amount of risk to go ahead and say, "Yeah. I'm gay." They say it's confidential. We'll see.

If a male is in a relationship with a man—oh, God. Don't—don't ever step on that one. Bad things can really happen there. And if someone knows that I'm in a relationship with a woman, they're going to make life rough.

It just needs to be a more comfortable environment. I was very, very accepted until I complained about offensive language in roll call. I didn't even complain—the lieutenant heard that this one officer was constantly using language referring to gays and lesbians. He complained and had me make a statement. There was a hearing. From that point on, I've been ostracized. Silently.

I can walk down the hall and they'll walk the other way or they'll look the other way. What happened to me about six months ago, I was coming out of my office. And one of the guys, he's in patrol, and he was one of the vocal ones at the hearing, he came walking out of another office at the end of the hall. He didn't have anywhere else to go. He turned around, he wanted to go back into that office, like he looked around like, "Gee, I forgot something. I know I did." But he just kept walking, and his eyes were focused on the wall away from me.

And I just kept looking at him. I thought, "Fuck it. What is it?" You know?

The psycho sergeant. This is going on in another precinct, but it was written about in our newsletter. Apparently, this male sergeant is harassing many of the women, but one in particular is filing a complaint against him. And, believe it or not—when I heard this, I couldn't believe it—the men in the precinct are supporting the woman. The *men* are backing her, and that is really unique. That's how bad this guy is supposed to be. I mean, this guy must be *hated*.

From the information I got, there was a female sergeant that convinced this woman to come forward and make a complaint, and then this female supervisor disappeared on her, wouldn't even back up the female that came forward. That's terrible.

The men gave the female officer, from what I understand, a standing ovation at roll call the next day.

There's a sexual harassment case pending. And what's very interesting, what they brought up . . . This woman is filing a sexual harassment case against a particular boss. And I understand that this woman dressed extremely provocative going both to and from work continually. After she was finished with work, she would hang out at the desk and talk to the guys and she would prolong her stay beyond the tour in very provocative dress.

Apparently, what happened was, she was dating a boss and he was treating her special and the guys . . . anyway, they *did* sexually harass her.

The thing that's interesting is that the commander asked a female supervisor to have a discussion with her. And one of the things the female supervisor brought up with this woman was that she felt that her dress was inappropriate. And what I find interesting is the fact that—I truly doubt that anytime in the history of the New York City Police Department that a male supervisor has sat down with a male police officer and said, "I think your dress is inappropriate. It's sexual." It's kind of a sad commentary. We have a double standard.

You would not believe what some of these women go to work in. It's not just them. The guys, too. The guys wear thong shorts—ass shorts—and spaghetti shirts to work. And then they change to uniform. And the women with the halter tops and short skirts and thongs—I tell you what it is, it's as small as a headband.

There was a female in the Major Case Squad that brought a sexual harassment suit against a sergeant. What the Police Department did was to take him from one side of the partition and put him right next door to a squad that had five women.

I happened to get along very well with him. But, one day, in fact, more than once, when I went into his office to say where I was going on a case, he'd say to me, "What? You never wear a skirt. You never wear a dress in here," he says. "I don't think you like men." So I said to him, I really was taken aback, so I said to him, "You know, sergeant, I don't dress for your pleasure. When I come to work, I don't know if it's gonna be a kidnapping, I don't know if I'm gonna get stuck with a collar . . . I wear what I feel is comfortable and appropriate attire." I said, "You'd like to see me . . . you'd like to see me in a short skirt with fishnet stockings and high heels, wouldn't you? I'm not here to dress for your pleasure." He was like taken aback.

We had a wonderful relationship until . . . One night, he says to me, "Why don't I come over to your apartment? I'll bring the lobsters and wine." He was starting to get a little . . . And this was the guy who has a sexual harassment suit hanging over his head! And they put him in a squad with five—they didn't punish him—they put him in a squad with five women.

You become more and more feminist as you go along in this job. God help you if you started out as one! Men in my office say, "Well, you're just a feminist." And finally I said to one of them, "Tom, what *is* a feminist?" And I waited . . . I waited. He never answered me.

The thing is, they'll call you that and yet, what is it? Is a feminist to them anyone who won't put up with men's bullshit? That stands on their own?

They label you and yet they're not able to tell you what it is.

When I was promoted to P-III, training officer, a division in South Central L.A., my first day of roll call, I walk in. I sit down with a bunch of people. They all get up and everybody sits on the other side of the roll call. I was the first female training officer in that area. They all got up, and they went to the other side of the roll call. That was, congratulations, you made training officer.

And when the sergeant passed out my mail, he threw it to me. That was tough.

They're all gonna know this is about them. And you know what? I don't care. It's true, and it happened. If this opens some people's eyes, I don't feel too bad about it.

I was transferred to an FBI office in Kenosha, Wisconsin. It was going to be seven male FBI agents and myself. I found out later, that before I came, the supervisor sat them all down—"Give her a chance. All you ever have to give anybody is a chance." I really appreciated that guy. And I've always tried to have that attitude. You know, it's true. That's what we owe. We owe everybody a chance.

Station behavior has changed a lot. In some ways, things have really improved. Compared to when I came on, things are a lot better. And probably, compared to the people who came on ten years before I did, they probably thought things were a lot better for me. A lot of people really feel like "Wow! We really have come a long way for women in law enforcement and in general." And that's true. We have— compared to where we were ten years ago or thirty years ago—we have come a long way.

But in some ways, that perspective really detracts from what we're trying to accomplish. Because what we're trying to accomplish is fair and equal treatment for *everybody*. We've come a long way, but that's not to say we're where we want to be. It's where you're honestly rated on your performance, you're promoted based on it, and not on people's prejudices.

And if we compare it—you know, it's like comparing somebody who only beats his wife once a day instead of ten times a day. Well, great. He has improved. But the reality is, he shouldn't be beating his wife at all.

CHAPTER 5

THE LOCKER ROOM

A couple locker-room stories. A woman cop walks into her broom closet/locker room and trips over the body of a shotgunned rat. She knows if she screams, the cops outside will never let her live it down. She sweeps up the rat and secretly disposes of it. A woman in the Training Academy has to leave P.E. and run through the showers before the men finish class, making sure she turns on all the taps so they can have a hot shower, shower quickly herself, and, since at the time there *is* no locker room for women recruits, change quickly in the classroom before the male recruits enter.

These stories are from the bad old days, when women first were mandated on police forces as patrol officers, in the seventies. There are lots of these stories. Making women change in broom closets, or trailers, or in the men's locker room itself was a way of saying, "You don't belong here." Playing practical jokes on women and subjecting them to intimidation and harassment were ways of saying, "We don't want you here, and we're gonna make sure you know it."

Before the seventies, women police were expected to use the public/suspects' washrooms. The "men's only" atmosphere was unquestioned. Things got much uglier and more creative when women were legislated into equal pay and treatment.

In recent years, locker-room harassment and discrimination, like most forms of discrimination, have moved from overt to subtle (perhaps even unintended or unconscious). Male supervisors have separate locker rooms; many women supervisors are expected to locker in with their subordinates. Locker rooms are still scarce for women: the LAPD and the NYPD still have facilities with inadequate lockering for women. Many women across the country find themselves having to dress at home, change in the public restroom, or wait for permission to use the men's locker room. Women often locker alone and hurriedly. It can be a profoundly isolating, punishing experience . . .

The LAPD has always been very strict about grooming. My first year, I was made to cut my hair at every inspection on Friday. My neck is very short, so I had to get my hair cut extra to make sure it didn't touch my collar. My hair was so short it looked like a bowl went around my head. Every inspection, they would tell me, "Your hair's too long."

I'd go in the locker room and I'd look at myself from every angle—*Is* it too long?

Of course, I was the only one there. That first year, there was only me in the women's locker room. They had made a public reception room into a makeshift locker room. It was directly below the male officers' locker room. I heard everything they said before roll call through the air vent. It was so sad—I'm telling you, that was the loneliest feeling, to be the only woman, and not having any camaraderie or anything, but just hearing the men talk.

And they all got along so well, it was kind of neat. And then, of course, after the watch, you'd walk in and you'd be by yourself changing and you'd hear the guys upstairs talking away.

I was never one of them. And I believe that to this day. They talk about The Brotherhood. And I am a sister. And I know I am not a brother. I'm a sister. And sisters are not afforded the same luxuries as the brothers.

I was the only woman, and the only black woman, in our Academy in 1974. They held our Academy at the National Guard Armory. They didn't even have a women's bathroom there.

I was called in and I was told by the lieutenant in charge of the Academy that I was to be given no special privileges. And what that meant was, they took forty-two, there were forty-two recruits in all, ten of us blacks, and they divided it in half, twenty-one in a platoon. There were two separate locker rooms. I shared a locker room with twenty men.

So what happened was, they told me upfront, "You are gonna have to work out how you're gonna deal with this locker-room situation." Well, I made it real easy. I dressed at home and came to the Academy in uniform and I went home in uniform. Whereas a lot of the men came and dressed there.

In the morning, when I had to go get my books or something, if I left them in my locker, I had to ask somebody to check to see if it was okay for me to go in.

At Physical Training—this is where the problem actually happened. Because at the end of P.T., they gave us fifteen minutes to shower and get dressed and be back in our uniform and in the classroom. And so, what we did was, we could go through our P.T., and as it got close to the end of P.T., the guys in the platoon would start moving me down closer to the door to the locker room. And when they blew the whistle, I'd run in first.

Now, part of my responsibility was to go in there and turn on all the water. Then I'd take my shower, put my basic clothes on, my underwear and brassiere and stuff, and then run out into the classroom and then finish changing while the men came in and took their showers.

It worked twofold for them. When I went in and turned the water on, I was taking a cold shower because the water wasn't hot. Now *they* got in, the water was hot. And they got the full fifteen minutes.

I had to finish dressing in the classroom. Not in the locker room—because the men were coming in and taking off their clothes. It was an interesting situation.

What happened would be, the black guys would stand at the door of the locker room, just in case there was some guy that wanted to come and peek or something. So the black guys kind of took me and protected the door. Then I'd holler and say it was clear and the guys would come in.

We had fifteen minutes for this. But it couldn't take *me* more than five minutes because I had to do a quick shower and get out before the men came in.

When I was in the Academy, in 1984, women didn't have lockers. We carried these huge duffel bags with us with our study books and our Physical Training shorts and sweat suits and stuff with us all day long, all day long.

With our class, we had Physical Training at the end of the

day. When we'd go out and train, we'd throw our books in the trunks of our cars and whatnot. They told us the showers for the women weren't working. The men had showers. No problem. You know one of *those* things. They went home smelling fresh and sweet.

In my class in the Academy, I was the only one. There was one other woman in another class. The women's locker room was in a trailer. It was this filthy, disgusting little trailer. It had one shower that no water came out of and there were just beehives *all over*, all up in the rafters of this trailer, so there were always bees in there. We would tell people about it and of course no one would ever do anything about it—"Yeah, yeah, right, right," and nothing ever got done about it.

The NYPD Police Academy was built with *no* female bathrooms. It was built in 1964. The legend goes, on opening day, the mayor and his wife were in attendance and so was the architect. And before the ceremony, she had to use the facilities. So she turns to the architect and whispers: "Where's the little girls' room?" He goes, "Ladies' room! Oh no! We never built one!"

So the female bathrooms in the Police Academy have urinals. They have stalls, but they also have urinals. They were too expensive to rip out. It's funny. You walk in and you have urinals in there.

In 1990, I went to a district as a sergeant. They had four locker rooms there: one for women officers, one for male officers, one for sergeants, and one for lieutenants. My locker was with the other female patrol officers. Only men were assigned lockers in the sergeants' and lieutenants' locker rooms. When they built the building, they never anticipated there would ever be *female* sergeants or lieutenants.

By 1993, there were more women assigned to the district than that one locker room could accommodate, so they had to expand. They put the male sergeants in the lieutenants' locker room and the female officers and supervisors into what had been the sergeants' locker room.

There's a big old urinal there right as you walk in. Someone put a rhododendron plant in the urinal. It's flourishing.

When I went to patrol, I was the first woman that worked nights out in a very bad part of town. I mean, it was the worst part of the city, and it was nights. They didn't have a woman's locker room, so they ended up giving me basically the janitor's closet.

It was this tiny, tiny little closet with, you know, the light bulb in the middle where you have to pull the string to make it go on? And the first day I walked in there, I kind of looked around and there were *holes* in the walls. And I looked at the holes in the walls and thought, "Well, I'll never get dressed in here." I think the holes probably got put there. They were pretty nice holes. When you walk into a situation like that and it's nothing but men, you do . . . you look for stuff like that.

At the time, it wasn't depressing. It was just kind of hard. Like, "Oh, God," you know, "How am I gonna handle this?" It had no facilities whatsoever. If you ever *did* get your clothes on in there, you had to go find a toilet. Actually, the women . . . we ended up using the public toilet. It was the one the suspects used.

One day, I walked into my little janitor's closet dressing room, and, you know, you had to walk across the floor to turn the light on because it had a string and it was on a bulb in the middle of the room. And, God!, when I walked over there, I kicked something—"What? What's that?" So I pulled the string and I looked down and here is this dead rat.

And I mean, this rat was not a rat; it was like a dog. I'll tell you, this was the biggest goddamn rat I've ever seen. This was one huge rat. And it had been shot in the head with a .22 caliber bullet. It had this bullet in its head and it's lying there on the floor and I turned the light on and I'm practically standing on top of the thing.

It was everything I could do to keep from screaming, but my first reaction was, whoever did it is probably sitting out there, waiting for me to scream. So I said, "Oh, God," you know, and what I did was, I got a big paper bag and I got something—I think I ripped a piece of cardboard off of something and I just pushed it into the paper bag and I rolled it all up and when I left, I took it with me and threw it in a garbage can. I was afraid, too, that if I left it anywhere in that precinct, I was afraid it would show up somewhere again, too, so I wanted to get it out of there so I wouldn't run into the damn thing again.

And I never said a word about it to anybody. Never. And I think—I'm glad I handled it that way. I think whoever it was or whoever they were were just sitting there waiting for me—the woman—to go off or scream or yell or something. And the rat just disappeared and I think they probably thought, "Jeez, did she ever *find* it? You know—nothing happened."

It's kind of malicious, in a way, and yet they look at how you handle it and after a while, if you handle it well, they start ignoring or letting you do your job. I kind of hate putting it that way.

In the mid-seventies I went to Central, and then I went to North, and then I went to East Precinct in Portland, and *none* of them had women's locker rooms. I mean, we were changing in the public bathrooms and, you know, these little makeshift rooms. In North, I was changing in the Report Writing Room. I closed the door and quickly changed my clothes as people were battering on the door to get in and write their reports.

It wasn't till after 1982 that you saw women in great numbers on the NYPD. It wasn't till my group came out that you saw women *really* being put in patrol.

It was an experience for everybody because it was like the male officers were not prepared. The department itself was not prepared because we really had no facilities. My locker room was a combination Community Affairs office, Youth Officers office, Crime Prevention office, and then they stuck one locker in there for me. We had three male officers in there at all times because that was their office. That was also my locker room. So whenever I had to change, I used to have to ask, "Hey, guys? Could you please leave the office?"

And there was a bathroom in that office, and they would bring in the female prisoners to use the same bathroom. The men wouldn't use it because they weren't going to use the bathroom that the prostitutes used. They sent the media to that bathroom.

In 1986, I was at a district that had a women's locker room, but all the lockers were taken. I had to keep all my stuff in the trunk of my car. I was living in a nice area. I went out, and I saw a piece of the *Daily Bulletin* sticking out of my trunk. I just pushed it back down and went on to work. When I got to work, I couldn't open the trunk. When I tried, the lock came out with the key in it.

Everything was taken from me: all my papers, my uniform, my raincoat because I was living out of the trunk, going to work, because I didn't have a locker. So I had to go rebuy all of that, out of my own pocket.

They didn't have a separate locker room for women at the precinct I was assigned to. The first locker room that I had was actually a little anteroom in front of the bathroom, which was a unisex bathroom on the first floor. And they had put a little bank of lockers in this little room. One of the officers, in big letters, put "Carol's Locker Room" all over the door. But it looked kind of nice. I was kind of proud of it, actually. At least I had privacy.

But I had to give it up. In this area, we did this Haunted House for the kids to come in and they needed that space so people could come through. So I had to go upstairs. That's where the guys' locker room was. I didn't mind that too much because then I could be with—the guys—and not be by myself and isolated. I remember going up the stairs and there these two cops would be, in their underwear—these are good-looking guys; it wasn't bad—bikinis, colors, very nice. But they didn't get excited. It was like, they're my brothers. I would never change there anyway. I just needed a space to put my stuff.

A male state trooper I used to date once pointed out to me that in the locker room, overhearing other male troopers talk about working with a female, it was the nudges and the grins and the winks, like, "Are you gettin' any out there? How is she, huh?"

And I said, "Oh, come on. They don't say things like that." He goes, "What are you talkin' about? You don't think they talk about *you* like that?" I said, "But I don't give them any reason to." And he goes, "It's just because you're a woman. Don't you think they talk about you like that?" And I'm, "I don't—Ahhh, bah-fffft!" No! You don't want to think that.

I was the first woman on the SWAT Team. I could get dressed in the women's locker room. But they put my locker in the men's locker room. And the reason they had to do that was the bags, the Emergency Response Team bags with all the equipment in them, were in the men's locker room and they had nowhere but there to put my bags, too.

I had to go in that locker room; my bag was in there. And I'd have to knock on the door. "Can I come in? Can I come in?" I'd have to wait outside the door to be able to come in. And all my equipment was in that bag and all my clothes and I'd have to stand there and wait or get some guy to go in and get my bag for me and bring it out or wait till everybody was gone to get my bag.

I mean, God, there were pictures in that locker room that would just—and there were *Playboys* all over the office. No effort was really made to stop any of this.

And, on the one hand, I didn't *want* there to be an effort to stop it. I didn't want to walk in and say, "Okay, the women are here, dammit. Clean up your act." Because I don't believe in that. I just don't believe women have the right to walk into something and say, "I'm here. Change." And yet, on the other hand, really no effort was made to stop any of it, either.

We have locker rooms now, but when I came on in San Francisco, in 1976, I'd walk into the locker room and there'd be guys in their underwear and they'd say, "Hello!" My attitude was "Doesn't bother you, doesn't bother me. Who cares? Big deal."

I was smart. I always wore a T-shirt and my police pants to work. So all I had to do was throw on my vest and my shirt.

The whole thing was to drive women out. Thinking it would. But it didn't, and it won't.

When you move up in rank as a woman, particularly as a sergeant and lieutenant, you're absolutely alone and you locker alone. You no longer locker with the female officers. And you're not with the male sergeants—you're all by yourself. There are still so few of us that are sergeant or higher that it's very isolating.

A lot of the relationships occur in the locker room. When the male sergeants go in to change clothes, they talk about the officers, and they'll identify problems—where they're not sharing that information with that female sergeant. She has no one to talk to or to hear what's happening.

Each time you go up, you're alone. Women come to me with that, mostly—they say it's so lonely.

Being the first woman . . . you had no one to talk to. You had no other women to go to and say, "Jeez, did this ever happen to you?" Or "How should I handle this?" Or anything. You're kind of left out there.

When I came on the job, we had a little closet. Now we have a locker room, with showers and room to turn around. If all of us, I think there were seven of us that came to the district out of my class, if all of us—well, not all of us *could* get in this closet at one time, but, I mean, if half of us got in there, you could not all turn around at the same time. We had to literally dress in the locker.

The new women don't realize what we had to go through just to get to where we are. And now they're at this point and they're like, "Hey, I deserve more," and yet they have *no* idea of what we had to go through when we first came in.

I'll tell you, because I'm from a different generation from the women who came on ten, fifteen years ago, I'll tell you what it was like when I walked into the women's locker room. It was 1986 when I joined. Before this, I had come from a unique setting of sports where everyone was supportive, always in team settings in women's teams and always supportive. And I thought, "What better group than a bunch of women police officers? I bet this is going to be the *best* support team!"

Then when I walked in that locker room, it was like BAM! No one would talk to me. And I could not believe it.

I listen to everyone talk about how bad the men were. I found that the men were the most supportive of me in my first year and a half to two years on the job. And I understand everyone has to put themselves into this job, that's the way it should be, but it was like no one would go out of their way to open themselves up. It was hard. I thought that women would probably be the most supportive group because it was a male-dominated profession and women would kind of stick together. But it wasn't that way.

When I came on, in '79, and I know other women who suffered the same thing, the women that were only six months ahead of you, or a year ahead of you, or two years ahead of you wouldn't talk to you. It was everybody for themselves. It's better now because there are more women.

But you'd walk into a locker room and they wouldn't even say hello.

You get the cold shoulder from the older women officers. The older women—you get the "You had it easy when you came on." It's all "I, I, I" with them.

I have very little allegiance to the newer women. I see them. And I don't have respect for them. I just feel that, from what I've seen, say from '86, '87 on—so many of these girls come on and—when I came on, the bosses gave us a hard time; everybody gave us a hard time. They did not want women.

The same bosses that did not want us now have their daughters, granddaughters, nieces, all of them coming on the job and protecting them from everything that we went through. You know what I mean?—automatically getting them into a unit. I really believe that you should do five years on the street, and I believe that you should do your time and not get in these nice little cushy jobs that other people are in. Earn it.

If I see some woman who has an inside job and has never been on the street, it irritates me. I feel like a white male in that respect. It irritates me. I don't think it's fair. I did twelve years on the street. I was the first woman in my department to walk a beat. And now, there's about six of them on foot and not one recognizes that I broke the ground for them, you know what I mean? I've heard other women say that, too—in that respect, we feel like a man. We agree with them one hundred percent on that.

I get recruits now. Before, when I used to be out there, we used to be concerned about doing things right. The priorities have changed. Now I get asked about pension, maternity leave, sick pay: what do you have to do, how do they check on you, what are all the inside scoops on playing sick, how long can you drag it out?

When we came on the job, we had the same problems that exist now. There were some of us that had young children, some of us were going to school, some of us had sick relatives, anything you can think of that was going on now was going on then. But we didn't even think of coming in, going, "Well, I can't make this because, you see, like I broke this nail last night? See my artificial nail? It broke my real nail underneath here, so I've got to make sure I get to my beautician so she can put a new nail on top of this?" This is a true story.

If you go through the ranks with women in police, I would suspect that most of them that have done real well are good athletes and have some type of background of athletic participation. Then you know how to pace yourself emotionally, you know how to communicate, you know how to turn it on when you need to, you know how to work with people, you know how to be a team player. Those are all overall elements that go into police work. I very much identify with the team concept, and that fits into what's going on with policing now, especially with working with the community, with community policing.

I think the older generation—they weren't brought up on team sports, it's only really recently women have been brought up with team sports. The older women just aren't team players. The ones that have been on fifteen, twenty years, you come into their station, oh, my God!, they will not talk to you, *you are invading their territory.* It's like "You have not been through *anything* I have been through." They are very hostile towards younger women officers.

Especially if you are very capable and very competent, they will not talk to you. You're a threat to them. It's like if anyone does anything to overshadow them, they get real catty. Someone gets a promotion and it's "Oh, she slept with so-and-so to get this." And, of course, it has nothing to do with they're very intelligent or they studied a lot, it has nothing to do with they're excellent cops—it's always, "Well, she doesn't have ten years on the street like I did." Okay—then you do it. You know the process, you know the game. Then play it.

And, again, it goes back to their basic "You have not gone through what I had to go through." Well, things have changed, okay? Get over it. We're here.

Some women do not support other female cops. They will walk out of a locker room and disparage other women to the men out there. I've seen this over and over again. It may be only one or two in a precinct, maybe it's not a lot of women, but I've seen it over and over again.

Recently we've been going through a lot of rumors about altercations between lesbian and straight officers in a locker room in one of our precincts. And we started checking into it, and talked to some of the officers, and found out it wasn't true. There had been one incident of inappropriate touching that had been dealt with months before.

But now the rumor has gone through the entire Police Department and the rumor mushroomed to where there is open war in the locker room over the line of demarcation between the lesbians and the straights. In our department, no male gay has come out of the closet. But the lesbians have. And I think that this rumor that has gone through the department is a two-pronged thing: One, it's always been to divide and conquer the women anyway, and if there's a feeling that they're fighting amongst themselves, then you perpetuate that. The other part is there's a great deal of fear among the male officers—male officers don't deal well with gays, they don't deal well with that concept. And I think they have a great deal of fear over what's going to happen with the gay officers. So this is kind of a prelude to what can happen to the male gays.

What this told us, as command officers, is we need to get women back together again. Women are not real good about supporting other women within the department in light of sanctions by the male officers. If a woman is being talked badly about by male officers, women officers are not likely to jump in and say, "Knock it off" because of the ostracism that they feel will come back on them.

I think it's better now. The past four, five years. Just as the men have changed, so have the women. I find that now women are trying to be more supportive. Even the women that have the old-timers' attitude of trying to pay their dues are trying to look down and say, "Well, we want these women to do good, too, so we'll try to be a little more supportive." It's getting better, but it's gradual and it's slow. But women do need to support each other a lot more than they do now. If we don't support each other, we're gonna go downhill.

I went to an NYPD patrol precinct as a sergeant in 1979. The numbers were so small for women who got promoted during that time; there were five of us and only eight or nine female sergeants in the whole city after *we* got promoted. That was tough, too, because they had never experienced a female sergeant before.

One of the things . . . I went to the precinct and they wanted me to locker in with female police officers because there were no facilities for sergeants, except for men. So I went to the captain and he told me, "No, I'm not going to ask for you to have a special room." So I called down to Building Maintenance and I made my complaint. There was nobody to complain to. Now, today, they would not have the nerve to say this. But the captain—"No, I'm not gonna give it to you. You either locker in there . . . I don't care what you do." And that was that.

It took *another* court case, going into the Human Rights

Commission, for women to get the separate facilities that they needed.

See, if you look at the history of the New York City Police Department, you will see that the department—and when I say the department, I mean the administrations that run the department—has never *once,* never *once,* given women anything. Women have always had to get it from outside. Any benefit that women have ever gotten on this job, they had to sue for or officially complain about it, or go to an outside politician, or go to the wall with these guys. It's interesting. No kidding.

A lot of women supervisors in the NYPD *still* don't have locker rooms. They didn't build the facilities with the expectation of us coming on. Many times, they do things like locker us in broom closets.

I just *came* from that experience. I was the only female supervisor in the district. All the other supervisors in the entire district on all three shifts were male. They only had a locker room for male supervisors. They had none for female supervisors.

The day I arrived there, we had an orientation with the captain in the district and then the inspector for that division came down to talk to us. And shortly after he finished, I was speaking with some of the officers from the other districts who were there. I noticed that all the sergeants that arrived when I did for that district disappeared out of the room. The captain's aide came back in, got all of them, and took them in and told them, you know—"Pick the lockers that you want. And just give me your locker number."

When I came out, he came over to me and said the captain said we don't have a locker for you. He said, "If you like, I can take you upstairs and you can try to move one of the female police officers out of their locker and you can share." I said, "No. I will not. I'm a supervisor. I will have a locker, a supervisor's locker." He said, "Well, there are no more left." I said, "These guys were permitted to take two and three lockers. *Somebody's* gonna give up one locker."

Not that I was gonna change my uniform in that locker

room; I chose just to wear my uniform back and forth to work. But it's still a pain. It totally is. Because where I live, most of my neighbors had no idea that I was a police officer. You don't want them to know.

I got the locker. But I was sharing this locker room with twenty-some male supervisors. I had to open the doors just a little if I heard anybody in there—"Are you decent?" If not, I had to wait. Did they give me that same courtesy? No. They would just walk in.

The male locker room had a separate male bathroom. And I had to use that. None of the females there had a bathroom of their own. If the females in the district had to go to the bathroom, they had to come in, go upstairs—some had keys for the restroom upstairs—others would have to get the keys from the detectives, in order to go—to the bathroom. You use the buddy system when you go—"Will you watch the door for me when I'm in there?" Even for me, if I went into the supervisors' locker room and used the toilet facilities in there, I would often hear the locker-room door open, the guys come in. So I had to announce *my* presence in there. So you usually found some place out on the street like a nice hotel or a few all-night restaurants. But you hated doing that—using public facilities.

I got to experience firsthand what I had received so many complaints about from the female officers. Always before, where I worked, there were separate locker rooms. But there are still districts in the city where the males and females have to share locker rooms. And there were complaints from the women. It's a problem.

This is true of only some of the districts here, not all of them. But it shouldn't be true at all. We should have our own facilities in every district because there are females in every district.

It's the very thing that South Jersey is filing a grievance about. They do not have separate locker facilities *or* separate bathrooms. They don't have separate toilet facilities. They have to share them with the guys. They're pushing for separate locker facilities now.

But the bosses are still saying, "Well, we haven't gotten around to providing them." Come on. Women have been on the street in uniform in this area since 1976. And you mean to tell me you haven't been able to put up a partition by now? And we're just supposed to take it.

Supervisors in the Seattle PD have a locker room now. But it's so packed, because they ended up with six of them, that when two or three of them are on the same watch, they can hardly change their clothes at the same time because if both bent over to put their pants on at the same time, they bump rears.

The LAPD is still adding women's locker rooms to some locations. There are some places in the LAPD where they brought in a trailer or the women would have to get dressed at home. But that's just like a daily reminder that you don't belong.

Not having enough locker rooms for women officers *means* something. To not acknowledge us negates us. It's a "Maybe they'll go away" attitude. It's a way of saying you don't belong. The psychology is phenomenal.

On our SWAT Team, the majority of business gets done in the men's locker room. Decisions are made in their locker room. I mean, the sergeants are in there with the guys; they're all in the same locker room, the talk goes on in there, the decisions are made. You're continually left out.

In other units, guys don't spend that much time in the locker room. In a uniform unit, you come in and put on your uniform, you leave. People come in at different times. And in almost all other units, the male sergeants have their own locker room.

But in the SWAT Unit, there's so many different changes of clothes—you have the ERT function, the Emergency Response Team function, and you have clothes for that, you know, your black Sneaky-Modo clothes . . . These guys are so proud of these black Ninja clothes—they are! They love these black outfits. I always say SWAT Teams are made up of black and Velcro. Oh God, it's so funny. They just love this black stuff, you know. They're like women with fashion, but they won't admit it. They have to have this particular T-shirt and Velcro this and Velcro that.

We aren't always on a call-out; we're not always responding to a hostage situation. So when we're not doing that, we could either be working plainclothes, going after narcotics guys, or we could be working uniform, or we could be working dignitary protection—that could either be uniform or a nice suit. So basically this unit has so damn many changes of clothes it's unbelievable. They have so many outfits, you know. The SWAT guys spend a lot of time in that locker room.

I noticed that at a workout club I belong to. I noticed that at lunchtime, all the businessmen come there and the businessmen play basketball together, they play racquetball together. I would listen to these guys and I would realize that a lot of business decisions were being made out there on the basketball court. Now, of course, the women are excluded from this. If you're a woman and you're trying to network or get ahead or be involved in the decisions that are being made, you're *not* involved; you're not. These guys are out there on the basketball court making decisions and you're not playing.

A lot of decisions are made in the SWAT locker room and you're not included. I used to really have the feeling down there all by myself down in my own locker room, if there was something like we were all getting dressed to go do something, I'd get dressed *really fast* because I was afraid they'd forget me and leave without me.

Because you're not included in it. You're not there. You're all by yourself in this little locker room. I used to always think, "God, they'll forget me. They'll forget I'm even here and they're gonna go without me and leave me here."

CHAPTER 6

THE CAR

In 1974, a Chicago newspaper ran a cartoon: a CPD squad car, bubble lights on top, "We Serve and Protect" emblazoned on the side, and frilly pull-back curtains on the squad's windows. Throughout the year, station houses were flooded with calls from citizens reporting the sighting of squad cars driven by women; the citizens assumed the squads must have been stolen. And in the early seventies, as police jurisdictions scrambled to hire women as patrol officers in accordance with the 1972 Equal Employment Opportunity Act, Police Wives Associations all over the country held emergency meetings protesting the imminent death or seduction of their husbands.

Men and women in cars together. *Alone* together, facing boredom and danger for entire shifts, even working the *midnights* together. Pretty volatile stuff, or so it seemed in the early days of women on patrol. Police cars became the focal point for male cops' and the public's anxieties over women cops being given equal pay and equal access to two male bastions: cars and guns. And the specter of illicit sex loomed as large as the backseat of an old Chevy over the police wives', the public's, and even male cops' idea of what it meant for men and women cops to work together.

A lot of battles were and are waged in the interior of police cars. Male officers used to treat women officers as dates—the men were the ones who drove, who opened (or tried to open) the passenger door, who got out first at any scene. Other officers simply ignored the women they were assigned to work with, making the woman cop the ultimate third wheel. But some, the ones most respected by the women, said, in effect, "I don't like you here, but I expect you to do the job same as me . . ."

* * *

138

I had a partner who used to read me poetry in the car. Poetry that he had written. I used to go, "Oh, my God," you know, "What have I gotten myself into?" But he was very nice; he never came on to me. No. But he would read me poetry.

I had one guy who always used to roll the windows up after he passed gas. He was known as "Rotten Reggie." You'd say, "Jesus! What are you doing?" He goes, "Hey, it's human. It's natural."

They put me in the Planning Unit of the Portland Police Bureau just before Mount St. Helens erupted. As soon as it erupted, they called me: "We have to have a volcano plan."

The first time it erupted, the ash all went east, but after a few days, they decided it was going to go again; they were studying the wind patterns and decided Mount St. Helens might dump it on Portland.

This caused tremendous policing problems—you can't drive squad cars in it because it sucks all that ash into the air-filtration system, and the cars die. So I had to come up with a plan of what to do if the volcano exploded again and it came our way.

It drove the department a little crazy when my volcano plan included putting a pair of pantyhose in everybody's squad car. I found out that if you put pantyhose over the air filter, the ash can't get in. And so the guys, you should have heard the comments about that one. But it worked.

We put a pair of pantyhose, a surgical mask, goggles, and a pair of paper coveralls in every car. The officers would have these goggles and protective coveralls on so they wouldn't get the ash in their eyes or guns or respiratory systems. Then the first thing they were to do was to drive to an underpass and jump out and put the pantyhose over the air filter.

I took a lot of ribbing about the pantyhose. But when I tell that story, I think of one officer and he said, "Now what man would have thought of that?" And I think that's true. Women bring a different way of looking at things. We're not afraid to try new things, and we're practical as well. This volcano plan was practical—and cheap. You could get L'eggs for just about a dollar back then.

My first five minutes on the job. We get in the patrol car and all of a sudden there's an "Officer Needs Help" call. You know what that means? Everybody flies.

Now, I'm brand-new. My equipment's hardly in the car. I don't even know where to sit, basically. My partner yells, "Get in the car!" I jump in the front seat and away we go.

And what we did was we went down to the housing projects where there was a suspect on PCP and all of a sudden, we are driving over these people's front yards. I'll never forget it because I said in my head, "We are driving on people's front yards!" And that was a culture shock. "Why are we driving on their yards? I'm afraid we're gonna get their yards wrecked by the tires!" We're driving through people's yards and under the clotheslines and my head was kind of ducking—"Boy! I think we're gonna hit this clothesline!"

Two minutes later, we were in foot pursuit and we were wrestling with a man on the ground. My first wrestling match. And I just remember thinking, "I can't believe this! We just drove on these people's yards, now we're in foot pursuit, and now we're wrestling!"

And that's what I kept telling my parents when I phoned them back in Minnesota: "We went and drove on people's front yards tonight. And nobody cared! We went up over the curb and on people's yards. Yeah. 'Cuz we're the police."

The biggest adjustment I ever had to make was moving from being an anonymous member of the public to being a cop. Even driving down the street, I remember thinking to myself the first week, "Why are all these people staring at me?" And I'd forget—Oh, my God. Look at the car you're in! And I'd forget that I was driving in a police car.

It's really strange. These people—nothing wrong with them, but I used to walk across the street to avoid them; you know, you see certain things about people, you just cross the street. All the people you try to avoid through your life, good God, now they come up. But as a police officer, you can't avoid them. You have to face it dead-on.

This whore in our district used to jump on squad cars. If you pulled up at the light, she'd jump on the squad car, spread her legs—and she didn't wear underwear, either—she'd jump up and spread her legs right up on the windshield. And a real filthy lowlife, syphilitic . . . She mustn't have had anything too terminal, though; she's still around.

I stopped a girl for a traffic violation. She blew a red light, almost broadsided a station wagon with about six little kids in the back of the car. That kind of got me a little bit, about the kids, that really could have been a nasty little incident. And I wanted to bring this to her attention.

She didn't want to hear anything I had to say; she started cussing and screaming and hollering. I asked her for her driver's license. She said, "I'm not giving you my license and I'm not stopping and I'm not getting any traffic tickets and you're not taking me to jail and you're not doing this . . ." so I reached in and took the keys of her car out while she's steadily telling me what she wouldn't do.

And when I took her keys out, then she ripped. Stuff was flying all out of her purse and everything, she starts grabbing me, starts choking me, the claws come out, both of us are going at it, I had to wind up calling for an assist, the assist came over. They had to drag her out of her car, they got her into the back of the squad car—she starts chewing up the backseat of the squad. She's chewing it and tearing it up with her nails—chunks are coming out of the upholstery. I said, "We're gonna charge you with damage to city property."

She's still ripping up the backseat of the squad car and tearing it up and when she finally gets into the station and they ask her, "Why did you do all this?" she says she thought that's what you're supposed to do when you run into the police. She said she'd always seen on TV the people fighting, carrying on with the police like that—she thought that's what they were supposed to do. That's when the cage cars first came out, because this woman ripped up the backseat of the car.

She said, "That's what I thought you were supposed to do. You mean I was supposed to go calmly? I was supposed to go with you calmly? I thought that's what everybody did." "Uh—Noooo. It'd be much simpler if you'd have just given me your license. You'd have got a little ticket and you'd be on your way by now. Now you're going to jail."

Policemen and women do not like change. Don't change. When they brought the portable radios in—oh, my God, the crying and wailing. Always, everything is going to be dire results.

When the first women came on patrol, in the seventies, the older policewomen who had never been allowed to be on patrol did not like it. They felt things were going to change for them. And they did.

This was 1973, before women came on patrol here. I was riding to dinner once with a woman. She had twenty-five years on the job already in the Youth Division, and I was a rookie.

The only time this woman ever left the office was to go to dinner. She was a huge woman; she had to be packed into her uniform. She had so many chins she couldn't put her own star on. So every day, she worked steady four to twelves, she would come in with her star in her hand and have somebody put her star on for her. And every day, there were barbeque-rib stains on her shirt. I can still see these rib stains down the front of her uniform shirt. I mean, she was an embarrassment.

I was driving; she was riding. She was so rotund she could not fit behind the steering wheel. We were in a marked car, in uniform. And this man staggers off the curb, covered in blood, waving his arms: "Help me! Help me!"

So I pull up next to him. This policewoman I'm with rolls her window down about two inches and she says, "You'll have to call PO 5-1313 for this. You have to call the police for this." I'm going, "We're the police! Get out of the car."

That was so typical of the mind-set then.

* * *

The news media didn't make it any easier. On the editorial page, one of the Chicago papers had a cartoon of a squad car with little chintz curtains on all the windows. It was lighthearted, sort of cute. But, naturally, that was cut out and posted on the wall in every police station in town.

Obviously, there were men who were supportive of the idea, even if they were a little bit nervous about us. They had honest and sincere feelings of fear that something would happen to the women—it's like this whole thing about women in combat. And yet we had policewomen working undercover already; things could happen to them, working Vice. But, somehow, that was different.

I came on as one of the first women in patrol. I remember the first day at roll call when we were assigned the FTOs right? They're all saying to the FTO assigned to me, "Oh, hey, you're gonna get lucky." And for weeks it went on, "Are you banging her?" In front of me. And they'd do it to all the women.

But he was such a good example and such a good guy, you know, and happily married and everything, he just taught me the right way. And he was a big guy, which helped, so they weren't gonna mess with him too much.

But things went on. We rode around in the squad car one night with a "Just Married" sign on the back. Never knew it till the inspector stopped us. They would put Vaseline under the door handles of the squad car when we'd go in to lunch. Just to toy with you. You know how cops always pull up next to each other and talk in squad cars?—you'd be talking and they'd squirt you with squirt guns. They were squirting both of us, but of course, I'm on the passenger side, so I get it the most.

They all turned out to be my good friends. You know what I mean?

You won't believe this. When we first went into patrol cars, in the early seventies, there was such an uproar with the wives that they sent us to the Fire Academy for a tea and a coffee to meet the wives. Oh, my God. Oh, God, police wives. The Police Wives' Association. At the time, they were very powerful. They were very organized and very vocal. They did not like us. We were the honeys that were gonna take their husbands in the bushes. Or, as they liked to say publicly, we would not be able to protect them.

Now all these women showed up. They were four thousand pounds and Capri pants and you know, the hair out to here, and there's about twenty-four buzzing bees in their beehive hairdos and they're all married to these slugs that you wouldn't look at on a *bad* day and they're all worried we're going to seduce their husbands. They're like, "Well, we don't want them working with our husbands." And I'm thinking, "Yeah, this is the idiot that's got an alarm clock and a pillow in his briefcase for the midnights and I'm supposed to worry about him?" I was so aggravated, I can't tell you.

I said that to a wife. I'm saying, "What would ever possess these women to think we'd want their husbands? I'm working with this asshole . . ." I didn't know I was talking to the wife of the guy I worked with.

One of the wives was just great. She used to tell people, "Look, if this woman can stand my husband for eight hours, you can have him. God, I can't stand him for eight hours. If you can, he's yours. If you want to work midnights with him and sleep in the car, go ahead—I can't stand sleeping with the man."

She wasn't threatened. But a lot of the wives are. They're afraid of the unknown. They think for sure when we work midnights that their husbands, whoever that might be, you know—that there's something magical about that midnight shift!

Yeah, right. It's real magical to watch your husband with his fat, flabby cheeks against the door—snoring and drooling. That's pretty doggone magical. Yeah.

I wasn't one of the first women on the street in Dallas; in fact, there were many. But the controversy was getting louder with the police wives being very vehement that their husbands should not work with a woman.

There was a Police Association meeting one day and the wives showed up. There was an older woman there and she started, "By God, this organization was built by men and they have certain ideals and we want this organization to do something about our husbands having to work with women. Women are going to get them killed or they're going to be cheating on us. We just don't think it's right. If women want to be on the police force, by God, they ought to work together. Women together—men together."

I just stood it as long as I could. So I stood up and asked if I could talk. I said, "Ma'am, let me tell you something. I've worked with one guy who is the husband of somebody. And at the end of the shift, I thank *God* he goes home to someone else because I wouldn't pay *anything* to have him. So get that across, okay?"

Oh, my God, you should have seen it. The guys wanted to clap, they looked like they wanted to clap, but their wives were sitting there. I just went on, "Look. I hope you got what I just said. Who would want your husbands? They may be good for police work, but I'm sure they're not good for a damn thing else." I didn't even think about what I was saying; it was just kind of a reaction of "Ig! Who would *want* these guys?"

The police wives never spoke about the issue again.

I was married to a cop before I became a cop. I was on the Board of Directors of the Police Wives' Association. When I went on the Police Department, I lost every friend I had. Suddenly, I was the enemy.

And, you know, quite often, they're right. Because, see, partners share a relationship that cannot be shared by anyone else living or dead in this entire world. The person that you work with like that becomes a true partner—you put your life in their hands. You don't do that with a lover, you don't do that with a spouse, you don't do that with a relative. But you do it with a partner.

And it's very easy to cross over that line—it's a physical response to an emotional need. And, since we're not working with rocket scientists, that's the way it goes.

The wives' fears are very well grounded. Because if it's a true partnership, you've got to have a very, very strong relationship with your spouse to survive it. And all the stresses of the job make that almost impossible. They *should* be worried.

There are women that come on that really establish a bad name for all the women because all the guys want to work with them. Because it's so much fun! They're party girls. They'll date every one of their FTOs that ask them out—they're the fun ones to have. And it just makes it bad for the other women, who have worked really hard to establish a working relationship, when the rest of the police see what's going on and they paint us all with the same brush.

I think women should be allowed to fool around as much as the men, but we're the minority. It's a tough reputation. I mean, there are women who have gotten that reputation over the years, they see it, and they change their life, and they try to get away from that bad reputation—they can't. It usually sticks with them forever. Their past good times.

I've worked with partners whose wives were very comfortable because they know that I'm a lesbian. It was kind of like, "Well, I know I'll have no problem with a lesbian."

I think the lesbians are accepted more by the men than by the women. Imagine riding in a radio car. You know, you spend eight hours in a car with your partner. Chances are you might hook up with a female, so you think you have a lot in common, and then she tells you she's gay. And now she's trying to tell you the better side of life—"I know how to make you happy; I know what you need." This goes on. This goes on.

I mean, I've had these encounters myself. And it's tough. I was sending out the wrong message—I had short hair. I don't have short hair anymore.

Kind of my first introduction to racism . . . I come from a mixed background. I have a black father and a white mother. There was not a racial thing in my family at all. There was just the right thing to do and the wrong thing to do; we don't care what color the person is doing it. Race never made up a big issue in my family; it just never did. I didn't even catch racism in school. But, coming on this job, I did catch it.

One of the things your FTO tells you when you're getting ready to come on patrol—"It's time for you to start looking for a partner." So you start sending the feelers out; you watch how other people are working—well, first you gotta decide yourself whether you just want to kind of lay back and it's just a paycheck or do you want to contribute something? So you've got your working police officers and then you've got the people that are just kind of present.

I started looking out for somebody to work with and fortunately/unfortunately, I picked a white officer. Nothing to do with the fact that he was white, but because he was a working police officer.

We worked very well together. If he got the color of a car, I got the make. If he didn't know if it was a two-door, I'd know the doors, and he'd get the license plate. Anything one of us seemed to miss, the other would pick up on. Really teamed up well together. And that was the only reason I picked him.

I was then semiostracized by the black officers with the "Oh! With as many black officers that there are in this district, who does she have to work with? A white officer. She doesn't like to work with the black guys, obviously." It was like, I obviously think I'm too light to work with the black officers.

Some even went to the point where they wouldn't even speak to me anymore. And I just had to come up to them and say, "What's your problem?"

"Oh. Well, I didn't think you wanted to speak to me. You see how dark I am, right?"

"What's that supposed to mean?"

"Word's out that you don't want to work with anybody black."

"What do you mean the word is out? I didn't say anything."

I got that for a while. The only reason that it kind of wore off was, I guess, I became really productive. There were times when one of the very black officers' butts was out there on the street, hollering for help or needing an assist with something. I was the first one went over there and helped them. So that kind of wore thin because I was just there and I was doing. They just ran out of things to say against me.

A big thing at the beginning was men drove. Men would drive; the woman could only ride. That was a big thing. With some men, it still is.

Five hundred times. How many times have we had to go through this same exact scenario? You get in a squad car with a guy, okay? And I would try to set him at ease because they would feel very awkward, too. They didn't know what to do. There's a certain way you treat your wife and your girlfriend, and now here's a female but it's a cop, so what do I do?

And some of the guys would come right out—"Am I supposed to open the door for you?" That was a big discussion. And "Do I have to buy dinner?" And some of them would. It was like it was a date.

So initially, every new person that we worked with—we knew that we'd have to set their mind at ease, okay?, joke a little, swear a little, act like one of the guys a little, and everybody can calm down about this. But some . . . were so ingrained in how to treat women that they simply couldn't do it. They were very uncomfortable with it.

I worked with one partner who would absolutely insist that he had to buy dinner: "I've never had dinner with a woman in my life that I didn't pay for."

Different time now! No shit!

But that put you in a subservient position. It really did. The same with opening the doors. And the same with—a big problem was male partners overreacting when people would get in our face. Same as your husband would. Somebody would scream at me, he would overreact as a man, not as a cop.

There were all those little things to work out.

When women came on, in 1974, they sent us to the two easiest districts. What they should have done was send us to the tough districts, and somebody would have gotten knocked on their ass. Then the police, men and women, would be better than they are.

But they sent us to these districts where there basically was no crime. And they circled our squad cars with red Magic Marker. I was down in Dispatch one day and I saw my squad car was circled. I was like, "Why is my squad car circled?" They're like, "We can't tell you." I found out that they didn't want any of the girls to get hurt. So we weren't allowed any in-progress calls or any dangerous calls—it was unbelievable what they did.

It's not that they should have wished us to get hurt, but they should have allowed us even to fail. Either do the job and fail or do the job and succeed, but don't give us this false atmosphere to work in.

When I first came on, they assigned me to a part of town I was totally unfamiliar with. I grew up in the university part of town and we were told never to go north of there. So when they sent me over there, I just figured they assigned me there to get me killed.

They put me on midnights in a one-person car. I'm out there all by myself. None of the men wanted to work with me—I mean, you know, nobody volunteered—so they didn't give me a partner. They didn't make anyone work with me.

It was real interesting because I'd always take ride-alongs [an officially sanctioned ride in a police car] so I'd have somebody to talk to. But the first thing ride-alongs would say when they came into my car was, "Why are you the only one without a partner?"

I tell people to this day, when they question what kind of cop I am—the only cop I am is what I taught myself because I didn't have anybody to teach me. I mean, I had to go and do it myself; it was right, wrong, or indifferent.

Initially, when women came on patrol, a lot of the women didn't do anything. I know an incident, male and female team, she was new on the job, went on a call. They were battling real good up there in this apartment. She ran downstairs with the radio, locked herself in the car. She locked herself in the car. She had the only radio—at that time, there was only one radio per car. She had the only radio and her partner's up there battling it out.

But, see, that was an isolated incident. That doesn't happen very often. But—it only takes one incident like that for all the guys to go, "Well, see. Typical female. Typical female." Now everybody has got to fight that. Now it's—we *all* don't get involved in a fight. We *all* don't know how to help. Just one incident like that, it can spread so fast.

We had a male probationary on our unit last year. We called him "Patches" because he wore those carsick things behind his ears in the squad car.

He was a little, teeny guy, so soft-spoken, so coy. This guy was white, white, white, white, white, almost an albino. The gang members would knock him down and start running. He was a danger to us.

One time, he was doing Narcotics and Gangs with us. We were involved in a pursuit; we were chasing a violent gang member. We had to race through all these houses that were known to have guns.

We're chasing—and Patches, he's in the middle of the street, standing next to the squad car. He won't leave it. He points—"He went that way." He's supposed to be in on the chase, but he won't leave the car. He said he had to make sure the squad car was secure. His female partner is chasing with us, but he won't leave the squad car.

The thing is, if a woman did that, you would have heard about it throughout the whole department and throughout her whole career. There's a big difference in the stories that go around about women and what goes around about men.

If people don't like you or have a grudge against you here, it gets to be serious because you're in a profession where your life depends upon the help of someone else.

We had a case here just recently, it was sexual harassment, where a male detective exposed himself to a female detective—he allegedly came out of the washroom with his pants down and he had an erection. This woman complained to her commanding officer, and once she made her complaint, the trouble started.

When she made her radio transmissions, they were keying her out on the radio. They were not responding to her calls for assistance. All of a sudden, she calls a 10–13, everybody has a job; no one can show up.

When you have a situation like that, it can be deadly. This is what keeps some women from complaining. Because your life depends upon how well these people like you.

Absolutely the worst thing that happened with me was with this nutcase copper. We had to pump our own gas into our squad cars. You pulled up at the outside of the station, big overhead garage door, little garage door next to it, and then an opening in the wall; the pump was inside this little cement room and you'd pull the hose out through this opening and then you'd pump it in your car.

Then you had to go back into this little room—you had to make out a ticket with your mileage and all that kind of thing, stick it in the gas pump—traditionally, everyone would just set the nozzle on top of the pump because the next cars are all lined up; you just leave it on top till the next guy comes in.

So I came in to get gas, thinking nothing of anything. This nut was there before me. He filled his car up; he put the nozzle on top of the tank and left. So I came in, I made out my ticket, I put it in the tank, and I turned the handle.

I was—drenched—with gasoline. He had left the clip on, you know, keeping the hose nozzle open. And I had a cigarette in my hand. And I want to tell you, gasoline comes out like a fire hose. It literally knocked me back up against the wall. I was wearing contact lenses at the time—full in the face, full in my eyes—and I couldn't get out because the pressure is so strong it's like being pinned to the wall by a fire hose. And I started screaming and I staggered backward out of the room. I was screaming. My contacts were melted into my eyes. I was screaming.

A sergeant came running up from the back—other people—they dragged me downstairs, to the women's bathroom. And I remember, they kicked the door open and this woman cop was sitting on the toilet; she's screaming, "Just a minute! Just a minute! I'll be out in a minute!"

They dragged me over to the sink and just ran the water

and shoved my face in it because I was scratching at my eyes.

They took me to the hospital. My eyelids were blistered, top and bottom—the insides of my eyelids were blistered. They had to pick the contacts out. My eyes were bandaged for six weeks. Six weeks. I didn't know if I was gonna be able to see.

And no one can tell me that that motherfucker did not do that on purpose. Because . . . when you fill a car, when it's full, that clicker clicks off. You would have to physically reset it and set it back up there. He had to turn off the pump entirely—go in there and turn it off and then reset that clicker. That's exactly what he did. That's exactly what he did.

Six weeks. My little boy had to lead me around the house because I had my eyes bandaged. Nice, huh?

With the police officers—the majority of the ones I worked with were just terrific. They were really good and really positive. There were, out of the twenty officers I've worked with, there were one or two that made it very clear to me, from the moment I got in the car, that they didn't want me to do anything; they wanted me to sit there and be quiet; they didn't think women should be in the car; women shouldn't be police officers at all.

The majority of them not only let me do stuff—they *wanted* me to do it. They were very positive about it.

I have to say, most of the cops are great. Most of the guys I've worked with through my entire career have just been wonderful. The problem is, and I think this is true in any profession, there are always a few strategically placed jerks.

What they did to me—this was 1975; I was working solo, one-man squad. So every morning I'd come out, get in the squad car—and taped around the steering wheel was a centerfold of *Penthouse* magazine, the scratch and sniff, and you know what part of the anatomy you had to scratch and sniff. So I'd take it off, crumple it up, throw it away.

And next morning there'd be a brand-new fresh one. So by that time, I figured anyone willing to spend five dollars or whatever for a new magazine a day, Hey! Knock your socks off. Doesn't bother me at all.

It took a good year for that stuff to simmer down and for some of the guys to stand up and say, "Hey, enough. Those broads are okay."

It was funny—the first day I worked, I was assigned to a patrolman, I won't say his name, but this guy was a psycho. A legitimate psycho. They assigned me to him. You hear your names called out at roll call and you look over to see who it is. This guy looked totally normal, absolutely normal.

We get in the parking lot. He told me, "Get the radio," so I went up front and got the radio and I've got my clipboard with all the reports on it and the radio hooked on it; I've got all the equipment I need, my ticket books and my flashlight and all that junk, and I go tooling off to the squad car.

And I open up the passenger door and he says to me, "You fuckin' cunt! What did I do to have to work with a goddamn broad! You goddamn bitch, blah, blah, blah. I didn't ask, blah, blah, blah . . ." And I went, "Uh, okay," and I got in the car and he said nothing more to me. And I answered the radio, he drove to the calls, I took the reports, never spoke a word till about six hours into the tour, and finally he said, "Where do you want to eat tonight?" And I went—I just kind of shrugged and went—"Mrrmmrrmm?" I wasn't going to say anything to him. And he said, "You can talk, you know. I'm not gonna bite you." And I was like—you could have fooled me.

And here I thought all policemen were like that. I really did. I had nothing to compare it to. So I figured that's the way all policemen were. I thought, "Holy cow, it's gonna be a long career." I just thought, "Okay, I gotta work with policemen and find ways of adapting."

That's the thing about women on this job. A woman—especially ten, fifteen years ago—if you didn't develop a thick skin, you were out of luck. You were out of luck. Because not only—it's human nature, people pick on you even more when they know that you have tender points, but you couldn't survive it; you couldn't put up and be sensitive to abuse for an eight-hour shift and still survive. So you just develop . . . I've got a skin like a table. Nothing bothers me. I just made up my mind that I had to take it and live with it and just move on from there and that's what I did. Truly, truly nothing bothers me jobwise.

All they do when you're working in the squad car is drool at women all day long. And I say, "How can you do your job? If I looked at men all day—I haven't seen too many to drool over—but if I looked at men all day, I'd never get anything done."

There was a picnic the other day, right? And all the guys were looking at the women. They came back and told us what the women looked like, who had the least amount of clothes. They come back, they're telling me, I say, "Look, if you can't tell me what the men look like . . . What makes you think I want to know what the women look like? Come tell me about the single available men and then we can talk."

I worked as a civilian in the Police Department before I came on as an officer. It was like I was okay and everything was just peachy-keen until I became a patrolman. The very people that had been smiling in my face and being real nice to me suddenly didn't want to work with me. It was like, "Well, she's nice enough to work as a little secretary, but I don't want to work with her."

That was a part of the job that hurt my feelings. That really did. The same people that had depended on me when I worked as a civilian in the PD, suddenly, when I became a police officer, I'm not on the same level as them. I was told, "Women should not be on this job. I'm not gonna work with a woman. Women cry at the drop of a hat and then we'll have to go through the periods every month." Seriously. Then—"What's it gonna be? Let's stop every five minutes so I can go check Kotex?" Some guys will tell you that. "Oh, is it Kotex time now? That why we gotta stop?"

I'd be out with my partner, working nights, we'd be out in the boonies somewhere and he'd say, "I'm gonna go out and look for some burglars." So I was fixing to get out of the car, too, and he said, "No, you stay in the car." So I got back in the car—"Why the hell did he make me get back in here?" He was going to the bathroom! When he came back, I said, "Take me to a fire station."

As a woman, you can't drive down a dark alley, come out the other end, and feel better. That's why I've always said that the Fire Department saves lives. The fire station—it's the only bathroom in town at two or three in the morning. One thing about being a woman in the Police Department, you know where all the fire stations are.

You can't really use public washrooms because you've got to take the radio off, then the baton, then the flashlight off your back pocket, and then do the gun belt. You put it on the floor next to your feet. And then the person in the next stall—"What's that? My God! It's a gun belt!"

I had a woman report me to the manager one time. I was in a public washroom and I was standing with my back to the door of the stall taking off all my equipment. All she could see was men's shoes and a gun belt on the floor. She thought there was a man with a gun in the stall next to her. So the manager comes barging in—"Hey! What's going on here?" "Wait! I'm a cop!"

When I started, I had a very rude and crude trainer, but he was a very smart police officer. He was bound and determined that either I was going to learn or I was going to be out.

First day I reported to work, we got in the car and I thought, "Okay, here we go." And he said, "Before we get out on the streets, I want you to know the three rules of this squad car. First, whatever happens in this squad car is between you and I, nobody's business. Secondly, we are here to work and I just don't want to hear anybody wanting to socialize while we're supposed to work. And thirdly—I don't know about the bathroom situation, but I'm gonna have to tell you: Don't start this 'Please take me to the fire station to go to the bathroom' because we are just not gonna do it."

I thought to myself, "And who does he think he is? I don't have to go to the bathroom for eight hours. I'll show *him.*" And so, I didn't go to the bathroom on duty. I drank coffee. I just didn't go to the bathroom. I was gonna show him that, by God, I could do it.

I was new in a district, and I was the only black. And I got a female white for a partner, and she thought I was just a big, dumb black woman. And she treated me like that. She acted like I was a big, dumb black person. Well, I acted like a big, dumb black person. You know, you act the way people treat you sometimes.

I didn't know my way around the district because I never worked up north. I had to have my map out in front of me, and I didn't know where I was going and she totally disrespected me all the time. And I let her. I always felt bad that I never said anything to this woman. I just looked at her, I never talked to her, we never said anything to each other. We were just stuck in the same car.

Now I think I would have something to say to her. But then I was new and I thought I better be nice. Because I was out of my district; I was somewhere that was very new to me.

I guess I've always hated the radio because when we first came on, that's how people would get to you. It still goes on. You know, they'd key you in, key you out when you were transmitting. Oh, God, it would make me a nervous wreck.

You hit the key to transmit and if somebody else is speaking, it cuts them out. So, like, "Squad, can I have a name check?" Then you get keyed and the dispatcher would say, "Go into the station and get a new radio. There's something wrong with your radio." And there's nothing wrong with your radio.

Or other cops would say something—"Shut up." Or when we were on midnights—"You should be sleeping."

One dispatcher would never say 10–4 to me. He would say, "Yes" or "Okay." Or "Yes, dear." "Yesss?" You know what I mean? It was like a woman couldn't be the real police.

It still goes on. Policemen do it to each other. It's just one more way to get people.

The women civilians who work Dispatch hate women cops on the job. They hate us. It's not so bad now as when I came on, in '83, but it's still bad. Back then, they looked at us as not belonging. They were bigger male chauvinists than the men, I believe.

Requesting Code 7, requesting lunch, the women in Dispatch would ignore me. They would never answer me. My partner would have to get on and request Code 7. And they'd answer *him* right away. So I went paranoid—Do they hear me?

Of course, the other guys won't answer you. You're talking car to car? The guys would ignore you because you're just a woman. My partner spoke most of the time because they would ignore me. So I would basically think that no one could hear me—not the women in Dispatch, not the other cops out there.

And another thing for the guys was the shock of a woman's voice other than the dispatcher's—a woman cop. It was very hard for them to handle that. And, of course, I have a small, high voice. They would tell me my voice is too high. And I would say, "I'm gonna take some steroids, but I worry about the hair on my chest." That was my big line back then. You know, I'm sorry, I'm a woman. My voice is different than yours.

I knew it was their way of saying they didn't want me on the job.

I remember this one male lieutenant. I was a detective in Homicide, LAPD. We were on a surveillance one day, and I would say something on the radio—he would grab the mike from me and repeat it in a different fashion. I didn't believe it! I mean, the guy had probably three years on this department. And I probably by this time had more than fourteen years on the department and was much more knowledgeable tactically and had much more experience— I had worked in the Intelligence/Surveillance Unit, basically Criminal Conspiracy, *for years.*

I was so angry. He was saying, in essence, I know what I'm doing and you don't.

When you first come on, sometimes you have a day or two after the FTO program before you have your first permanent assignment. I worked two days in another precinct before I got my first assignment. Half your squad has a roll call at a different time than you do. So I was out on the street for a couple hours and another car wants to meet with me, which I thought was totally absurd—people still weren't talking to me, so why would anybody want to meet with me?

These two guys pull up next to me after I gave them the location to meet; they pull up and they go, "Oh. It's you. We heard a woman's voice . . ." They were not in the roll call and they heard a woman's voice and they thought that they had gotten a woman in their squad. And they were devastated. They were devastated. They said, "Oh. It's you. We, we thought we had a woman in our squad. We wanted to know what was going on."

I said, "Don't worry, guys. I'm only over here for a couple days and then I'm gone. No problem." They were very upset to hear a woman's voice because there were still no women there.

Guys are very pleased if they're on squads with no women. That's a real victory.

I can remember my FTO, the first second we got into the car. He sat in the car with me, turns to me before he even puts the car into gear, and says, "I'm gonna tell you right now. I don't like the fact that you're on the job with me, but I'm stuck with you. If I get into a fight, you get in a fight. If I get hurt, you better be on the gurney next to me." Welcome to the department.

But I sat there and respected him more for spending that ten minutes with me before we started patrol instead of a copper sitting in the car with you for eight hours and not saying a damn thing. In fact, we became very, very close friends.

That helped. And then, the very first fight we got into that night, I was right down there, getting dirty. I loved it. I can't remember much, but I know it was a good humdinger of a fight. This was a guy who just didn't want to get arrested. And I remember when we finally got him cuffed, there were twelve coppers that came to our defense and they're all standing there, in amazement that I was fighting. And from that point on, every copper knew, "You can trust her." If you have to work with her, even though she's a woman, you can trust her.

And you only have to do it once, too. After that, you're one of the guys.

I came on in '83. The thing that was probably the most surprising to me was realizing that I was not wanted—women were not well received; you were not wanted. That didn't hit until I actually started doing the job because when you're actually going through the recruiting process, there is absolutely *no hint* of that. And I had worked real hard at keeping myself in shape, so none of those barriers was a consideration. I had a lot of other jobs that had been traditionally nonfemale as well, and I grew up with six brothers.

And then you get here . . . It was getting here and realizing it wasn't an individual thing; it was—men are accepted until proven differently. Women are *not* accepted until proven differently.

It's true. It's very true. One of my first partners I ever worked with, he came up to me, he was assigned to work with me against his choices; he told me, "I don't want to work with one of you." Fine. That's fine. It didn't really faze me too much.

For the first four hours in the car that night—he was driving, of course, God forbid he let a woman drive, right?—and I asked him how to spell his name because everyone has unique spellings to their names, you learn that in police work right away. He said, "Just as it sounds."

That was the entire conversation until we got to a disturbance where it turned into a fight where the suspect got injured so we had to go to the hospital. And he was so surprised that I did what he never anticipated a woman doing, and that was basically participating. I think it was that I was rolling down the cement steps with the suspect.

Later, we're sitting back in the car and he says, "Would you like to review my statement before writing yours?" And that was the turning point. A few months later, the sergeant asked this guy who he wanted to work with in the squad and it was me, out of all the people.

They do come around, but initially, it's you're not accepted till you prove yourself.

When I came on, in 1981, I was not talked to. My own training officer did not speak to me in the car until we had it out one time. I said, "I am human and you treat me like that." And we really had an argument.

I used to have to go in and carry his stuff to him from the car. He would talk to other officers about me as if I weren't there.

And then, what happened was, we got in a physical disturbance where this guy was resisting. We ended up in a knock-down, drag-out fight with this guy and I was caught in the middle. I don't know, he really must have thought that I was just gonna stand there and not do anything—what was I gonna do, buff my nails?—but I had the guy over the hood of the car. I turned around to my trainer to say when you're ready, let me know, so I can get out of the way and you can cuff him, but it came out, "Whenever you're ready, just tell me." And he said "Okay" and I got my mouth busted open by another officer during the struggle—that often happens when police get in the same pit.

The thing is, after that, every single person in that precinct spoke to me. And I was no different an hour before. But from then on, life was okay because I had gotten in a fight. It's like all of a sudden, you're okay. You're one of the guys. Which is totally . . . insane.

I have worked both in a squad car on patrol and in the Mounted Unit. People *love* you when you're on a horse, but if they see you pull up in a car it's like, "What did I do wrong?" Oh, it's true. You and your horse can stand on a corner in downtown Boston, especially during Christmas-time, they'd have us down there, and people would flock to the officer on the horse. Kids would come up and pet the horse. People would ask a question—"Gee, that's interesting!" And then they'd ask you another question. They think you're really a person, a human being.

The officers on foot—no one cared. And if you're in a car, they're intimidated. There's a barrier there.

You know what really keeps you on this job?—and it doesn't happen very often—it's hearing one person say thank you. Nobody ever says thank you to a police officer.

We're sort of like the lepers. People stay away from us. They don't think we're human. We're all we have. We have to take care of each other.

A lot of women think it's beneath them to work the beat car. They want to be in an office; they want to go out for coffee; they want to shop. You tell people who work inside you work a car—"Oh, God." Like there's something wrong with you.

I think there should be a difference in pay and a difference in benefits for people who work the cars and people who work inside. I've had friends killed in narcotics raids; my best friend was killed at a school. I don't think there should be the same benefits for somebody who sits in an office. What's the danger there? Are you gonna be attacked by the killer paper clip or get hit by a runaway typewriter?

You're not taking the same risks as I do. I've been cut on crack vials. I'm around people all the time who have gonorrhea, syphilis, God knows what else—"Officer! Ack-ack-phlugh! Officer, come here!" I search women and men and some farm animals, it seems. I've had everything from my shoulder dislocated to my arm broken in two places. God forbid—I've lost count of the cuts and bruises and bumps and shoves-around you get when you're kicked in the shins and the knees and the everything else. You don't even keep a tally sheet of those. That's just par for the course, comes with the job. It just happens.

But how can you feel you are on the same level as me when you're sitting in an office and the worst thing that happens is maybe you grab a cup of coffee that's too hot and you have to set it down real quick?

So many women come on this job and just scurry inside and get desk jobs as fast as they can. It bothers me. It really sticks in my craw. If the main thing is to get out, why come on?

Being a cop is so frustrating. The good and bad is so mixed in. It's so frustrating. But my attitude is—you take one bad guy at a time. And if you make a difference in just one life, if you just do one thing to make that difference, then your whole life is worthwhile.

I know it sounds corny, but to me the thrill is knowing that by being a cop I'm actually *doing* something.

Being a police officer is the finest job anybody can have. I truly believe police officers *do* make a difference. I've seen it proven time and time and time again.

The rewards—are different. It's not the big burglary, the big robbery, the big coke haul—that's *rare*.

You look for the small rewards. That's where a lot of officers, especially the younger ones fail—their expectations are too high. They think it's like TV; every day, a big-time arrest.

It doesn't work that way. It's the small things. And they *are* there, every single day. For example—one type I hate is the person who drinks and drives. I've been to too many scenes with dead children. I do my best to take the drunks off the street, and God only knows how many lives might be saved by that simple action.

It can be as simple as writing a seat-belt ticket. My daughter got a citation a few years ago for not having my grandson in a seat belt. Because of that officer doing that simple thing, they've never gone without a seat belt again.

Two years ago—her second son—my daughter was in a head-on collision and the impact was on this child's side of the car. Because he was seat-belted, his life was saved. There's a ten-, twelve-inch space between where the dash ended up and that little boy. If he had been an older boy or an adult, he would have been crushed. As it was, he sustained head injuries.

An officer came up—he had just stopped a speeder and was coming back. He put my daughter and my grandson in the squad car and took them to the hospital. With that action, he saved my grandson's life because the ambulance took another thirty-five minutes to show up.

So those are two situations where two officers made a difference. A simple citation for a seat-belt violation and a traffic stop on a speeder. These two officers saved my little grandson's life.

So many times the things we do out there, we don't see the results. But they *are* there. And to say I have a lot of pride in what I do—you bet.

I met my husband in a squad car. We didn't like each other. In fact, we disliked each other a lot. Our conversation in the car was limited to "See that guy?" "Yeah." "Want to follow him?" "Yeah." "You want to surveil that woman?" "Okay."

It got to the point where I woke up every morning and dreaded having to go to work and sit in the car with this man. It turned out he was thinking the same thing.

The only way we became friendly enough to even talk was when we realized we weren't gonna make it as partners and we were about to request a partner change. We gave one last shot at communication and went to a bar after work and sat and talked. Two kids later . . .

Once we started to talk, police work went better. And what really helped—he saw I could fight. We'd be in a fight and then he'd say, "You know, you can really handle yourself." There's just something about violence. When men see that you can do violence, it's okay.

When we were first partners in the squad—I had one year on him—I'd look at him and think, "Rookie." I found out later that he was sitting there, looking at me, thinking, "Woman."

CHAPTER 7

HOME

Police enter unimaginable worlds. How do women police keep the psychic filth of these worlds from muddying up their own homes? How do they locker up all the tragedy and despair so it doesn't haunt them? And how do they keep all this at bay when, in their private lives, no one ever lets them forget that they're cops? Relatives and friends constantly ask them to be their own personal police, and anyone who finds out they're cops feels compelled to offer their own assessments of police. As one woman cop says, "Everyone is so careful to be politically correct these days, *except* about police."

The ways men and women police find to cope with the job from which it's almost impossible to escape can determine whether they survive as police and as people . . .

I'm a forensic artist. I do skull reconstructions. I love the work. It satisfies my artistic needs; I put the skull on the base and build up clay around it. It's sculpting.

I bring the skulls home. I keep them in the garage, and then I do them in my sewing room. The first time I did one, there was still a little bit of flesh on him. I had to clean him up a little. I was thinking, "He looks a little sad." I'm cleaning him up; it was real late at night. Everybody was in bed and I'm sitting there in the sewing room, cleaning him up. It's real quiet. And then I think—"What if a ghost comes?"

There's one I did last year, he was real young. He still upsets me. Dentally, he was about twelve. Skeletally, maybe sixteen. He had a real unusual nose. He was found in a wooded area surrounded by apartments.

You realize when you do this kind of work—there are a *lot* of bodies out there. So many runaways, so many transients, so many just *dumped*. Whenever I'm driving on the highway, out in the secluded areas? I always think, "What's out there that's never even been found yet?"

My son hates the boxes I bring home with skulls. He calls them my deadheads. The first one I did really stunk; it was really nasty. My son came in the room: "Mom, it smells! It smells!" I'm sitting there eating cookies; I didn't even notice.

There's one in my garage now I'm fixing to do.

I'm a singer as a sideline. I do weddings and funerals, serious music. My father passed away in 1988 and I sang at his memorial service. People say, "How could you do that?" Well, I'm a professional singer. You put your professional *persona* on.

I've sung a lot of cop funerals. And that's really tough. Really tough. Particularly when I know the officer well. Oh, God.

One time, I was singing a funeral mass for an investigator whose life's work was missing children. He passed away, and this sheriff was speaking right before I sang. And he's looking at the casket and saying, "You know, Jeff, the little boy that you were looking for? Well, we found him." He's talking to him like he's there. Oh, my God. I mean, I got this lump in my throat and I'm—How am I going to do this? But I, you know—pushed it right out of my mind and sang. But tough? Oh yeah.

I was sent to the hospital one time on a child abuse case. In the old days, many times, if the nurses were busy, we would bathe the children. Here was this little two-year-old. I had a son the same age. It was like seeing my son on the examining table. This little guy had been beaten by his father and thrown out a second-floor window. He was brain-damaged. They wouldn't let the mother get him for two days.

Now, I was having trouble to begin with, washing this little guy, because of my own son. He looked like my son. And then he reached up and touched my cheek and started stroking it. I completely lost it. I started to cry. I left the hospital and refused to follow up on the case.

I honestly think that that might have been the incident that turned me around, that made me realize that if I was going to be a professional, I'd have to turn off all my emotions. The only emotions you keep are the ones that help you do your job. Everything else you shut off to surface later.

When I got home, my kids could tell by my voice that something was wrong. I thought, "Who do you protect if not your kids?" We're supposed to protect everybody else—What happens if we can't protect our own family? The hard thing is, in trying to protect them, a lot of times, you cut them out.

I was called to an apartment building. It was one of those buildings that's got a very small foyer and there's—my God, I can remember this so clearly—like little insets in the wall where flowers and vases used to be when they first opened up the building and it was still a good neighborhood. And it had like a marble floor. And—see, I started shaking when I saw that movie, *Silence of the Lambs,* and saw that deputy that was skinned alive—because that is exactly what it looked like. It was almost like this kid was lit up because there were lights behind him.

What happened was, somehow, he was about eight years old, seven or eight years old, they'd been playing in the lobby. And in the older elevators, you know how there's the door, but in front of the door there's the metal gates that close? And he somehow—it had to be the steel closing first and *then* the gates—somehow he got stuck in between—it was the steel closing on him and then the gates—and the elevator went up—and he was this tiny little hillbilly kid, he was tiny enough that he could do it. Somehow, the elevator—I don't know if he had pushed the button or there were kids in the elevator because I didn't stick around long enough to ever hear what had happened. The elevator went up, he was caught in the middle, and it completely flayed him—clothes, skin, everything. And he was plastered like this, with one leg up, and his head was turned to the side, and everything was missing.

And when I came in—you could see what had been *underneath* the skin, but the skin and the clothing were gone because it had been completely flayed off of him. And his head was turned to the side, his head was facing south. And it was my job to tell the mother what had happened because at that point she was coming to the scene.

And the mother . . . took it like a ghetto mother would. She cried, but it wasn't desperation, it was almost a resignation. It's sort of like battle shock because they deal with tragedy on a day-to-day basis. One day, their kid's friend is there; the next day, the kid's friend is dead. Their grieving is a grieving of resignation.

And I was devastated. It seems like three days was the time for me where I would allow the stuff to brew inside of me until I get drunk and then cry and get it over with. And that was all it took: two glasses of wine, I'd cry, and it was okay.

And I don't remember at what point I stopped needing the wine. And I don't remember at what point I stopped crying. But I'm gonna say it was probably five or six years into the job where I decided you were either going to cry yourself silly and be totally dysfunctional or learn to accept it and go forward.

There were two children living in an apartment where the adults were dealing dope from. And the dad was so worried about the competition coming in there and stealing his dope, what he did was he took a loaded nine-millimeter gun, and he placed it on top of the refrigerator that was right next to the door. Cocked it, had one in the chamber, left it on top of this refrigerator, so if someone came in and was trying to get his dope, he could just reach up there and get it and shoot the person at the door.

So they've got two children in this household. One of the kids—I guess they had been doing their transactions, they forgot to feed the kids. So the kids are small; I think the oldest was five and the other one was two, I believe. They had learned to be somewhat self-sufficient and take care of themselves. So they decided, they hadn't had lunch, they hadn't had dinner, they were hungry. So they did the best thing they could. They went over to a cabinet and got a box of cereal out. And they poured it in two bowls. And then they went over to the refrigerator to get the milk. Well, the five-year-old kid tried to open the refrigerator door and I guess the door was stuck, so he yanked it open. He got the milk, he poured the milk, and then he went to close the door. Well, he closed it and it opened back up. And he closed it and it opened back up. And he closed it and it opened back up. So finally, he just hauled off and *slammed* the door. Well, when he slammed the door, the gun on top of the refrigerator went off and shot his brother right in the head. This five-year-old's got to live with the fact that—he came in and, you know, this happened. Shot him right in the head.

You go in there, you see that—here's this two-year-old baby lying on the couch, waiting for his older brother, fix him a little bowl of cereal.

Again, your mind goes back to—How many times have my kids gone and got a bowl of cereal, you know? Just think—they could have been in this same type of environment. How many times can you remember your kid getting a little bowl of cereal? *Of course,* every kid gets himself a little bowl of cereal, fixes himself a little sandwich or something out of the refrigerator, grabs a piece of fruit, and closes the refrigerator door. How we take these common everyday things for granted. I know my refrigerator's like a swinging door—"A piece of fruit, Mom, an apple, Mom, juice, Mom"—and you let them go and do it. But take that very same incident and put it in a different location and a different environment, and it's a tragedy. Tragedy.

The things we just take for granted every day. Turn it around. Different hands.

I worked as one of the investigators on the Green River killings. One of the jobs I had was the analysis, doing a definite stop-and-start time for the killer, which involved reading through all the unsolved homicides where women were victims since 1972 in the state of Washington. It included all of Ted Bundy's stuff. You got sick to your stomach after looking at some of those autopsy pictures after a while and seeing some of the things that we saw.

The other thing is, anytime an unidentified body was found murdered anywhere in the country, we normally would get a Teletype of that. It got to the point where even the guys in the office would cheer if the unidentified body was a male. Because you got so sick of seeing "Unidentified female's body," "Unidentified female's body," "Unidentified female's body."

It was just like you were so tired—the victimization against women was so overwhelming, it was like, "Is there anything else? Is there *anyone* normal?"

I was just telling the people in my current squad that working in the unit [Green River Task Force] . . . any naiveté you had about what people were capable of doing soon disappeared. You realize people are capable of doing some really horrendous things.

I have some nightmares, and I've always put it off to—oh, this happened back in this period of my life or this happened or something. Until finally I had someone bring up the fact to me that "You've seen a lot of ugly shit. Maybe *that's* why you have nightmares once in a while." And I thought, actually, that could be. It was a hell of a good experience, but I got really burned out on seeing dead bodies. Would I do it again? You bet.

All the exposure we have, and yet you'd do it again in a heartbeat, for the experience and for the exposure. It sucks you in. And that's where you get the real conflict with what you see and what it does to you.

The ironic thing is that it's a love/hate: You know it's probably not the healthiest thing to do, but you wouldn't trade it for anything. But you do lose perspective.

I've been told it makes you a paranoid parent. My kids think I'm overprotective. I had two children before I became a cop, and I raised them to be independent. But my two younger children—my eleven-year-old. She can't go to school by herself. She hasn't even been on the bus by herself. She doesn't even go get the newspaper at the corner store, you know? She bikes—"Mommy, can I go bike riding?" "No. I'll take you to the park and you can go bike riding there." Because I don't know how I would feel if someone stole her bike or pushed her down. My oldest daughter says, "Is she ever gonna grow up? You never did us this way." I think, "Am I ruining them?"

I compare myself to my sister. She'll go to the automatic teller, take out money, and walk back to the car with the money out. I'm frantic—"Put that away!" She's like, "Come on. What could happen?" "You never know." I'm paranoid because I see what can happen.

Most units you go into, the victims are women and your suspects are men.

And sometimes, though, you think, "I don't want to know any more." I've heard enough, that's enough, thank you.

I talk to my mom; she had seven children. She's a fairly naive, normal-type person. And she thinks about now, all the things that have gone on—and the media now is much more open about things, too.

And there's a real conflict. You don't want to know. Because if you know too much, you'd be paranoid. I'd be the worst parent in the world. I'd never let the child out. He'd be one of those ones that'd be shackled to the . . . you'd read about the ten-year-old who was found shackled. Because you know so much. And it's hard to keep perspective that this is actually a very small percentage of the community.

If there's one thing I've learned, and I tell people this all the time—that if you're a cop, no matter where you are, you have to have another life. You cannot let police work be your life.

A lot of cops do it. They allow police work to be their life. And, my God, that will kill you.

When I was on the street, I was involved in martial arts and I was going around the world competing and I was training a lot. That helped quite a bit; that would put your mind completely into something else. Then I got shot and I couldn't compete anymore, but I still worked out a lot.

Then I got into weight training. I got into embroidering and creweling. You just—I started taking piano lessons. I've always consciously done that. I've always thought—okay, I have to find something else to do so I don't go home and think about this. I would consciously come up with things *like* piano lessons where I can't think about work; I have to think about hitting the right keys, which I never *did,* but . . . And I've been very fortunate in my life. I've always had very good friends.

Women are better at doing this than men are. Absolutely. Men have very shallow friendships. They have trouble finding things outside. I think it's true of all men, not just male cops. But it's worse with male cops because it's such a macho profession. I taught in the Police Academy and I taught right at the beginning, right in the beginning when these guys would show up their first day at the Academy, and you could just see it in them—my God, this is their life! They're so excited they can hardly stand it. I used to lecture and lecture and lecture and say, "My God, you just have to find something else in your life," and they would look at me like, "What are you talking about?" That *is* their life. And they're cops twenty-four hours a day. They don't make really good friendships with other men. And they don't have other interests—well, yeah, a lot of them like eating potato chips and watching football.

And it would be really hard to explain to those guys that there is another life.

That's why the men police officers have the drinking problems, the heart attacks, the strokes. They have no life and a lot of times, they'll reach retirement age and there's *nothing else in their life.* There is nothing in their life.

Men don't know how to talk. So they internalize everything. I have a lot of male friends; they don't talk to their wives. They can be married twenty years and the wives never know what they did for a living. Men do not know how to communicate.

Now, put that on women. Put a group of us together and we know how to communicate with each other. It's a natural-born thing in us, that we *have* to talk to each other.

With a man—"Talk to me." "I *am* talking to you." "You're moving your lips, but you're not saying anything."

You have to learn when to leave the job. I don't mean just leave it physically in the sense where you walk out of the station and you go home. But you don't take your job home with you. When I get home, I'm a sister, I'm a girlfriend, I'm a mother, I'm a grandmother, I'm a friend. I'm all these things I was before I got this job. That's my . . . life. *That's* my life. The Police Department—is a job. Just like a teacher, just like a nurse, just like anybody else that's got a physical *job* they've gotta go to—factory, anything. There is no difference. There *is* no difference.

I think a lot of people have that conflict when they can't sever the two. They can't make a distinction between the two. You don't go home and start chewing up the old man about everything he's doing wrong—and that can happen. We have bad days when everything'll just get to you.

There *are* things that just get to you. I had an incident when I first came on the job about a lady that cut her kids up. She was a mental. And she literally dissected her baby. She cut the baby up like you would a whole chicken if you would go to the Jewel and you would buy a chicken and you would cut the arms here and the legs there. And not only did she dissect the one, she had a three-year-old there, too, and she stabbed him repeatedly. She didn't cut him up; she just stood over him and stabbed him in his chest repeatedly. He died also. She killed two kids. When we got there, she's stabbing at the wall.

And you see that. But you can't be a mother; you can't be sympathetic. You've got a job to do. So what do you do? You handle the paper, you make your notifications, you call the coroner's, you notify your supervisor, you take her into custody, all the things that you have to do. You do what you gotta do.

And then when you get home—as in this case with me—I handled all of this, seeing all of this, *to the letter*—and it didn't bother me, never shed a tear.

Then I got home. And I walked into my children's bedroom and I looked at both my boys. Safe and sleeping in their beds. And I lost it. The tears. The whole nine yards. Everything cut loose. The ghosts. You see it.

And you know, you think how safe they are, what good shape, how much they're loved, how much there are people around that love them. You learn to appreciate the things that you sometimes take every day for granted. Like walking into your kids' room means nothing. Okay, they're in the bed, you go into the living room now and have your time. But there are times that just those little things like that—all the many times I would walk into their room, I would never just burst out into tears. This got me. This just absolutely floored me.

You see something like that, and the first thing you do, you think of your own. And just seeing them—safe, and sleeping, and secure, clean. It just gets you. It really gets you.

I used to work Vice as a decoy. What bothered me was, for every one arrest, there were at least another ten circling the parking lot. And this was an all-day thing. I mean, we'd go out for hours and do these sting operations. Most of them are married, most of them have families—they are not what you would consider the stereotype person, you know, the old, lonely guy or the guy who's too unattractive to get a date. That wasn't the case. It was, actually, quite the opposite. And there were all professions.

And I also worked the dance clubs at night. And to see what you'd see—part of it, you'd get so frustrated with women that would allow themselves to do this—they'd dance naked and sit in guys' laps and stuff. And it's just like, it's just so many men. It's like—Is everybody like this? Is there anybody out there that has any respect for people? For women? You do lose perspective. It was not a healthy unit for me to be in.

And there'd be people circling my block who I knew when I was growing up as a kid. And I told my parents about it—"Do you remember this guy?" It's like . . . Wow! It's kind of an amazing world out there.

And there are just so many men. We're talking doctors, lawyers, men who have this picture-perfect family life, right? But then, at noon hour, they're down there circling blocks looking for a whore. And there are so many! I tell you, I used to work that decoy assignment a minimum eight hours a day, at least one day a week in this particular area of town, and we'd have parking lots full of people circling. And for the ones that get arrested, there's probably ten for every one.

And, of course, that affects your personal life, particularly if you're single. You get to the point where you don't believe or trust anybody because of what you've seen. And it's not that personally you've been affected, but professionally, you've just been so exposed that it's hard to maintain too much openness in your personal life.

Girlfriends call me up. They give me his name and date of birth, I run them. Or my boyfriend will call me up: "By the way, I'm looking for an old classmate of mine. What's he doin' these days?" He gives me his name and date of birth. I call him back. "Well, he's doin' six to ten in the state pen." I've said, "I am more to you than just some information service."

You become the family consultant. Your family is always—"What shall I do about this incident where my car was hit?" "Somebody broke into my house." Or—"These people are harassing us—what shall we do?"

That's what else you become. You become the family consultant.

Or you sit down to Thanksgiving dinner. "Well, what can you tell us today?" So now I'm the family social service representative. Like, "Don't leave your kids with anybody you don't know. Have you checked out your baby-sitter lately? Have your kids come home with marks on them that can't be explained?"

And they're at Thanksgiving dinner, looking the kids up and down. "Do your children know the difference between a good touch and a bad touch?" "How often do you talk to your children?" I got them all talking to their kids.

I used to tell the elderly members of my family, "Don't go around with all that money on you." I said, "They pat your breasts down now. They're not satisfied just to snatch your handbag and run. They figure old people are smart now, they're not gonna put any money in their handbags. So now they're ripping the old women's bras off, throwing them down on the ground so they can feel their breasts. They make the men take off their socks and shoes to make sure they're not hiding money in their socks and shoes." I tell them, "These criminals are so sophisticated now, you just can't be safe. You just can't be safe, no matter how you try to camouflage it or whatever. You just always have to be so aware and so careful."

I just went to a family reunion. And this is one of the reasons I don't go to them. It's always, "Well, how are things in the Police Department?" They try and make me the center of attention, which I do not want to be. There are times when I don't mind talking about the job with people that aren't immediate family. But it gets really old really fast. My husband's aware of it. That's why we don't go to large parties where I don't know a lot of people or, if they're not cops, I avoid them.

This family reunion—one of my aunts came up to me and she brought her two granddaughters up to me whom I haven't seen for many, many years; last time I saw them they were babes in arms. And she very proudly said, "I wanted to introduce my granddaughters to you. And I just told them that you're a cop!" And she was so proud of that. And it was like—now I'm supposed to perform? What am I supposed to do with this information? So I just smiled like, yes, that's nice. That's why I hate large gatherings of relatives.

They threaten their kids with you. Our neighbor did that to us not too long ago. We were talking and he was saying his nephew was over and he wouldn't buckle himself up into his seat belt, and he said, "There's two police officers live over there. And if you don't buckle up, they're gonna come and arrest you."

We hate that. It puts us in a really poor light. And all these little kids are thinking we're the bogeyman. That's not what we're all about. And we're not there as disciplinarians for their children; that's *their* function. Even though they try to involve us. They cast us in that role. And we don't care to do that.

The worst thing that I've come across is that everybody's got a bad cop story. No matter where you are. In fact, I hate to tell people what I do and I *won't* tell them what I do until I really get to know them. Like the woman who cuts my hair. For the longest time, she only knew I was a city employee.

But this one—he's the husband of one of my cousins and because I like her so much, I don't put him down. But, man! If he was by himself, I'd really lay it to him. Because invariably, he will tell me a horrendous cop story.

One time, he was talking, saying something bad about cops, and I said, "Jim, what do you want me to say?—'Yep! We're all no good, we're all worthless, that cop did the stupidest thing I ever heard'—What do you want me to say?—'You're right? This proves it? You convinced me, Jim. I will no longer be a police officer.'"

I have a friend, she's a writer for a magazine here, and we'll go out and she always wants to know, "Well, what gory things did you work today?"

Or we'll be somewhere, we'll be at a bar or something, talking to guys, they'll say, "Well, what do y'all do?" And my standard answer is "I work for the city." I never tell them where I work, anything.

But my friend—"Aw! Tell 'em where you really work!" I don't like to do that. Because people are put off by it. And sometimes the guys *may* like it or may *not* like it.

I never tell them. But my friend'll keep on—"Do you know where she works?" And I want to *kill* her. I can't break her out of it. I tell her, "Not everybody is thrilled or interested. Some people get disgusted even knowing that that's a cop they're talking to." And with guys, I guess if they're not real confident or sure of themselves, they might get a little intimidated by it. I don't like to do it. I guess my friend is proud of me. But I told her, "Not everybody is."

* * *

Dating as a police officer. You get used to people lying to you on the job. Everybody lies—suspects, victims, witnesses. So, in your personal life, if ever anybody tells you the truth, you're amazed. You always think they're lying because people always lie.

If you're a single woman cop and you meet a guy, it's a three-month thing. That's it. Three months. At first, they love the fact that you're a cop. Then you notice a change. What's the matter? They're intimidated, they're disturbed that you're capable and intelligent.

Well, try to understand. They work nine to five. They go home. You go out on midnights. You put on a gun so you can protect people. That's intimidating.

They think they can handle it. But that's bullshit. They can't handle it. They're gone after three months.

Now I don't tell people what I do.

It's hard for our personal relationships working in a situation where we don't trust as much. You know, we work with the men, we know the stories, we know the lines, and the first time your husband or boyfriend says, "We're working late," we're like, "Yeah, right, honey." We're always waiting for men to fail on us. We're waiting for them to be less than perfect. No one *is* perfect, but it's hard for us to accept that.

Dating is very difficult. It's very hard for men to handle that you're a cop because it's such an authoritative role.

There've been times where I've been talking to a man I've just met and, as soon as I tell him I'm a cop, I could visually *see* him drawing away.

You gotta watch the guys you date, you gotta watch the guys you meet, because men are just intimidated by your job. And then not only are they intimidated, some of them are resentful that you're a police officer. They're *really* resentful.

And some of them will try to like—"Okay. What can you do? You're such a bad son of a bitch, or whatever," that's what they say, and then they want to *fight* you and stuff. You're like, "Why?" They're just *unbelievable*. Some men take that kind of attitude. They want to take you on. "Well, what are you like without your gun?" I'm like, "Whaa? You wouldn't come on to a *man* like this." But they come on to a woman like this.

So lots of times, prior to my current friend, I'd meet a guy and, especially if I didn't know he was a cop or anything, I put him through the nth degree; by the time I dated him, I ran him for records and stuff. I wanted to find out all I could. Because women have to be careful in any kind of police job—in our department, they don't want you associating with known criminals. You have to be very circumspect in this job. So many times, you have to be very careful who you date, and you gotta run them, and also, sometimes they just haven't been caught yet. You just gotta be *real* careful.

Some policewomen have it tough . . . where they're abused. You've got some women who work hard and they're being beaten by their husbands. They go home and hang up their gun so that the husband can beat them up and throw them around the house. Can you imagine that? Now they won't take that crap off of a stranger in the street, but they go home and get beaten up by a "loved one."

They come to work and hide it, or take a couple days off sick so they can hide the bruises. Because you're not allowed to come to work . . . in our department it's you're not allowed to come to work bruised up. You can't come to work with a black eye or a slash on your face or stuff like that, you can't come to work all scratched up and stuff. You gotta take off sick or wear sunglasses or whatever you gotta do, but you cannot come to work looking like you've been through a war.

We have people who won't take that stuff off of a stranger on the street, but they sure are taking it from a loved one at home. A few years ago, we had two female officers killed by boyfriends or significant others. The one woman, she was constantly being abused by her daughter's father. She'd gone to her coworkers and even some supervisors for assistance with this man. And they told her to leave him and not have any dealings with this man. I guess she was sort of torn because he was her daughter's father and the kid loved her father. The bottom line was, he was a crack addict. She came home once; she'd gone out on a social function with the squad or something—the man was hyped and he just ended up shooting her with her own gun. Fortunately for her, she was supposed to go and pick up their daughter, but because it was so late she decided to let the child sleep over at her grandmother's. But had she brought her daughter home, the child would have seen her father killing her mother.

And then, not even two months later, we have another officer, she is dating some guy, and he's an ex-con, I don't know whether she knew it or not. But things didn't work out. He decides he wants to slash her up. He stabbed her numerous times. He really mutilated that woman.

The ironic thing was, she worked in the Hostage Negotiation Unit of our department. So everybody's looking for her murderer and four days later they traced it up to him and—Doesn't the Hostage Negotiation Unit get a job? And who is it who is suicidal? Her murderer. And so they had to try to talk him out of killing himself. Because he had already killed—he had gone to hole up in his ex-girlfriend's house, but the ex-girlfriend's mother didn't like this man. So what he did was went off and shot and killed this woman right off Jump Street. The girl managed to get out of the house, but the guy was holed up in the house. So now he's got two corpses under his belt.

So here, her unit has to try to talk him out of killing himself. Really, they wanted to storm the house and kill him. So you talk about a tough thing—needless to say, the man killed himself anyway. The inspector for that unit ended up having to hire a psychiatrist for the squad. It was just too devastating for them. They really held the girl in high esteem, and then to have to talk her murderer into turning himself in? It was wild.

So, like I say, being a policewoman, this job also has other social aspects.

I just got on estrogen-replacement therapy. I didn't have a period for three months. My doctor said she didn't want to put me on the stuff till I missed my period for a year. I told her, "Look. I'm crabby and I've got a gun." She gave it to me.

There's a lot of two-cop marriages. I think it's dangerous, myself. Because cops are controllers. Especially if you've got somebody that's overbearing and both of you are overbearing. Who has the control? Who has the upper hand? And then if they have a temper problem, or they've had a rough night, or maybe they're abusive on the street, maybe they're overly aggressive on the street. Well, they're gonna be overly aggressive at home. And if you're like that and your spouse is, "Well, I'm not taking that crap from you," that could lead to some bull. Next thing you know, everybody's pulling out their jacks and if that doesn't work, then they're pulling their guns.

And on top of everything else, so many cops are philanderers. Especially if you've got a cop for a wife and she knows all this and she suspects you to be a philanderer, then uuuuggh. Cop wives know the excuses, they know the squad goes out together, they know about the parties. It'd be too dangerous. Too dangerous.

I've heard, I don't know how true it is, I've heard that now we have cops that are in these cop marriages, they're getting restraining orders against each other and domestic dispute crap. It's dangerous. It is really dangerous. I wouldn't marry another cop. I would never do it, not in Philly anyhow. I always say, "Two guns in a house is two guns too many." Only one of us can have a gun. Only one. And it better be me.

That's why my friend, he's a fireman, so—he can have his ax. But I've got the gun.

CHAPTER 8

THE CLUB

I love being a cop. It's a lot of fun. It's just me and my buddies and we have a lot of fun. You're out there, you're laughing with your buddies, it's an adventure, it's a good time. It's like Boys' Night Out.

—Male police officer, Seattle Police Department

It is a men's club. It really, really, really is. If you get a woman in, you're concerned. You think—Are we gonna have to watch what we say? Is she gonna be one of the guys? Is she gonna have enthusiasm for the job? Or is she someone who should be selling dresses, but she's a cop? Is she gonna quit when she breaks a nail? Is she gonna always be messing with her hairdo? I don't know.

I think women cops really do belong in law enforcement, but if you're a woman, you've gotta be twice as good. You're judged twice as hard. I've seen women who were worthless cops persecuted and just as many worthless male cops were just . . . let slide. It's a double standard. We've gotten some good women in here—once you establish what they are, no problem.

—Male police officer, Upper Peninsula, Michigan

You're at a terrific party. You're in a circle with like-minded people—high hilarity, great insights, wonderful camaraderie. Things are going great, until in walk one or two people you don't know. Pretty soon they try to crash your group. What's your reaction?

Probably the same as males in law enforcement since women were legislated in. Or the same as men in any organization who had come up and thrived in the Good Old Boys' Network. And while the reaction may be understandable, the results can be pernicious . . .

I was the first woman in the Canine Unit, the only woman they had ever had in the Canine Unit in our department. The guys really didn't want me there. A couple of them did, but the majority didn't. They put me where nobody else wanted to work, on a team with a sergeant and four other guys who didn't want me.

I'm Italian—my first language is Italian. In training, the sergeant would always bring up olive oil and ask me if I wanted an olive-oil body rub. He'd always do this in front of the other guys.

They'd give me a hard time about fighting the dogs. We always had to take turns fighting the dogs. I always had to fight the biggest dog. They were like, "Let's go look at the girl. Let's watch her fight *this* dog," you know. And a couple of the dogs were big enough and strong enough that when they hit me, they knocked me down, they knocked me down completely.

You put on the sleeve, it's a big protective arm you put on. If we were gonna do a call-off, you'd run and they'd send the dog after you. The dog is trained to go after the arm. Then an officer would tell the dog to halt. You would stop and the dog would stop. Sometimes they did; sometimes they didn't. The dogs didn't always mind.

One time, when they sent the biggest dog after me—I mean, this dog would knock the *big* guys down—this time, he knocked *me* down and took the protective arm off me and knocked me to the ground. But I just stayed still, and he didn't do anything.

The only thing that saved me was this dog knew me really well because his master was my primary training officer and this officer told him to halt. He listened to his master.

I never had a problem with any bad guy in the street. You have more problems with the people that you work with than you do with the bad guys on the street.

I'm a senior officer with the Department of Corrections. I look back over the years, the problems I have had have *not* been with the inmates—it's always been with my fellow officers. That's where our problems come in at. The inmates—they know what they're there for, they know what they have to do. But it's the staff that gives us a rough time. I didn't see it at the beginning.

They used to tell us women, "You will have to fight every day when you get a job like this, and you could get killed." And it really wasn't like that when you got inside; you *didn't* have to fight every day. Or they would say, "What are you doin' here? Pretty girl like you? You should be home raisin' kids"—you know, all this dumb stuff that you didn't want to hear. You're here to support yourself, and they tell you, "What are you doing here?" "I'm here to make some money . . . if you'll let me."

They used to harass me so bad. I mean, they treated me so cold. I had this job I'll never forget, called "The Court-yard." All you had to do was supervise the area so no fights would break out, anything like that. Rain, sleet, and snow. It was like they give you those jobs nobody else wanted, shit jobs. Nobody really wanted the job, so if you were on their list, you would wind up with something like that. And that was just to belittle you, or degrade you, or get you mad enough to quit. That's what they wanted. I know because they used to tell me, "Before this year is over, we'll have you out of here."

And I'll tell you, many days I was so hurt and so bitter, but I never would let them see me cry. I would go out to my car in the parking lot sometimes, and I would sit there—I mean, it just hurt so bad the way that they treated me, you know.

I tried to come inside a couple of times from The Courtyard to get coffee because during the wintertime, it gets cold here, so cold you feel like your toes are gonna break or your fingers, right? So I tried to come in a couple times to get something warm to drink. And they would report me for being off my post. All I wanted to do was go get the coffee and go back out in that area. Mind, no inmates are in the yard; they're all locked up.

Or just to stand in that doorway, get a little heat. Because a lot of times, you can just warm your hands up and go back. But they'd report me for that, too—it just shows how nasty. I couldn't believe it. I felt, "Why are they treating me like this?" I think it was because I was a woman. I really wholeheartedly believe that now as I look back over the years. Women were just not accepted during that time. The men kept everything for themselves—the best days, the best jobs. Weekends off for a female was a no-no. Mind, you could do the same job, same function, but you just couldn't . . . They had it so locked in.

We women were working side by side. When we had our feedings for the inmates, we were all in this big mess hall and had our positions to take to supervise the feedings. So we were basically together. And, in the visiting programs on Saturdays, when the families come to visit, we would work together.

We had just us to confide in because any complaints that you had, who did you have to go to, you know? The other girls. Because the guys didn't want to hear it. The things that we were talking about didn't exist and we were making this stuff up. But it was real. It was real.

And even now, the job I have right now in Corrections, I

have had many jobs working with people, but I didn't realize people could be so cruel. It happens. It happens.

In 1968, we were assigned to particular station houses. We didn't get out of the house unless it was to go process a dead body or go stand on a picket line.

It was customary that when a neighboring precinct would call the station house looking for a female because they had a deceased, they would very often try to rattle your cage.

This one day, I get a call, I'm going to get picked up, I have to go do a search, and all the way out of the house, this sergeant is telling me how gruesome and gory the search is gonna be. So he gets in his car and he says to the officers who are gonna take me, "Bring her over. I'll meet you there."

So on the way, I ask the guys if they'll pull over; I had to make a stop. So I made my stop and I proceed on to the location.

The procedure was: You would go in, you would search the body, remove any jewelry, money, personal effects, and turn them over to the sergeant. And then he would voucher them.

So I go in—the sergeant's outside—and before I go in he's telling me again how gruesome and gory this is gonna be in an attempt to scare you, intimidate you, and because I looked twelve years old, I was easy prey. I go in and I'm blowing up my gloves so I can get my hands in them and I do my search and I come out and I say, "Sarge, I have some property for you." And he puts out his hands and I place in his hands some chicken livers and gizzards. This man almost fainted right on the spot because, of course, he took it with his bare hands.

And I looked at him and I said, "Don't ever threaten another female." And he just looked at me and everybody had a good laugh—because that's what I stopped to get. I went to the butcher and got the chicken parts.

They never did that to me again. Because I was so tired of being threatened and intimidated because sometimes you did go and the scene *was* particularly gruesome.

And you learned how to deal with it. Mostly, it was the smell. So you'd learn to take sugar and put it in the bathtub and set fire to it—so the carbon would permeate the air and would kill the smell of death. Or you would do your searches with one hand while you kept a handkerchief doused with perfume over the other hand. Or you'd shoot ammonia in the room, spray ammonia in the room. Anything to kill that stench. And sometimes you would go in and the bodies were in various stages of decay. Or, when a body fills with gas, if it's been around too long—it explodes, like a balloon.

So, some of these things were not pleasant, even if you went in with an open mind. So to have some clown telling you this all the time and hyping you up—I mean, this guy really needed to be taught a lesson. And I really think he learned because he was the joke of the borough for about a month—"We can't believe that pipsqueak did that to you!"

I go to a call. They send another male officer and then another male officer. The attitude is—get a *guy*. I'm there with the one male officer and when the other guy shows up, the first male officer says to the second, this is right in front of me—"I'm glad you came."

In SWAT, we go to a shooting house, where you shoot targets, it's part of a qualification. It's just an old thing that was built on a range and it's just walls, and you can move the walls inside to make different types of rooms, put up targets of good guys, bad guys, guys that have guns, cops, or maybe somebody holding a bad guy. You have a certain amount of time to go through the house, and you have to go through and shoot the bad guys and not shoot the good guys. It's part of a qualification exam, so there's a lot of stress on it.

The guys go through there and every once in a while, they'll get going too fast and screw up and they'll accidentally shoot a good-guy target.

I was out observing one day. And I noticed that when the guys went through there and accidentally shot a good-guy target, it was kind of a Good Old Boys' joke. Captain would slap them on the back: "Hey! You shot a good-guy target. Hahaha." They'd laugh.

But when this woman new to the unit would come

through the shooting house and do that, there was a whole different feeling about it. It was like they looked at each other like, "Gee, would you want to work with *her?* She just shot the good guy." *"I* wouldn't want to work with her." It's like, she screwed up; we *knew* it!

I don't know exactly how to put it in words, but there's a real subtle line in there where if the guys do it it's okay because they're part of the Good Old Boys and it's something funny, but if a woman does it, she did it because she's a woman. It's a real subtle type of thing in there. Kind of like the glass ceiling; it's a real subtle thing you can never do anything about, but it is definitely there. It's there.

My brother and I are in the same department. He's had a totally different experience than I have had. He's 5'11", he's a white male. He's perfect, he's nice, he's just what they wanted. He has had not one bit of turbulence throughout his whole, entire career. He floated through the Academy; he had only four and a half years on the job and he ended up in a very elite unit. He's a great guy, by the way. But as far as any of the experiences I've had, he does not understand it in the least.

I'm very small. When I was on probation, I noticed that if you're all small and petite, they figure you're not worth a shit. But the Big Guy! There was a guy on probation with me, he was 6'4", 200 pounds. A big, dumb guy. And at deployment meetings, the training officers and sergeants are fighting to see who will get him in their car. Maybe he can't walk and chew gum at the same time, but if he's big, he's already accepted.

Have you heard of the Good Old Boys' Syndrome? It takes on a Southern connotation in Texas. You've got the *redneck* Good Old Boys' Syndrome. There's always the attitude to the "little ladies," "darlin's," things of that nature. The atmosphere down here, it just seems like the country boys in this area—the woman needs to be barefoot, pregnant, and in the house, and if she *does* work, it needs to be a secretary's job, or a nurse's job, or something that women are good at, that doesn't threaten them. It's a blatant insult.

I came into law enforcement in 1985. I knew what I was stepping off into. I knew some of the women police officers and I knew the scenario, basically. I don't mean to lump all men in one category. I'm working with one guy now who is the best partner I've ever had and I've known some terrific men who have been my mentors. But the basic mentality is there.

I had a supervisor that flat ran me out of the warrant section to transport prisoners. That evolved into me being sat down at a desk as a clerk. I was considered a warrant deputy, but they did not want me on the street. And they were paying me deputy salary, when they could have been paying a clerk *half* my salary to do the same job.

So the basic redneck scenario in law enforcement is there are some that believe women cannot take care of themselves on the street and would actually sit there and say, "I'm not working with a woman because I'm not gonna get my ass shot because she ain't gonna do nothin'. She's just gonna stand there and cry." And they can infuriate you so much that you *want* to cry, but you know if you do, they're gonna say, "Well, that's just typical."

The name of the game on the New York City Police Department is to belong—to get behind that blue curtain and to secure that we're a solid force—no one's gonna leave rank; everyone's gonna stay the same and be the same. And I think that's probably true in any police department.

We just have encountered a major corruption scandal. The cop that turned said that he got out of the Police Academy and came to the precinct and said he got into corruption because *he wanted to belong.*

I mean, there had to be some sort of leader in that group. But how many cops were drawn into it because they did not have the courage or the strength, if you will, to be an individual?

And, in fact, do we *want* individuals to work for the New York City Police Department? Or do we want just a bunch of puppets?

Another interesting thing about this corruption scandal is that, I heard, the only two people off of this whole tour that were *not* included in this whole thing were the two women that these men neither liked nor trusted. Now, I don't know these two women, but what I'm curious about is—Did they not like them and trust them because the women were willing to stand on their own two feet? Or were these women really people who could not be liked and trusted or were they simply women who would not go along with the program?

I was talking to the fellow that works for me, and he's one rank under me, and we were talking about it and I was saying my whole . . . my whole *craziness* with this job; I was saying, "Don't you see that it's the whole administration— don't air our dirty laundry—the club is here. The club is in every rank. Don't you see that this is just a progression? This kid and these people learned from *us* that *we* want to belong to the club; *we* don't want to embarrass the department; *we . . .*"

And he said to me, "Well! We *all* want to belong." And he could understand perfectly. And if he could understand perfectly, then every man on this job can understand perfectly. I have absolutely no understanding of that because I have *never* belonged.

Now, I ask the women officers on the NYPD—you tell me, have you ever really belonged? Belonged to the *system*—feeling that you were a part of it *all,* that you were a part of the New York City Police Department? Do you feel like . . . if you ran into a problem, they'd be there for you, they'd support you if you felt that you were right?

Would they call you to ask you, "What do *you* think about this?"

One of Joel Rifkin's first victims—guess who pulled her out of the river? My partner and I did. And the squad says, "Suicide. Looks like an OD." It came over on 911 like this: "There's a box floating in the Hudson River and there are two legs coming out of the box." So we go down to the Hudson River and sure enough there's a box floating in the river with two legs hanging out of it. So we pull the box out of the river—and the detectives kept referring to it as a "he"—and Mary and I, my partner, kept saying, "Not for nothing, but, ah, those are a woman's ankles."

My precinct squad wasn't there yet, so the neighboring precinct shows up. And the guy says, when I say it looks like a woman's ankles, he says, "Well, you know, this *is* Greenwich Village, and the men—ahhh—" I say, "You know, if you go through an operation, you can shave your Adam's apple, you can have breasts put on, you can have other things removed or put on—but you don't change your ankles."

So they argued with me about that. All we had was the ankles to go on because she was in a box, wrapped in a plastic bag in a box—tied up. I say to one of the detectives, "Do you think this possibly might be a homicide?" He says, "Well, you know, down in this precinct, you get some junkies—somebody ODs in a shooting gallery, the other junkies have to get rid of the body, so they just tie it up and carry it to the river." Okay, that makes sense. And it *does* make sense.

But what if that's *not* the case? It was officially classified as undetermined, and they just left it at that.

My partner and I tried to convince these brilliant detectives. We said, "Why don't we treat it as a homicide anyway?" And they said, "Listen, kids, leave this to us."

So now, two years later, a detective came to me and said, "Remember these pictures?" "Yeah, I remember these pictures." "Do you remember what kind of box? Because we can't read the writing anymore." I said, "You know, you didn't want to ask me this two years ago, but two years later, you want me to remember what kind of *box* she was in."

The entire investigation was screwed up. The detectives, two years later, now want me to answer questions they should have asked me two years before. The only reason they even know that she is one of their victims is because Rifkin told them—they had no physical evidence. They had no physical evidence because they threw everything away. They didn't treat it as a homicide. And now, not only is it a homicide, it's the biggest homicide this state has ever seen.

And you know, me and my partner, we were just two

broads in uniform, so we didn't have anything important to say, so let's disregard that.

Seattle is a very politically liberal city. If the city of Seattle and the politicians hadn't mandated affirmative action, there would be very few blacks, and very few Asians, and there would be even less women on the force today.

When I came on, there were very few women. It was very outwardly hostile by some people. They were very verbally abusive and tried to discourage you every chance they got.

Where now, I find, that the discrimination is a lot more subtle, a lot more insidious, actually. It's political correctness now. It's p.c. It's p.c. to say, "Yes, we want women, yes, we want minorities, yes, we want this cultural diversity—we want to appreciate *everybody's* diversity." And everybody mouths the words, but I don't feel that they're quite living the words yet. It's kind of like, even abusive parents tell their kids that they love them.

I don't know about other departments. But the San Francisco PD is *stubbornly* progressive. I think because society has changed so much the PD has found itself having to change—against its will—but still change. The men who claim not to care about any issues of sensitivity involving women and minorities, they tend to voice their opinions. The men that are more in tune to what's happening in the real world tend to be the ones that are in power and they know how to keep *their* opinions covered up and quiet.

More gay officers now. More women now. But the women that tell me they've never had any problems as a female in the Police Department—I don't think they're real smart; I don't think they'd know a problem if it hit them in the face. It's like a black person saying they've never experienced racism. I figure they've been living in some cave somewhere.

The male black officers, I'm sure, were just so glad to see the women coming along. Because now officers are happy to work with black guys so they don't have to work with a woman. Same thing with the Hispanics and then—the short men were so glad to see women come along.

And I'm just equally positive that the women are so glad to see the gays come along. Because now, the males would rather work with a female than work with a gay officer.

It's like a hierarchy. The white males are on the top. Then the black males and any other minority males are the next best accepted. Then probably the white females. The black females are the least accepted. Except for the gay males—they're at the very bottom.

Gay men are at the bottom of the ladder in the police hierarchy. Straight men don't want to be the prey; they're the predator. Men don't want to become us. I mean, God forbid anyone should want to be a woman.

I know there will always be people that don't want to work with me, same as there are times I don't want to work with certain people. But their reasons might be different than mine.

People don't want to work with me either because I'm an African-American female, an African-American, or a female. It might be, oh, any combination of the above.

Black females on the job get a lot of flak from the black officers. You would expect them to be supportive of us, you would truly expect them to be, after what *they* had to endure. And then we come on—when females came on, white, black, whatever, it was like, "Phew! Okay, they're after *them* now." The attitude was "We're not the ones being picked on anymore."

Don't get me wrong. There are male black officers out there who totally support our cause. But you also have that faction, the dinosaurs, the guys that came on in the sixties and seventies—these are black males and they have an attitude toward black females. It's just *there*. They don't accept us on this job. They take it as you're taking their job. You're taking a man's job.

Case in point. There was a black male that got promoted to lieutenant and he went to another division. He went there and the only people he was disciplining, the only people he was reprimanding, the only ones he was doing it to, were black females. It was for things that the white male officers were doing and he would not even speak out regarding them. If a black female would speak up to him, that was the worst thing—one woman did and he called her "uppity."

When you're a black woman on the force, it's a double whammy. You've got two strikes against you. It's hard to be a woman on the force, *and* it's hard to be black. We get it both ways. There's no doubt about it.

Something dawned on me recently about a saying that we have always said, and you have probably heard this. If a woman gets a compliment, sometimes people say, "Man, she's got balls bigger than any man I know."

Why is that a compliment? Okay? I have said that a million times. I have said it myself. Where it hit me, I picked up the paper about right after Waco and this guy wrote a letter to the editor and it said, "I'm not a fan of Janet Reno's, but I will say this for her. At least there's one man in the White House." It's like this hand came out of the paper and slapped me in the face. It's like all admirable traits belong to men—if someone shows courage, decisiveness, any wonderful trait, then they're a *man*—they have balls.

I have done it a million times. To give a woman a compliment, we say that she has balls. Now, *why* is that a compliment?

See, we're our own worst enemies. We buy into it. That's what the guys say, so we say it, too.

It's a boys' club. Absolutely. You're excluded from the grapevine. And you're excluded from a lot of the socialization.

There was a guy who started a month before me. It was hard for me—well, I was jealous of him because they'd have poker parties or something. And here's Tony, and he's always invited. Here's me and, "Well, you know, my wife wouldn't really like it if you're comin' around at midnight to play poker with the boys." That's hard. Everybody wants to be liked. You know?

* * *

The Good Old Boys' Network. A big part of it is socializing. That's where a lot of the information is shared and relationships formed. But it's difficult for a woman to join in—they might brand you either as a drinker or as a loose woman. You run those risks. It's really . . . it's difficult. Because you want to go out and have a good time and share these experiences. The *guys* do it—to share experiences and to kind of get over some of the stuff that's happened to them and also they gain knowledge that way. That's how they exchange information is they go out and have a few drinks.

In our department, we call it "Down Under," going to Down Under. There's an industrial area in our city with some underground parking garages and we just take them over. So, you know, they'll go Down Under and, you know, you just bring your beer and pizza, and you get together with your team and maybe you invite some other teams. So you'll have three or four teams down there partying and, you know, we turn up the stereo and nobody knows you're there; you don't bother anybody. So you party for a couple hours and then you go home.

But in the meantime, you've told war stories and laughed and giggled. Part of the war story thing is you're picking up on tactics people use to make things happen. And some of those things are really funny.

If you don't go Down Under, you won't get a lot of this information. But if you're a woman and you *do,* you run the risk of getting a rep.

We found it necessary to have our own social gatherings, just the women. Sometimes it would be at someone's house or we'd go to some restaurant and basically raise hell. We formed a Women Police Officers' Association. That was a big threat to the men. But we told them, "Hey, don't worry about it. We just go out and drink and have lunch, you know."

But they *did* worry about it. They felt it was political, and they put us down for it and all that. We just shrugged it off. Men don't like women to organize. Not at all.

As long as they thought we weren't griping about anything *they* were doing, that we were just telling war stories, everything was okay. But once we started talking about serious things like women being accused of something they didn't do, or stories getting around about women and their behavior that just weren't true, or women being mistreated, and we started getting serious about those kinds of concerns, then it became a threat.

Right before I made lieutenant, the captain in the Vice Division wanted me to come back to Vice as a rookie lieutenant. He asked for me. So the big rumor was out that I was gonna get the Vice job.

Well, the chief of police came in the office one day, just wandering around. He looked at me and said, "You gettin' ready to make lieutenant?" And I said, "Yeah." And he said, "I'm not gonna send you to the Vice Division." And my heart just sank. "Why not?" And he said, "Well, rookie lieutenants don't get good jobs like that. You have to go out into the field and pay your dues." I said, "Okay." "You gotta do your dues and then you can apply for a job like that."

A month before that, though, one of the sergeants had just got promoted to lieutenant and they sent him to the Special Operations Unit, one of the real elite units. Of course, that was a man, don't you see.

I didn't say anything about that, but what I did, I went to an assistant chief I knew—"I want to know what the real reason is I'm not going to the Vice Division." And he said, "Okay. Let me see what I can find out." And he came to my office a few days later and he shut the door and he looked real sick. I said, "What's the reason?" And he was very hesitant to tell me. He said, "The reason that you're not going is because . . . you drink too much with the boys." I said, "What?" He said, "You know when you go to the Police Association Club a couple nights a week? That gets back to the chief." "But you know what? *You're* over there every day." He said, "I know." He said, "You drink too much with the boys. You're too close with the boys." And I said, "Okay."

That was the first time that I really got angry. Because if I was one of the boys, I'd have been in that Vice job. They would not have ever told a man that he couldn't drink with the boys.

I might be one of the boys, but I'm not *ever* gonna be one of the boys.

Every time I've gone up in rank, I've gotten a jealous reaction from some men. Every time. And I really thought that would go away. And it has happened every time. When I made lieutenant, before we got the list back as to who was where in rank order, one of the guys came up to me and said, "Wherever you are in the list, I just hope that I'm one in front of you." And I said, "Why?" And he said, " 'Cause you know they're not gonna pass up an opportunity to promote a woman. And they have to get to me to get to you." Little comments like that. Little comments like that.

Generally, promotion stuff is a big thing and people take sometimes three or four weeks off prior to the test. If the bosses have it in for you, they won't grant vacations or days off. But, of course, it's all based on workload, right? They can always justify.

I know a number of women where that happened. But it also happens to some men. So, see, it's their way of supporting the people that *they* want to promote and not supporting the people that they don't want.

There are other things they can do: meet with you and talk about your work performance right before your oral interview or right before the test. Shake you up.

I've been a captain for about five years now. I do the duties, I run around the streets, I get really good reviews from the division inspectors—because I'm a worker, I'm a smart girl, I do what I gotta do, I stay till it's finished—but they never call me and say . . . They never include me in the meeting. Never. They never stop and say, "Oh, Mary! What do you think about that?" They'll never say that. And if I make a point in the meeting, I can't say it's well received. I don't have ten guys going, "Whoo! Yeah. Uh-huh. Yeah. Uh-huh. Hey, she made a good point." It's ignored. It's ignored. It's absolutely ignored. It's almost like . . . "What are you here for today? You didn't have to pick up your kid at school?"

The glass ceiling is bulletproof. You're always on the outside.

Women don't support you, either. It's like crabs in a barrel. Crabs in a barrel—one of them's trying to get up, the others are pulling him down. It is so true. So true. Women are their own worst enemies.

You would think that, there are so few of us in supervisory positions that if we came into a detail over men, the women would rally to the higher-ranking woman's side. No. It becomes: "Who does she think she is?" God forbid if you look a little bit better than the rest of them. "Who does she think she is?" "Look what she's got on today." "She's wearing . . ." "She's talking different." "She's a slut." I have had things said about me, and I'm like, "Oh, yeah? What do you have on me today?"

Something that happens to a woman that doesn't happen with men. It's a matter of degree. So, if a man gets promoted to sergeant and he gets transferred to a new precinct and he's put in charge of a squad of people on a shift, they're gonna kind of watch him for a while and he's gonna have to prove himself, prove that he's got the ability to do it. Put a woman in the same position? She's gonna have to prove it and prove it and prove it and prove it and prove it. You never stop having to prove yourself. Never.

That's why a lot of women are reluctant to take promotional exams and start all over from ground zero. A man doesn't have to start from ground zero. He brings his reputation with him. So if he walks in and they say, "Gosh, I heard he was really a good sergeant over there in Precinct Twelve," they'll watch him for a few days, a couple weeks— "Yeah, well. He's fine." And that's over. A woman—it doesn't matter how good she was in Precinct Twelve. She's got to start all over again in the new precinct and prove herself every day for years before she's . . . tolerated.

There was an incident where a male and female were working together and the female had her gun taken from her. And this went around the job like wildfire.

And then about a month later, two cops, male cops on Staten Island, had *both* of their guns relieved. And that was okay. What a contrast.

If a man makes a mistake—no big deal. But if his female counterpart makes the same mistake, it's a major thing. It gets around the whole job.

They're always looking to see a woman make a mistake. And if she does, it becomes a major catastrophe. If a woman screws up, it's like, "What do you expect?" But the worst male will be embraced by the Good Old Boys. The worst boss, the worst male detective, if he screws up it's "Well . . ." There are all these excuses, even if they know he's a piece of garbage. If they have to pick the worst male against the female, they'd rather side with the male. But it's changing slowly. Now we only have to prove ourselves 110 percent instead of 150 percent.

The overall attitude is so pervasive, historically, that it affects even the younger men coming on. They are the nephews and sons of the ones that have been giving us all this crap in the past, okay? They grew up getting all this stuff fed to them all these years.

It doesn't change that quickly. They may *see* themselves as more liberal, more progressive, but they've been fed that all their lives. So their attitude—it may not be that they make the blatant jokes or that they touch you or say things to try to hurt you or even overtly do something—but when it comes time to make decisions, to handle cases, whatever—they will go to another *man* instead of to a woman with a better outlook on the case, or more experience, whatever.

Because, to them, the person to turn to is a man. You're in trouble? You get a man to help you. That's just something they automatically do. That's where the worst part comes in. It's because of attitude. And they don't even *see* it.

It's survival of the fittest. They don't want you here anyway. If you're weak and you can't hang, they got you.

My attitude is—I'm leaving when *I* want to leave, not when *they* want me to leave.

I've seen girls crying; they tell me they can't take all this. They're resigning. I say to them, "This is what they *want* you to do. They *want* you to go home and take care of the children. If you do that, then they've won."

When I got to the specialized Narcotics Unit, it was pretty well known that they don't want any women up here. Certain teams are all men, and they want to stay that way forever.

I got along with all the guys except the sergeant. He was a drunk, and he could not stand women. It was just—every day, I just tolerated his shit. I just put it out of my head, didn't say anything to anyone, I would ignore it, handle it, but go home at night sometimes, just shaking and crying. Because I can't fight it. What am I gonna do with the sergeant? It's either me or him, and it's gonna be me that's gonna leave, not him.

But it would be things like—I would be in the car with a couple of the guys and the sergeant would call on the radio—"Oh, ya got the kid with ya?" And we would joke about—"Yeah. She's in the baby seat in the back. We're giving her a Melba toast right now, she's teething." I mean, we would just make jokes about it. He'd pinch my cheeks when I'd walk in.

It got to the point where he started shitting on me with my work in a way that was becoming dangerous. Whenever I had something going—a buy—suddenly, no one would show up. We'd all be planning it the night before—meet at one o'clock, let's go here, let's go there—one o'clock, one-fifteen, one-thirty . . . There'd be one or two guys that would always be there for me—"Come on. We're here with you. Go do it." But I *know,* you should be out there with a *team.* I shouldn't be doing what I'm doing out there by myself with this one guy or two guys. And they'd be like, you know, "Just *do* it!"

The sergeant would be too drunk to come in to work and then you would beep him a hundred times, he wouldn't show up. He let the other guys know ahead of time, "Whatever you have to do, go ahead. It's okay. Judy will be fine. Someone'll help her."

And then you're running around looking for other teams to help you, which makes it look bad now because what's wrong with your own team? And you don't want *that* to get all over the place.

Afterwards, everyone would come in with the same thing: "Oh, we thought so-and-so was coming; we thought so-and-so was coming." But when it's *their* shit: "Oh. We're all here for you; we're all right behind you."

He would just frustrate the shit out of me. I'm not stupid. I *want* to work, I *want* to be the police. And if I fail, I fail. I don't need a pat on my back, but please, just leave me alone and give me a chance. You've got two other drunken assholes on this team I wouldn't want *anywhere* near me on *anything* I do because they're so damn dangerous.

Five guys on the team were great. I loved them. They were good to me. They would teach me—if we'd knock down the door on a warrant, they'd give me the hammer, they'd give me something—"Go ahead. Learn to do it." Where most guys would say, "Get in the back. You're watchin' the backdoor."

But this sergeant. We'd go on a warrant and we'd be saying, "Okay. This one'll do this. This one'll do that"— he'd say, "Well, Judy, you stay right behind me." And I'd go, "Oh. Okay. But don't forget, you know, I am a . . . just a female. I might trip and my gun might go off and shoot you in the ass or something."

And the thing is—as much as these guys would be on my side and help me out, the shit would hit the fan?—Fwoosh! They're all out the door. No stand-up. They talk like they are, but they'd kiss the sergeant's butt. I found a lot of that. The guys are more the kiss-butts and the women are more "I'll stand up for myself."

I remember one time, I had a guy come up to me and say—he had a couple women pining after him. This guy came up to me; I said hello or something, and he said, "Gosh! I thought I was gonna have to hit you upside the head to get you to ever speak to me." Because these other women were basically sitting in his lap, getting to know him.

And I took offense to that because I want to do my job

and I want to be looked at as somebody who's just here to do the job; I'm not here to play with all the guys.

Because that's what they think. They think that a lot of the women come on the job just to play with them, that we're here to be their little playmates. And there are a bunch that *are*. It sets all of us back.

We had a situation. It was written up in the paper here. There was a sergeant who allegedly fondled a female officer's breasts at a bar when they were off-duty; a whole bunch of them went out for drinks. Subsequently, allegedly she made a complaint. Later, she had to call him to come to a job, that they had a dead body, it was up on a rooftop, and allegedly he threatened to throw her off.

The newspaper article was about: Isn't it wonderful that all these cops have all come to this woman's defense? They're closing ranks around her and they're all going to testify against the sergeant? This columnist was making this assumption.

It was funny because I had this discussion with a male sergeant. And he said, "Hey. Absolutely, you know. When they see something like this happening, you know they're gonna close ranks." I said, "No. The newspaper columnist was wrong. They're *not* gonna close ranks. They'll close ranks easier around a male officer than they will around a female. They'll close ranks around a female *only* based on their perception of her. If they think that she's a good worker, which means that she has to be superexceptional, then they'll close ranks around her. But if they think, or if there's a hint, that she might be a bimbo or she might sleep around with other people, or she's—or she has a sex life— then they won't. They won't be as prone. No matter how heinous the crime might have been—because allegedly the sergeant fondled her breasts very publicly—they won't be as prone to support her."

It's funny because—the sergeant I was talking to disagreed with me, and he has two females that work for him and he asked them. And they said the same thing I did: It all depends on the officers' perception of the female.

But with a man, the support would be automatic. Automatic. Unless he's a real, true, out-and-out jerk. It's more ordinary for them to close ranks around a male than a female.

If they're gonna criticize a cop, if the cop they're criticizing is a male, the other cops will always criticize—"Oh, he's a terrible worker, you can't rely on him, he can't back you up, he's a coward . . ." They always critique and attack his working ability as a cop.

If they're gonna attack a female officer, they'll attack her sexuality—"Oh! She's a whore, she's a sleep-around, she's a hose-monster, she's a dyke . . ."

You're either a sleep-around or a lesbian. Because I guess in their minds they automatically assume that you're not good as a cop anyway.

You're tested over and over again. Absolutely. They don't care *what* I have done. I am a woman. That's number one.

This is the best one. I was nominated for Woman Officer of the Year. This was a nationwide thing. All it said in my commendation—and I had accomplished a bunch of things—but you read this commendation and it was: "She's very nice. She's very good with people." All the woman things. I wanted to puke! I mean, I just went, "This is so sickening." Why would I win? I can't win with this.

I tell you, I was mortified. I didn't even show up at the banquet. It was embarrassing—"I'm nice. I'm sweet. People like me." No way. I have developed all these inner-city things and solved crimes, my crime rate went down fifty-six percent—and I'm nice? I'm sweet? Please.

It was a lot worse when we first came on. When I was going through training, the guy training me did not think I could do the job. One time, we were going through the projects to a call of a laundromat vandalizing. We got there—there's water all over the floor, washers and driers are tipped over.

My training officer said to me, "You should right them. Right now. All the washers and driers. Come on." I'm like, "You're kidding. I could get shocked." But I did it.

He gave me a low score. He wrote that I spent a long time

fidgeting. That's the kind of pressure we were under. It was like—How high should I jump?

I was the first woman in the Mounted Unit here. I was treated like shit. But I understand that because when I went on the Mounted Unit, you had to have five years of patrol experience to be on it. It was a brand-new unit, they started in May of '74. Here were these guys who wanted to be on the Mounted Unit, all over the Police Department, and they couldn't because they didn't have five years on the job. I had a year and a half. So there was resentment, and I can understand that.

But—my instructor wouldn't talk to me. Makes it real hard to ride a horse and get the training when your instructor won't talk to you. The men wouldn't talk to me. I walked into the roll-call room one day and they spat on the floor and they all left. I never cried there, but I cried every day on the way home, I was so frustrated.

Some of my closest friends to this day are all those guys that gave me a bad time on that job because I just stuck in there and didn't give it back to them.

I was sitting on my horse right in front of the aquarium and I was waiting to use the phone. And I see this car across the street—it's one of the inspectors—and he's watching me, and he's watching me, and I'm waiting to use the phone. I'm on my post, there's no problem, you know. My horse decides he wants to take a pee, so I kick him in the ribs and I back him up because there's a woman wanting the phone and it was gonna run right through her, you know? Well, the ground was real dry and it *did* trickle on the sidewalk.

So this inspector comes around, he writes me up for allowing my horse to pee on the sidewalk. I said, "Excuse me. You make $63,000—this is back in '76—you make $63,000 a year as an inspector and the best thing you have to do is to tell me my horse peed on the sidewalk?"

Later, I got a call from my lieutenant—"What did you do to that inspector?" "I didn't do anything to the inspector. I asked him how he could possibly justify his salary." He's like, "Ohhhh. You get in here right now and you gotta leave yellow paper [an internal report]." And he asks, "Do you have any witnesses?" "Yes, I do."

So I typed up two reports. One from me and one from my horse. The report from the horse was classic: "She kicked me once and you want her to kick me again! I had to go. You guys know how it is when you have to go! Not only that, but they cut my balls off! And I *really* had to go!"

I had him sign it. We paint the horse's feet, we put this dressing on the hooves to make them shiny when we go out, so I painted his horseshoe again and had him step on the paper. And I submitted it downtown. I never heard anything more on that beef.

It's gotten better, but it really hasn't. Now you get subtle discrimination. They haven't stopped discriminating against women. They've just gotten smarter about it.

Last year, I decided I wanted to transfer to a tac team. I work very hard to maintain a high level of physical fitness. I run; I lift weights. You have to if you're gonna work on the streets. I've always vowed that I would only stay on the streets as long as I know I can protect myself.

I called to find out about the testing requirements for the tac team: Calculated according to age and size, they require that you can bench-press seventy pounds—I can do one hundred twenty without even trying. In every physical requirement, I could already do more than is required.

So I had a discussion with a high-ranking officer on the tac team about my coming on. The first thing he said— "Well, it's really, really a physically demanding job. They have very strict testing." I said, "Yes, sir. I understand that. Like you, I was concerned about this. So I thought I better check it out. You know what? Surprisingly, I'm well above the standards already." Then he said, "What I really meant was it's so *mentally* stressful. The demands are just so high." "Well, sir, I couldn't be in a better position. The kids are grown and my husband is very supportive of this." There was nothing more he could say.

What if I had been a younger officer? I project myself back twenty years and I wonder—How many women have been discouraged from even trying?

They do this in different units, and then when the bosses say, "Why don't you have any women over here?" they can say, "Well, we try, but they just don't join."

It's discrimination. It's subtle. It still exists. We've come a long way, but things haven't really changed.

It's subtle now. They don't say anything that they can be called on, pretty much. It used to be real direct. Right to your face—and to your back and to your sides.

The tests, I think, now, are much more things like they're not gonna openly say anything against you as they will sit back in judgment and test you and more or less put you in a situation and sit back and watch you—"Are you gonna be able to think your way out of this? Because I'm not gonna help ya."

There was a twelve-story scaffolding on the side of a building. We got a burglary call at about three in the morning; that alarm went off because they were working on that building. So when we got there, I knew it was a false alarm, probably, because they were working on it.

My partner wanted me to climb the twelve-story scaffolding to check the roof. And I said, "Yeah, I'll climb the scaffolding if that's what you want and check the roof. No problem." If he really thought there was a burglar up there, he would have got another unit to check the perimeters. But, no.

It took about an hour for me to climb the twelve stories of scaffolding. And then when I got to the top, I did kind of like the Rocky thing—"Dada*da*—Dada*da*"—I had my flashlight trained on myself and I'm dancing around with my fists in the air. I looked down at him and I said, "Well, I got up here and now I guess I gotta get down. And, of course, there's no burglar up here. Just me."

He just wanted to see if I'd do it, if I was afraid of heights. You know: "Women are afraid of heights." Not this one.

I got in a foot pursuit of three armed suspects. My partner and I were going up to an apartment, we thought it was just a family dispute, we were walking up and we were ten feet away from the door, we were typical cops, lookin'—"Where are they? Where are they?" *"I* don't know." "Oh, here's numbers." "Yeah—might be up there." We're walking, all of a sudden we see three guys come out. And they have their guns in the up position. We saw three guns very clearly. They saw us and they took off running. We went in and there are three victims tied up on the floor.

So we go in foot pursuit and we go over a big fence and they all three split up in three different directions, which is very smart. So you know, you only have a second to decide—Do we both go after one? Do we try to get two? What do we do?

My partner and I split up and I was able to corner one of the guys. My partner got one and one got away and we finally got one later in the night.

I don't know. I remember that night, that feeling, going over the fence, and chasing this guy, thinking, "Why am I doing this by myself?" I saw the gun! I know he's got a gun; I saw him running with it.

In pursuit, I couldn't see because it was pitch-black. I didn't want to put on a light because, of course, you would illuminate yourself. So you're running, just listening for noises. I thought to myself that I'm taking risks because I need to prove myself. And that's . . . a sad thing.

I continued the foot pursuit and I caught him going up a chain-link fence. You know, I was just lucky. And the guys—they didn't want to think I was okay, but that helped.

I think in many ways it's changing. I don't know if it will ever change completely or become the predominant atmosphere. For cops on patrol, not bosses, this is from talking about other people I know around the city, there are still a number of people who from the day they came on the job bought the book that if I'm a man I have to say women don't belong on the job. Regardless of any personal knowledge. There are men who still do that.

But there are also a lot of men who may have come on with that attitude, who, once they start working with women that *do* the job, will change their attitudes. I've seen this. I've seen it happen. There are a number of men out there that *are* supportive, men who are just police officers, not horses' asses.

A significant portion of them are starting to change their attitudes because they are working with these women every day and they are doing their job and women are moving more into positions of rank.

When I happened to be a supervisor in the Eighty-eighth Precinct, a 10–13 came over the air. Luckily, I was a couple blocks away. I was the first one on the scene, I jump out, I'm in the middle of the tussle. And as everybody else rolled up, they were like, "Oh, the boss is here rolling on the ground?" They were amazed. I said, "I'm a cop. I don't care what my rank is, I'm a cop. If I hear somebody call for help over the air, I'm gonna respond. I'm not gonna sit back and say, 'Did they do everything right? Did they get out of the car with their hats on?' Bullshit!"

I had the guy, the guy who radioed for help, come up to me afterwards, and he said, "Oh, Carol, you can't believe how thrilled I was to see you come around that corner. Thank you."

This is my point. I think that generationally things are changing and that men, because they're working with women every day now, they're starting to change because they see that the women actually *are* doing the job out there.

Fights are your proving ground. They judge your worth on whether you can fight. That's true of men, too, but with women, it's even more so.

For the longest time, and, you know, it may still be that way, the telltale deal was "Will she fight?" "Will she fight?" And it didn't matter where you went, that was the deal. "We're gonna see if she'll fight."

Well, the odd thing is, every new assignment that I have had up until the time I became a lieutenant in the Audit Unit, which was my first staff job, every assignment that I have had, the first thing that happened to me was I could get into some kind of fight that always turned out well for me. We're talkin' pure dumb luck.

When I first came on, I was with a trainer that trained all the women because he was an older "Daddy" kind of guy. His name was Bubba. Bubba had done twenty-five years in the military and was on year number ten in the Police

Department. Bubba never let his rookies do anything the first week they rode. All we were supposed to do was get used to listening to the radio.

Everything was smooth until Friday. We got a call on a family disturbance; it said, "A man is beating his grandmother." Bubba recognized the address. He said, "Man, I know this guy. He beat the hell out of Sergeant Ortega last week and Ortega had to put out an assist, so be prepared to shoot. This is one bad ass."

So we get up to the front door—Bubba was very protective—and Granny comes out of the house and she has been beat to hell and she says, "He's inside. He's got a gun and he's gonna kill the first person that walks in the door." Bubba says, "Okay." He looks at me and says, "You go around to the back."

He's gettin' me out of the way. So I walk around the back and the garage door's open. And I've been standing back there maybe a minute and this guy comes walkin' out of the house. It's very hot, it's June, and he's got on a pair of cutoffs and nothing else. He's got tattoos all over him. He's got something wadded up in his hands, like some kind of material, a shirt or something.

I figure he's got a gun in there because of what Granny said. So I draw my gun and point it at him and say, "Put your hands up. Drop whatever you got in your hands and freeze." He looks at me and drops his shirt, so I see there's nothing in his hands, and he says, "Bitch, put that gun up. You're not gonna shoot anybody." And I did. I put the gun up because I wasn't. I could see that he did not have a gun. I said, "Come on. Step up against the car." And he's like, "Fuck you." I said, "No, you really need to do this." He said, "No." The fight was on.

It was pretty humorous. I'd love to have it on videotape. When I say the fight was on, the fight consisted mostly of me trying to get ahold of him—he was very sweaty and every time I tried to grab ahold of him, it was like—greased pig. And he wouldn't run away and he'd ball up his fist and take a swing at me and I'd duck and try to grab ahold of him and then he'd pull out. And this went on and finally I said, "This is getting ridiculous." I got him on the ground and we rolled around.

The deal was, I was screaming the whole time for Bubba, right? See, I know what Bubba was doin'—Bubba is methodically searching the inside of the house, okay? He can't hear me; the central air conditioning's on. And he's doin' a real thorough search because there's a maniac in there with a gun. And another officer's in there with him. And I'm screamin' this whole time: "BUB-ba! He's out here! BUB-ba! He's out here!" Well, I mean, nobody's comin' out here.

The guy who lives across the alley, there's an apartment complex across the alley, this guy drives up in a Coca-Cola truck, just got off work. He gets out, me and this other guy are rollin' around on the ground. He comes up, I look up at him—I'm sure I've got this terrified look on my face. I say, "You need to go in there and get my partner." He says, "Y'all need to cut this out. Really." And I say, "Look. Go in there. Go get my partner!" He says, "No, really. I don't want to get involved. I want y'all to stop this right now." And I'm like, okay, if I ever get ahold of *this* guy, I'm gonna beat the shit out of *him*. Not only am I gonna put this one guy in jail, but I'm gonna beat *this* guy to a pulp.

So, finally, I get this fool to get inside and I decide that I'm gonna put the old choke hold on the guy I'm rollin' around with. I've never done this to anybody, but I'm fixin' to. So I choke him. I put the choke hold on him, from behind him, he goes limp, which he was supposed to. But as I took my arm off, the fight was back on. So he was foolin' me. We rolled around again and rolled back up his driveway. Pretty soon, don't ask me how, but I ended up on top with him in handcuffs. Of course, I was exhausted and soaking wet. All of a sudden, you know, it's like—"Okay, *this* is what this shit is about! I'm likin' this now!"

So I pick him up. I walk up; he's being very nice now. I walk him around to the side of the house. I'm comin' towards the front, and Bubba and Rodney Jones come tearin' around the side of the house and Bubba stops and he looks at me and he sees I've got the bad guy and his eyes are as big as saucers and he says, "Where did he come from?" And I say, "Well, you know, it's kinda like, while ya'll been in the house? Me and him been rollin' around out back." And, of course, my uniform pants were all ripped; I looked like I'd been rollin' around. And Bubba says, "Oh, my God." It scared Bubba. It scared him really bad to know that I had been back there, his little rookie had been back there all by herself. I started tellin' Bubba about the Coca-Cola man? Well, he went ballistic. And he went back there, trying to find him—"Which apartment does he live in?" And I said, "We'll find him another time. We'll beat the shit out of him."

You would not *believe* the good press I got from that—when I get back to the station, it's like, "Well, lookee there! There she is! That's the girl—that's the girl that got the guy that beat the shit out of Ortega." It's like . . . well, we know she'll fight.

And it was instant acceptance. That's all it took. It was instant acceptance. It was bizarre. I'd never seen anything work like that. It was like—this girl's okay.

All it took was a fight because that's a man thing to do. And, obviously, I had proved myself to be a man. And that was a go. They loved it. They loved it.

And, you know, I did, too. Because my whole goal was to fit in, and I just did. I was in. And that had always been my goal. My life was complete. I was a happy little camper. This life was for me.

And I was *truly* accepted. It's so hysterical that that's what I had to do to be accepted. All I did was roll around in the dirt with somebody. It's like that old saying—"Never roll around in the dirt with a pig. You'll both get all dirty, and the pig likes it." This used to be a very popular little police saying; a bunch of people had it hanging on their walls.

It's not that I could go out and be nice to a person—it's that I had to fistfight with somebody to be accepted. That's a man thing. That is a man thing.

And the more I acted like a man, the more people saw me as successful.

Through sheer peer pressure and the need to survive—rather than the organization changing, it's the women who change. The women become more like men, rather than the women impacting the organization, when there are small numbers.

This is sad, but in some ways, some of our harshest critics on some issues are other women. Women who came through ten or twenty years ago and women who complain about some of the harassment *now*—well, that's nothing compared to what the older women went through! And *they* made it.

So women end up adopting the rules of the game rather than impacting them. They believe they're one of the boys. They *have* to be. They want to be. But they're not.

I'm a marksman in hostage-barricade situations. You have to compete equally. I really believe that. I decided at the beginning I will not make any exceptions for myself, you know, I expect it of them—I expect it of myself. I let it basically be known that I wasn't expecting any favors. I worked out. I made the obstacle course. I shot in practice shooting, and I shot as well as anybody else.

I think one mistake women make that I've always tried hard not to make and it's worked for me is—I am a woman and I'm proud of it. I don't want to be a man. And a lot of woman police officers, *especially* in the more macho units, every other word is "Fuck this," "Fuck that." They talk like truck drivers; they act like truck drivers. They think it will make them accepted.

And with me, it's like, I'm a woman and I'm proud of it. I like being a lady. I like being feminine. When it comes to gettin' out and rollin' around in the mud or having to go through the obstacle course, I can do that. I can sweat. I can work hard.

But when I get dressed up, I like wearing a dress with lace on it. I've always had that attitude. I will compete equally, but I like being a woman. I couldn't stand to be a man. God help me, I'd kill myself.

We're our own worst enemies. We really are. We're our very own worst enemies. No doubt in my mind. No doubt.

We're not unified. We have also fallen into the same traps that the men have as far as treating each other badly. We work around men so much that we start to act like them because that's the way to be successful, right? *They're* successful, so we act like them.

What occurs is we start doing the same things that they do. And one of the things they do is discriminate against women in very covert-type ways.

I remember when I first came on, they did that old "divide and conquer" thing where they'd say, "You're okay, but so-and-so's a real bitch" or "So-and-so is a real slug," and then you get to thinking, because you don't know any better and you're naive, "Huh! Well, I guess I *am* better than her." And then you realize it's all a big game. That she's just as good as you, but they're just seeing what kind of reaction they can get. Divide and conquer.

Women often put other women down, which I think is the worst thing you can do. I know a woman in the Minneapolis Park Police, she strongly believes—if anyone says anything negative to her about another woman officer, she will not participate. She will say, "Hey. I don't know where you're coming from, but I'm not going to say anything bad about her because I don't know anything." That's a positive thing. And that's a message we have to get out to the younger women.

Some of the older male officers—they resigned themselves to our coming. Their only question was, "Can they do the job and not get me hurt?" If they can do the job and not get hurt, then they can care less about whether it's a guy or a gal.

But with the women—sometimes you were the only woman in the squad. So all the guys belonged to you. Now a new woman comes into the squad, you're facing that old "Who are they gonna like better?" Which is sort of ridiculous. It's so high school.

I had a woman sergeant when I had been on the street less than a month and I was still in training; she was working the watch after me and she told me that she didn't think that women should be on patrol. She's a patrol sergeant! I found it really interesting and frustrating. She was the one that had the biggest hang-up for the new ones coming in.

* * *

Men are easier to work with than women. Women are bigger back-stabbers than men. They're petty, and they're back-stabbers. Men have this special camaraderie. They can work together. They joke around. I don't take offense— even the sexual comments, I'm just like, "Yeah, yeah. Right."

But women—they're always, "Why does *she* have this shift? Why did you give it to *her?*"

Women aren't *fun*. You know how men talk? How they can pick on each other and tell each other what sorry s.o.b.'s they are and no one takes offense? You can't do that with women.

I like women. I hope they do well in law enforcement. But I *like* working with men.

Men can hate each other, but they'll play softball together, they'll play basketball. Women—if you don't like that person, you're not gonna stand on second base and you're not gonna play first base together. It just won't *happen*. There's a lot of that.

I tell you, male police officers—they have a tremendous sense of humor. It's fun to be in their company. And when you leave that, you're lonely. You miss that.

In my life, I've met a lot of women that are extremely entertaining. I like people that make me laugh. But percentage wise—I have found more men who can entertain me than women. It just seems an ability to make others laugh. And maybe it's because women are not forceful enough to say, "Listen to *me*." I don't know.

But men *are* fun to be with.

Women don't organize. If you get a group of women together that have organized for a cause, these women are *furious* about that cause. It's not just gonna be something minute that they organize over.

We're really gonna have to make women *mad* before they organize. Because they don't have time—they're the primary caregivers in the family and I mean, it's gotta be a major deal.

* * *

There's a generation gap, too. A lot of females, once they got the job, forgot all the litigation and new laws that had to be put into effect for them to *get* the job. They forgot where they came from, so to speak. It's now—once I'm in, I'm in. I'm part of the group.

You kind of have to look out for women like that. You have to look out for them to keep yourself safe because they're not gonna support you. And they're not alert enough to see that they're being oppressed. They just think I'm a cop now; I'm one of the team, and they don't see that some people don't *think* they're part of the team. Sometimes they just don't see it coming. They just don't see it coming.

It's been an interesting evolution. When the first women were hired in patrol, it just caused a furor everywhere; *no one* wanted women in those positions. In Portland, for example, they hired three women and put them in three different precincts. They were totally isolated. Their fellow workers did nothing but harass them from beginning of shift to end of shift. They were told on many occasions, "You sit in the car. I'll take care of this." These women were harassed until they left patrol. So those three women went into specialty positions within the department. Then we hired five or six more for patrol, the men harassed them, and *they* left the streets.

Then all of a sudden, the men thought, "Wait a minute! The women are getting all these cushy jobs!" For the next group of women that came in, the attitude of the men changed and then it was "You're not a *real* cop unless you stay on the street." And they took these women and they made them into men. It was kind of amusing to watch, but it was pathetic in a lot of ways. They were rough-talking, rough-acting; I mean, they acted just like the men. And the men would tell them—"Don't talk to those other women"—all of us that were on already. They said, "They're nothing but troublemakers. Stay away from them. We'll take care of you." They deliberately cut them off from us. So these women wouldn't have anything to do with us because *they* were part of the men. They were *real* cops; we weren't real cops.

That was the tactic that they used for a few years. And the

women bought into it because they want to be part of the group, you know? But what happened was, as soon as one of those women did something "wrong" in the eyes of the men, they'd set out to crucify her.

And she had nowhere to go for support—except to us. We got most of them back because the men at some point would turn on them and we would jump on them and try to help them. This was true of women in Portland—it's not true of a lot of departments. In a lot of departments, it's just every woman for herself, but here, at the very beginning, we had formed together into a team and we had built a code of ethics that we would stick together.

Now we're in stage three. The men have learned to be more subtle, so it is more difficult, more insidious to figure out what's going on. The "make them into men" stage didn't work; it did for a short time, but not really. Now, as far as being accepted, it's more on an individual basis, which it should be anyway.

The men are still the ones that set the standards for training and what we do and how we act and there's still this macho mentality and the Boys' Club that you have to deal with on a regular basis. And the public has *no idea* this is going on.

Some women can be—sort of accepted. On the surface, you feel like you're being accepted. But when it really comes down to it—if they had to pick a person to throw to the wolves? It would be you.

The discrimination now—it's subtle and it's insidious. It's there. It's definitely there. But it's kept real quiet.

But, you know, it's like everything else—the fact that it's being kept quiet now is making it worse than it was. When you first came on, you knew what you were fighting. And now, when it gets real—kind of behind-the-scenes and real quiet, you can't fight it. It's so quiet.

So in a way, it's gotten worse, I think.

The younger women—they think everything is great, the men are great, there are no problems. It's *not* true, but they *think* it's true.

That's exactly the way I felt. When I first came on—this is wonderful! I just put this guy in jail, everybody thinks I'm a hero—this is *great!* I love it. They treat me great.

And I guess the truth is, they think it's wonderful because they're being treated like—a guy. They're being treated like one of the guys.

And that's okay. I like that. I had fun. They were my buddies. They were the people that I started hanging out with; they became my family. And that really is okay.

These younger women—they're not telling you a lie. It may be to the point where they haven't experienced it yet.

Because . . . my first taste of this started when I walked in the door and they didn't want to hire me because I was divorced. But I didn't know it was discrimination then. And I didn't know *any* of this then. Even when I was *being* discriminated against, I didn't know it. And I thought everything was great for a long time. I loved it. I was so accepted. It was great.

I spent two years out in the field, and I was the first woman assigned to the Vice Division two years later. And it was like, *man!* I'm a pioneer and I've got some major acceptance here because they don't pull any other woman and I'm the *only* one they're gonna take. And the reason is, because I'm such a good old egg, you know. I fit in with the guys. I cuss, smoke, dip, chew, drink, and I pal around with them. So I've been accepted. And life is *great.*

And it *was* for a long time. And the truth is, it still is. I love these guys. I do. I absolutely love them. I still love them.

But, see, they're confused. The rules have changed. Since Anita Hill, the rules have changed. And nobody's ever told them the rules. And people are just now telling them the rules. And they're confused.

They got away with so much stuff for so many years, and it never occurred to them that they might be offending somebody. *Should* have. *Should* have occurred to them, but it never did because we all laughed and took it, so it obviously must be funny.

And now the world has changed and they're confused. I feel sorry for them. Because I love them. I do.

* * *

I think women have a lot of denial. It's either denial or ignorance. At the same time, I'm not saying that it *is* everywhere. I was treated very well. I can't say definitely if a woman says she's never had that experience, she's wrong. But I think in the vast majority of cases, you either have denial or ignorance.

I honestly believe that women in the policing profession can come as close to knowing what it's like to be black in our society as anybody can. Because you can never be . . . one of them, one of the boys, never.

The thing that is just really hard to explain inside and may be easier to explain to the outside is that every day that you come to work, no matter what the situation you're in, you know that you are never one of them. You can work with a partner in a car, you can even get to be friends, but there's always, almost like an invisible line that you can never get past where you are one of this police "brotherhood." And I use the word "brotherhood" because that's what it is.

And so every day you come to work and that's there and you know it. But you work with it, you work hard, and you try to fit in.

But then things happen, and it's like somebody walks up and slaps you in the face and says, "You're getting too close. You want too much."

So when the special missions are formed, women are not asked to join. The district assignments—if a woman and a man both want a district, chances are they'll give it to the man.

And then when the real slap in the face comes is when there's some kind of sexual harassment case pending. That's when they really band, they really say, "Okay. You're not one of us and you never will be."

People work around it. Especially the new women coming on. They really try. They really try and they try to . . . talk like the boys and drink like the boys and do the kinds of things that the guys do to try to fit in. And some of them have even gone to the point of not having anything to do with the other women officers.

And they think it works for a while and then, after just so

long, they get an insight: "It's not working. It doesn't work. I don't get the district, I don't get the mission, unless it's a prostitution mission . . ." It's really slow to come around. You know, maybe the first thing that they hear is rumors about themselves or about another woman. And it's just the little things start sneaking in, and it's like you know . . . that you're not one of them.

The clincher for me was—I went to my first SWAT Unit banquet. Every year, they have this banquet for all the past and present members of this unit. This unit has the macho men of the whole Police Department; that type of a unit attracts a certain type of personality. A SWAT Unit will attract a certain mentality of male. This one sure did.

So I go to my first banquet. Here's all the past and present members of the SWAT Team. I'm the first woman ever in SWAT. There's about sixty men there. The police chief is there—this is what floors me: the chief is there, the captain of my unit is there, some very high-ranking majors and assistant chiefs are there because they had been in the unit before.

And I get there, and during dinner, they basically show, up on the *big screen,* while we're eating our dinner in this beautiful banquet room at the Westin Hotel, they show a porno film. This is a few years ago; we're not talking 1940 here. And I'm sitting there, eating my dinner, and I'm thinking, "How am I supposed to handle this?"

It was like a videotape they had put together that was like a spoof on other guys in the unit. I can't remember . . . but it was all sexually oriented. They had one guy supposedly making love with a mannequin on a bed. They had another guy going around, sniffing in the air, going, "Beaver, beaver. I'm looking for beaver." It was all revolving around sexual antics. It was worse than an actual porno film because these were actual guys in the unit doing all this stuff. Very gross.

I'm sitting there looking and I'm thinking, "My God, the *chief* is here! The chief of all police is here!" And here I am, sitting in here with all these people, and I didn't know what to do. I think that was one of the most uncomfortable times of my life—I'd gone into a unit, I'm new there, I'm trying to be accepted—and what kind of message am I being given where the chief himself is sitting there? The captain was sitting right next to me and watching this. What kind of a message is this?

And I thought of getting up and walking out. Then I thought, "God, you know, I'm the first woman in here, I'm sitting in here with sixty guys yakking it up, and I walk out. What do I say later?" What do I?—I just didn't know what to do.

I was kind of thinking, "If I walk out, they'll think they won. And then it'll be a running joke forever—we chased her out." I wasn't sure. I just didn't know how to handle it.

I think the thing that got me the most was—it was like I walked into the prehistoric unit of the world. Because it never would have happened anywhere else, anywhere else in the department. I walk into this place that has never been touched by any type of moral—I don't know—sensitivity. I mean, it's just a bunch of guys walking around belching and farting and being macho. And this woman walks in and— Hell! We're not changing *nothin'* for her.

What really got me—I was thinking, "This is the *nineties*. My God. All this stuff is supposed to be long past."

There's still the perception that women can't do the job, that women have no business being in here.

I don't know if this will ever truly pass until a generation of men has been raised with the idea that women can do the job. They've gotta see their moms doing the job—then maybe they'll believe it.

I became a cop for a really weird reason. In my family, when I grew up, there was a real definite division between male and female. Just for an example, the boys would get *paid* for working out in the fields and the girls would get nothing. Or the boys would get all the money that we brought in for selling sweet corn in the summer and then when it got down to my turn, the first two boys got the money and then it came down to me, my turn, and then the money went for the boys to get a boat or something like that. It's probably—I wanted to go into a male profession because I wanted to somehow be more equal or to show them—Yeah, I can do a good job.

CHAPTER 9

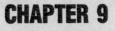

THE CODE

Twelve NYPD officers took their own lives in 1994, the highest year for suicides ever on the NYPD. But not unusually high for a police population. Those who study suicide say that in the nation as a whole, police commit suicide at a far higher rate than the rest of the population—roughly twenty-nine cops out of a thousand commit suicide compared to the general population's eleven suicides out of a thousand.

The code kills cops, some police experts say. Police still live and die under an inflexible code that dictates their every move. The rules of the code are simple: You don't rat and you don't complain. A cop is supposed to be strong no matter what—suck it up—and never to admit or complain about weakness in himself/herself or in other cops. With such a system, it's easy to see how discrimination, harassment, and the despairing isolation that can lead to alcoholism, drug abuse, and suicide can take hold.

The toll is especially high on women in policing since they are expected to adapt to a male world and take whatever the males hand out without complaint.

For you *can't* complain. You can't "grieve" (cop for filing a grievance, which also extends to not being able to mourn for fear of being seen as weak). The code has a clear-cut set of punishments for violations. And they are enforced. Those who violate the code, those who rat, those who can't take it are killed—sometimes fast and sometimes slow. The fast way is an act of omission—some officers may respond very slowly or not at all to an offending officer's calls for assistance.

Most often, the killing is slow and psychic. It follows the ancient Greek model of ostracism, the worst punishment the Greeks could inflict on any offender. Cops who have made enemies—or even one enemy, according to the code—are cut off, ignored, treated as if they didn't exist. You can have twenty years of no one talking to you in the halls, no one asking you for a meet, no one ever including you in. And your rep, and the punishment, follow you wherever you go. As one woman cop said, "You can grieve and you can win. But forever after? You're through. You're dead."

The beauty of the code is it's so embedded and the punishments so well enforced that police can—have to—flatly deny it exists to the outside world. It's only through the testimony of individual women that we get a glimpse of how the code works to keep everyone in line . . .

You've heard the term "eat their young," right? You've heard the term, right? The military does that a lot. So does law enforcement. They eat their young.

There's a code. Some will tell you there isn't a code anymore. Bullshit. There *is* a code. It's more subtle now and it's harder to deal with when it's subtle. The code is: You don't complain and you put up with their bullshit.

The code *still* exists. Most definitely. The code comes from the fact that often with police officers—it's us against them. Nobody understands us. As police, we become very insular and distrustful. So the code is if somebody breaks that trust, it's not a good thing.

The bottom line is everybody wants to be accepted. They want to be part of the family. And anything that threatens that acceptance, which means rocking the boat or confronting somebody on something that they've done, threatens that acceptance.

The whole idea is this is a very closed society and if you want to be part of it and you want to get along, there's certain things you gotta let go. And you let them go and you let them go and you *let* them go, and it's sort of like the Chinese water torture—it gets to the point where you just can't let it go any longer. And when you come out front with it, then it really destroys you on the job.

* * *

When I was president of our Women's Police Officers Association a few years ago, there was a gal who used to work for me and she went to an undercover unit. She was a good officer, very athletic, she had been very well known in collegiate running competitions. Very pleasant to deal with. She was supposed to work a sting operation, which was exactly what I worked. So she used to call me for advice.

Then I started hearing rumors about her and this guy she was working with, that they were romantically involved. She called me and I said, "You know, I'm hearing these rumors about you and this guy. What's the deal here? I don't think it's very professional, but if people want to do this, hey, it's none of my business, but not on duty." She said, "That's not true. I don't know where those rumors are coming from. I'm taking care of it. No problem."

Well, God, about two weeks later she contacted me at home, came out to see me and laid out to me how the guy had been harassing her and how she wouldn't go back to work anymore because on this particular occasion he actually physically attacked her; she thought he was going to rape her, he forcibly sucked her breasts against her will. I said, "What do you want to do?" This was a criminal allegation. And he was her supervisor! I mean, this was the guy who was going to evaluate her. And the attack happened in the course of their sting operation.

He was maybe thirteen, fourteen years older than her, he was this bachelor guy, and he was engaged. She said, "What bothers me about this whole thing is he's engaged, so I trusted him. And the little things that he would say to me, well, I just let them run off my back." But they got worse and worse. On occasion, she would tell him, "I really don't appreciate that." But then this attack thing happened where he actually put her down on a bed and that kind of crap.

We ended up reporting it, and it ended up going through all this big stuff. She ends up being ostracized in the department and basically driven out of here over a two-year period. The guy—they filed charges on him. It took, I swear to God, two or three years to resolve the court case because of all the delays his attorney went through. And his biggest supporters in the department?—the Police Officers Association. They took out an ad in our newspaper asking for donations for *his* legal bills. They didn't give *her* an attorney. They didn't give her anything. They didn't even give her the time of day.

She started experiencing harassment on the job. She was being covered on the air, which means you're trying to talk on the air and if somebody keys their mike, nobody can hear you. And you can't tell who's doing it—it could be anybody that has a radio. So she's saying, "I'm making a car stop" or "Some guy's running from me," and no one can hear where she is because she's covered. And they weren't filling for her. When you need assistance, what you need is a fill. No one was showing up when she needed assistance. So she figured they were gonna get her killed.

And I'm not talking about a large number of people, but all it takes is *one* person covering you on the air or someone who should fill with you and hears the radio—and doesn't go. It's not what they did in the affirmative, it's a lot of what they didn't do. Some people wanted to remain neutral so badly, and not get in the middle of this thing, that they wouldn't do anything either way. They stuck their heads in the sand.

The command staff was basically asleep at the switch, I think. Some of them really wanted to do something, but they weren't given sound direction on what exactly they *should* do. That all has to do with a lack of leadership. The chief did not tell people what rules he expected them to play by. Because he didn't think it was that big of a deal. Really. What the chief should have done was just gone to the troops and laid out what the policy is on sexual harassment and demand that they treat each other, no matter what side they're on on this issue, that they treat each other with respect so that they can do their jobs. I went in to the chief a number of times and told him, "She's being harassed. You've got to do something. You've got to go down there and tell them to *behave.*"

She was out there working a beat car and her harasser was on administrative leave, being paid full salary. That's what we do when they get into trouble because we don't want them working the streets. So instead of firing him in a timely manner, he was on paid leave for a whole year, doing whatever he wanted to do, on a sergeant's salary.

All of that led eventually to her filing a lawsuit against the city, going out on a stress disability retirement, and being granted a retirement; the city settled out of court. They were dead wrong. They were *lucky* to get off that cheap.

This was very debilitating for me, too. I was out there trying to get people to see this for the serious thing that it was and there were people in key places that thought, "Oh well, boys will be boys. And it's really no big deal. And I don't see why anybody wants to fire this guy."

What ended up happening to *him* was that—she's out, right? He got convicted. They let him plead to a misdemeanor sexual battery. He didn't get any jail time, he got a fine, and he had to go to counseling. He got demoted, which is the first time in our history that anybody's ever gotten demoted. And he's a regular police officer now; he's not a sergeant anymore.

But *he's* here. She's not. She's in some other state because she's afraid of retaliation. She's living in another state and is basically heartbroken because she can't be a cop because once you go out on a stress disability, you can't be a cop anyplace. You're through.

When you talk about the code? It's here. It's here in the federal agencies.

It means if you pay an informant $500,000 and there's nothing to justify paying it, they'll cover it up rather than confront—oh, it'll make one of the old-timers look bad, or *you just don't admit anything's wrong.* You go into a house and a suspect is manhandled and you don't see it. That is one thing you're not allowed to see.

What do you do? If you say anything, you're in trouble.

We had one deputy here that—a police officer wanted a case so bad he lied about affidavits. It had been going on for months. This deputy tried telling someone. No one would pay attention. It finally got to the point where they *had* to start an investigation, but this deputy—*she's* the one being transferred.

Women tend to see more in black and white instead of in all the shades of gray. That is a problem. It's a problem, yet it's one of our strengths, I think, that we're not able to do that. Men are far more forgiving of each other's weaknesses than we are.

I have a girlfriend who is now retired off the force. She was wearing her hair in braids. And this white captain, he told her something about wearing pickaninny braids. She asked her coworkers, "Did you hear that?" And they all said yes. To smooth things over, he gave her one of those nine-to-five jobs. He didn't stay much longer.

But he told his successor that this girl was a pain in the ass. And then his successor gave her even more hell than he did. So the captain got back at her. He got back at her anyhow. For *his* comments.

The rest of the squad had it in for her, too. What she did was, she said, rather than go through all this nonsense, I'll just quit the job. So she did retire.

You see, once they have it in their mind that they want to get back at you or make your life miserable, they don't stop until they go for the jugular. And they can make or break your career. If you get somebody in there and you've crossed them—it can be supervisors or your fellow officers—you're in for a bad time. I've known some women who have had bad times, and they just end up quitting. It's really a shame. It's a form of harassment. Some women, they just get in a bad spot and they get in with squadrons who are just not tolerant or sympathetic, or there's a clash of personalities. And once there's that personality clash, then you can forget it.

That's what I've always feared. That's my biggest fear. I've always said, "Lord, *please,* I don't want a personality I'll clash with." Because there's nothing worse in the Police Department than having to work with somebody that can't stand you. And they can make your day hell. They can age you in a week. Believe me.

It's bad enough, you're carrying a gun. But to have someone who hates you, or who wants to make your day bad, or your week bad, or your life miserable, give you unpleasant assignments day after day, week after week . . . And then they wonder why cops chew on their guns.

* * *

In the Police Department, we have all these rules and policies to the point where somebody could get you, could write a report on you for maybe one little thing that you didn't do—you maybe didn't sign the sign-in sheet in the right place or something.

So, whenever people decide they don't want you in this setting, then they start monitoring you until they find some reason. Then they'll write an anonymous letter to Internal Affairs, knowing that Internal Affairs has an obligation to investigate every complaint that comes in. Then, say, you're up for a transfer, well, there's an open case on you and they can't promote or transfer you while there's an open case on you. So even if it's something frivolous and Internal Affairs doesn't find any merit to it, it still might take them six months or a year to clear it up. And you've lost out on what you were going after.

And that's how they can do you. I know that happens constantly in this department. I have watched a number of people—blacks and women primarily—that have gotten charges on them, and I know a couple where it was to prevent them from going places.

It's vicious. They can do it anonymously. They can pretend to be your friend during the day and break bread with you and they're trying to set you up.

If you complain, you get ostracized. It makes no difference if you're black or white or whatever. There was a suit filed within the last year where a black female officer charged sexual harassment. It was a very hostile working environment. Very hostile. She wasn't getting the same type of assignments the guys were. And it was the nude picture thing all over the office. And they'd say, "If you don't like them, you don't have to work here. You can leave." There was a *lot* in her case. She went straight to the feds. A few of the guys who worked there got transferred out.

I was at a training session and I heard some of the guys talking about it. And the most outspoken ones as to what *should* happen to this female and what *they* would do to her if she worked for them—were the black males. I looked right at them and I said, "That's just the attitude that keeps costing this city money."

Their attitude was it's okay that they did what they did to

her. Those guys shouldn't have been transferred. She should be walking a beat somewhere because they harassed her. Don't punish the guys that did this. Punish the girl because she complained. That's the attitude.

In businesses and corporations, this would not happen. It would not be tolerated. But with police—it's like a little family. It's like when people do this kind of stuff in a business, they're gone—you're outta here. But with police, it's like, "Well, gee. Just too bad. We'll just put you over here. Expect you to behave."

I think in business, it's just more insidious. It's more overt with police. But it's *becoming* more insidious now where people are trying to be more politically correct now. But the biases are still there and they're acted upon. It's done behind closed doors. Very much.

A real recent case. There was a young woman working Prostitution and she got pregnant. Once you reach a certain point in pregnancy, you're taken off the street. She worked inside and then she had her baby. She was off for a short while after the baby and she returned to the Prostitution Squad where she had been.

The lieutenant called her into the office and said, "We're transferring you because you had a baby." She's sitting there in shock. She's in shock. "We're gonna transfer you out this week or the next week; I'm not sure when." She all of a sudden felt the tears coming because she didn't know how to respond. He says, "Come on now. It's time for the squad meeting."

He comes out and starts the squad meeting. He starts the meeting by announcing that she was being transferred because she had a baby. Whoa, now, wait a minute. This is the nineties. When are you penalized for having a baby? She was married; it's not even like a moral issue.

She was transferred. And she filed a complaint; she filed an EEO complaint. They're immediately—Whoops! He was wrong.

So he was sent to sensitivity training, which is an eight-hour course, doesn't mean anything, like *that's* gonna do it. She kept asking me, "Why isn't *he* being transferred?"

She pushed it. The deputy commissioner told her pick a unit, pick someplace where you want to go. Well, she was happy where she had been, in Prostitution. She went to Civil Affairs and she continued to pursue her case; it's still pending.

In the meantime, another young woman from the Prostitution Unit got pregnant and the lieutenant gets *her* transferred out. So, so much for his sensitivity.

We can't believe this man is still there. We can't believe he's still in charge of that unit. We can't believe he's still being permitted to treat women the way he's treating them. He's in charge of a unit that's predominantly female! You mean there's no other lieutenant that the PD could replace him with?

This just shouldn't be. It shouldn't be. We have to uphold the laws. Shouldn't we be held to the same standards?

That old thing about cops don't come forward if they see criminal activity? They don't rat? We don't see that in our department to that degree. But we're a small-town department. I think some of the big-city departments you might get that.

But there *is*, while it's maybe not ratting, it's not doing the person harm. Everybody gets mad at their supervisor sooner or later and maybe says bad things about him and maybe even goes to their lieutenant about him. But you don't put your sergeant in a situation where he could get demoted or fired. You don't want to be responsible for getting somebody else disciplined or maybe losing their job. That's a given.

It's more—okay, get mad, scream and yell, but don't cause this person any harm. And they don't stop to think of the harm when you see a sexual harassment victim—they don't stop and think of the harm that has been caused to *that* person; they just know that the accuser is trying to cause harm—and that's what shuts them out.

Twenty years ago, the old process things that were so visible were easy to attack. They didn't *seem* like it at the time, of course, but the difference in pay, the difference in assignments, the difference in educational requirements, all those kinds of things. They were there. They were written down. They were rules. So they were easier to attack because they couldn't deny these rules existed. I say they were easier—we filed suit in '72 and didn't settle until '78 just for equal pay and equal promotional opportunities.

The stuff you see now is the real subtle stuff that is very hard to put a finger on. It is the sergeants that seem to move women out of their districts because they "aren't performing," but if you look at the sergeants' history, time and time again, that is what they do, time and time again, every place they go.

The men in general have become more sensitive to what *is* discrimination and what *is* harassment, but with that sensitizing, the offenders have *also* become more clever about how to do it and not get caught. It's much harder to prove than these things used to be.

It's more insidious in a lot of ways. You can't meet it head-on and fight it because there's nothing there. It sounds like you're a malcontent that can't go along.

And when a woman does come out front about a harassment or something, she automatically becomes the goat. That's not just with the male officers—it's with a lot of female officers, too. Yeah. They're all, "Why did you put up with it before this? Why didn't you tell him to knock it off? It would have been okay if you'd just said something, but you're too stupid to say anything."

Even when we've done sexual harassment complaints, where a lot of women were involved, where somebody comes forward and then gives the names of other women so that they get interviewed, we've found that when we get them and we talk to them and we get all the information, we've found that when push comes to shove and it comes down to disciplining a male sergeant or a male officer for their actions toward the female officers, then everybody starts backing off. They want the situation to stop. They *don't* want to be responsible for getting somebody disciplined. So then, the women sort of back off and it wasn't as bad as it seemed. And then the poor woman who initiated the suit is ostracized.

It's a real no-win situation when you go out front to try to fight a harassment or a discrimination because you really are ostracized.

It's more than isolation. You rely on these people for your life. I haven't seen this, but there certainly have been allegations where people have failed to respond quickly to a backup request or have even *put* people in dangerous situations.

I have been . . . things have been said to me, I've been asked if I want to go out, if I want to do this or that, and what *they* can do, bosses have said different things, where they want to put this, where they want to put that—but I laugh it off, "Yeah, right, what else you want to do? How much money you gonna bring?"—and that's *it*.

Maybe it's because of my size, no one's tried to push themselves on me, or maybe I get it from my personality and nobody wanting to put me on that line because they know what would happen. Whatever it is, I've never had that problem with people continuing to bother me.

Any woman in any male profession is going to go through that. Did I report it? No. Will I report it? No. Do I ever think that I would have a problem where I'd have to report it? No. But then that's *my* personality. That's me. And I feel I can take care of myself. If someone attempted to touch *my* breast, I know what would happen. And I wouldn't have to go to the commissioner. Do you hear what I'm saying?

So, we *do* tolerate it. And we *don't* say anything. Because you don't want to make it a big thing. I look at it like this: We're women in a male profession. With that comes the negative statements, about women, the references to sexual parts, you know—I've heard it *all*. Do I have a thin skin? No. Do I say anything about it? No. Sometimes I even laugh at the jokes. It doesn't bother me, but some women it does offend. And if it offends you—that's what the law says—if it offends you, say something.

But most women don't say anything at all because they don't want the attention brought to them. They don't want to be labeled "troublemaker," or whatever the case may be.

Because in the end, it will haunt you. The Police Department forgets about *nothing*. It will stay with you for twenty years. They'll still be hounding you because you made a complaint. So a lot of women just don't say anything at all.

And see, it gets to be serious because you're in a profession where your life depends upon the help of someone else.

It's hard to be a female in an all-male group where there's a lot of bonding going on. In the PD, especially in New York, you really need to be close to the people that you work with because often it's a life-and-death situation. You need somebody to watch your back, to save you.

The Big Picture used to make a lot of us not say anything because we have to work with these people, we need them for our backup, and you don't want to have a certain label, you don't want to be known as a shit disturber or snitch because if you needed help out there, they wouldn't come. And you knew it.

On the converse side, I had a *female* supervisor I had a run-in with, and she said that if I ever needed help on the street, she would put the word out that *she* wouldn't respond. She's a supervisor today, too. I still see her every once in a while and I always think, "I'll never forget what you did." There's always some people you never forget. There's like five percent—I hated them yesterday and I hate them today. And I'll hate them when I go to my grave.

I would say it's different because now there's somewhere you can go. But I would say it's not different if you were someone who made a lot of complaints, as far as not getting help on the street. I think that still happens.

It's still done, but on a smaller level. There may be that person you had a beef with and a couple of his friends might not show up. But the sergeant out there would make sure some units showed up.

If you hated someone, you could conveniently not show up to help him. But because of Communications and the computers and everything, they would make sure someone would show up.

But sometimes—if there's only three people working the

midnight shift and two of them are your enemies, I can see where it could happen.

It's a hostile environment, the way men treat women now. It's not all of them. Not by any means. But it's more than enough of them. Some women can't take it—they prey on them.

Each individual woman has to set her own standards for how much she's willing to put up with. I've found in being involved in sexual harassment investigations that lots of times the harassers pick their victims not unlike a rapist picks *his* victims. They look for somebody who they not only have some power over, but who is less likely to stand up and say, "Knock this shit off or I'm gonna deck you." Or "I'm going to the captain." They have the same ability as a rapist does to know who they can go after with relative impunity.

And it's horrible. There are no winners in a sexual harassment case. When I have to meet with a female officer when she's about to file—and usually they file internally; we don't have a lot of women just marching to State Civil Rights or EEO and filing, they always try to go internal first—I always try to explain to them what they're gonna go through and that people are not gonna love them, but it's gonna be done. They're gonna have to go to court and they're gonna try to make you look as bad as they can. Whoever is defending the officer or whoever involved is always gonna make it look like the victim either overreacted to innocent things or that she caused it to happen. It's kind of like a rape victim in a criminal trial. It's your fault. It's hard for them. It really is.

In the real serious ones, we generally lose the woman, one way or another. Either they leave the profession, or they go off on disability. We generally don't keep them. It's just too hard.

I had a boss, he would kind of go out of his way to get close to me so he could rub up against me and then make these lewd remarks. I'm not a person that stands for lewd remarks. I'm not real shrewd, I'm not a schmuck, but I don't like dirty jokes, I don't like bad language, and I try not to use it myself. But I mean, if somebody tells a dirty joke, I don't make a big deal, I just try to leave the picture.

But if a supervisor comes up to me, rubs against me, and makes these lewd comments, and does it more than once, I would go out of my way to stay away from this guy. But it was like, next thing you know—he's there. And there was never anybody there to witness it. I made a comment to another supervisor and it was like, "He won't do that anymore." "Oh, thanks, that helps a lot."

So it wasn't real fun. I've gone throughout my whole life being able to deal with men and their problems, but when you confront somebody that's your boss that you have to deal with on a daily basis, and if you mess with him, that's gonna really come back in your face. It's gonna be your word against his, he's been around a long time, and you're just being a tight broad.

In general, women will come out and say: "There is no sexual harassment on the LAPD." It's just denial, that's all. I feel like saying, "Where are you *working?* Maybe there's no sexual harassment for you, but you have to be blind not to see it happening to others."

I took a lot of stuff that I wouldn't take now. Certain remarks would come my way that I would laugh off, but I would think—God!

You know, up until about '86 there was no sexual harassment. There wasn't even the term. I mean, most of the stuff we would laugh off. But if somebody did something to you really bad that you wanted to make a complaint about, there was no way. There was nowhere to go. All you could do would be to go to your boss and he would say, "It's okay, honey. I'll talk to him."

I had an incident once. I had a sergeant call me into his office. And he was mad at me for something, I didn't answer up on the radio, and he said, "All you policewomen are cunts, whores, and you don't belong in this department"—and he ranted and raved for about five minutes, and I had nowhere to go with it. And that was something I would have made a complaint about. But I couldn't. I had nowhere to go.

When I walked out of that office, some of the guys that were my friends said, "We heard him. We'll back you up if you want to make a complaint." And I said, "Where will it go? It will go nowhere." But today, if that happened, I could probably get a retirement, I could probably get a full stress retirement for that same incident. You know? And that always bugs me that I couldn't—where am I going to go with this? It's gonna go nowhere. And I knew that. *Now* you don't have to go to your lieutenant, you don't have to go to your captain, you can go directly to the chief or outside.

It's bullshit to think you can file for sexual harassment. *Nothing* will happen to that person. You can't file a complaint. If you do, you're punished. And the costs go way beyond what you would gain by complaining. Anytime you speak your mind, it's over.

We had a sexual harassment victim recently who filed against a sergeant and we ended up demoting the sergeant. Then he grieved it, and there's been a change of chiefs, and the new chief reinstated him to sergeant and suspended him.

But there was a letter in the union newsletter written by two women officers, not just supporting the sergeant as being a very good sergeant, but really viciously attacking the victim. It was a personal, vicious attack on her. And that's what happens. The victim becomes even more of a victim by complaining.

Once a female officer files a sexual harassment grievance, she can just about forget ever being welcomed into any unit again. Your reputation precedes you. It's always better if it's dirt than reality. No one ever needs to hear the true story— those three words "sexual harassment grievance" are all the men need to hear. In their minds, it confirms why we shouldn't be on this job.

I was raised not to tattletale, not to beef. If I believed in filing sexual harassment suits, I'd probably be a billionaire by this time.

The few who have filed complaints are *buried*. My attitude is, Let me handle it first. If you go through channels, it's never gonna go away.

I had a lieutenant, he put his hand up my dress. I knocked him on his ass. He grabbed my chest the year before, when he was a sergeant. Then I slapped him. "Why did you do that?" I said, "When you find someone you care about and they're treated this way, see what you do."

At least twenty people came up to me—"Why don't you sue?" I handled it myself. I told this lieutenant, "Next time, I'll kill you."

What I tell women is that you have to confront people and you'll find that they'll just melt. You just have to tell them, "Hey. When you do these things, this is what's going on. Don't don't do it anymore. I don't like it, and if you don't stop, then I'm gonna have to do something else."

Then you always get the asshole that will challenge you on it. But then you just go tell everybody else at the same level what's going on, and a lot of times they'll protect you because a lot of them don't like it, either.

If people don't like you, you'll have a harder time. But if you're liked, then the harassers have a really hard time harassing you.

You know what you'll find among women? Women have a hard time confronting people. There are things that are wrong that drive us crazy, something is wrong, but we're afraid to confront or we're afraid to go into the boss's den. We're not taught to do that. Men are taught to be the aggressor, to handle that. It's one of our weaknesses. How do we learn that?

The chief of police asked me to get all the women in the department together to hear their concerns. This was in '93. We organized two meetings, two separate times. We didn't get all of them, but we probably got three-fourths of them. And it was great.

But what we all observed—there is a definite generation gap.

What I'm telling you—back in 1977, I *expected* to be

harassed and I was prepared to put up with it. And if it got to be more than I could stand, then I would handle it. In that sense, I was not bashful. I expected it to happen. And when it did, I handled it.

This generation now—and I say this generation, I'm talking women in their twenties—not only do they not expect it, they are highly outraged about it and they want somebody *else* to handle it. Because the first thing they do is run and tell their supervisor.

My generation never did that. We never told on anybody. We got the person in their face: "Listen, motherfucker. If you fuck with me one more time, I'm gonna rip your balls off." You know, something they would understand. It had to be very basic. You had to talk in *their* language, get in their face, and say, "Leave me alone" in their words.

That doesn't occur now. You know what? They're not taking care of it themselves. What we're seeing is, these women in their twenties, if somebody puts up a Coors poster of a woman in a bikini, instead of saying, "Hey, jerk. Take it down," they run to their sergeant and tell on them and demand an investigation on sexual harassment. It's very much a generation gap.

We didn't tell on people. Because to tell—you would have been ostracized. You'd have been ostracized. You wouldn't be one of the boys anymore.

And the women now who *do* tell—they *still* are ostracized. Not by their own group, they're not—they're like, "Good for you, telling that s.o.b." But they're ostracized by the men. And they're ostracized by my group, my generation.

There's just this pervasive attitude of women now that I would never have considered having. I work in a district that's absolutely divided between the men and the women officers—I've had guys tell me that if a woman gets into a 10–1 [Officer Needs Assistance], she better be able to get her way out of it, or there better be some other women working that watch, because the guys are not going in. They're not going in.

They have been so devastated by harassment suits, sexual

harassment grievances . . . I mean, the guys can't do anything, the woman turns around and files a grievance on them. That's bullshit. You can't operate like that on this job.

And I don't blame them.

The men are so afraid now that something they do in the course of the job, the women are going to misconstrue, or misinterpret, and they're going to get a sexual harassment grievance, or file a lawsuit, or do something. Supposedly in one district the commander has got like three lawsuits and eight grievances.

I just don't understand it. What women are doing now is just so self-defeating; it's terrible. What man is gonna want to do something for a woman who he is afraid is going to misinterpret his every action? They're not gonna want to. You can't build up that partnership that is so important on the street.

And this might be a very masculine idea on my part. But I've been twenty years on this job and have I been approached? Absolutely. Only once have I ever considered filing a grievance, and I did and I won it. And that's in twenty years.

I'm not Roseanne Barr where any attention is a compliment. You should have the strength to say, "Please back off. I'm not comfortable with this." You don't fall back on a grievance before you try other things first. That's unfair. Women now are grievance-happy. And it scares the men, they're afraid to react, it's no good on the street.

The women I'm talking about are using sexual harassment as a tool to put their thumb on people. And that's not what this job is about. This job is supposed to be based on trust, not fear. And the men are afraid to do anything. And the white men more so than the minority men. The poor white men have been beaten so far into the ground now anyway.

You need grounds for a grievance. You say I've approached it in every other way, this guy is not listening, *now* I want to file a grievance. You don't first time out of the box say, "I'm filing a grievance, get away from me."

* * *

241

I take great issue with the whole sexual harassment thing. Certainly it occurs. There *is* sexual harassment. There are true, true cases of harassment against women.

But a lot of times, it's a *ploy*. It's an easy out for a woman to use if she doesn't get what she wants, if she doesn't get the assignment or the transfer she wants. They abuse the sexual harassment thing. It's so *easy* to claim. It's a one-on-one and a tough charge to disprove. Most often, people side with the women. And *most* of it is baloney.

I have a woman officer who works for me who's claiming one of the males also under me is harassing her. I know it's bullshit. This woman—I wanted to send her back on the street because she doesn't have enough street experience. She didn't *want* to go back out there. Suddenly, she's making allegations against one of my male officers. She saw herself going back to uniform and she wanted to be in a specialized unit.

Many times, what happens is whoever hears the complaint wants to make it all go away, so they say, "Okay. Give the woman what she wants. Send her wherever she wants."

This one never got to EEOC. I checked into her background and found that in another position, they were going to transfer her back to the street and she did the same thing. Now she's doing the same thing to me. I decided she's not going to use something like this to get her way. Thank God I'm a woman. A man would be too intimidated *not* to give her what she wants.

This kind of thing makes it difficult for bona fide cases. A sexual harassment complaint? It's a powerful tool. And sometimes it's misused.

Filing a grievance or filing a lawsuit isn't the answer for any woman's problem, though it may be a necessity. Even if you win the battle, you've lost the war for the rest of your career. Man *or* woman, it's the truth. If you stand up and you *really* stand up for what's right, that's it. You're done.

I'm living, breathing proof. I was a state police sergeant in 1980 and was made a MEG [Metropolitan Enforcement Group] director at that time, first woman ever to do that, and I worked for a bunch of good ole boys and they didn't want a woman. That was that.

I filed a sexual discrimination lawsuit. A MEG Unit is composed of all local communities, and the police chiefs of all these communities sit on the policy board and they dictate policy. When the man who was commander of the MEG Unit left, I said, "I want your job. I'm next in line." He said, "They don't want you." But they let me have the job. I had two or three people working for me at the time. In a nine-month period we confiscated three quarters of a million dollars' worth of drugs in a three-man unit.

But I didn't have the time, because we were so short-handed, to go drink coffee with the chiefs, and that's exactly what it boiled down to. They told me I wasn't doing the correct liaison work. I had a stenographer come to the meeting where they told me what I had to do to come up to snuff. I did everything. They told me they'd vote at the next meeting whether I'd be retained or not. I went on vacation, they called my boss and said, "She's gone. She's history." I went to the director of the state police after going through the chain and told him, "Not only have you hurt my pocketbook, you've hurt my promotional chances" because now I was back to being paid as a sergeant. I told him if he couldn't help me I'd have to go to court. He said, "I wouldn't do that if I were you because your life won't be worth a damn with the state police if you do that." And, by God, he was right.

Because from that point on, I have never had a promotion. I've gone from assignment to assignment at their whim.

I won my lawsuit. The guy who was my boss came to court on my behalf and attested to everything I was suggesting, that it was because I was a woman. My past boss told me, "It's because you're a woman, it's because it's an election year, and we can't help you." I was like, "I've been a good employee for eight years now. Come on now, give me a break." "No. Sorry." So I got a paltry settlement, and I do mean paltry, they paid me as an acting lieutenant for a short period of time with overtime, that was my settlement, and took all the negative paperwork out of my personnel file, which I'm not even sure they did.

So I'll leave here a sergeant and my heart is broken because I come from a family of captains and lieutenants and that was my goal. But sergeant's the best I'm ever gonna do.

My intention was to make a statement, not to make a big monetary settlement. I've been punished ever since.

The attitude is "Don't rock the boat." It's like, "Honey, you're lucky enough to have this job. Don't complain."

It's—don't complain about the wrong thing. Don't complain about the wrong thing. You can complain and commiserate along with everyone else, but don't say it's because you're a woman ever. Ever, ever, ever. Your friends will stick by you, and they'll say, "Yeah. It's because you're a woman this happened to you." But if you say it to the wrong person, you've just sealed your death warrant.

If you're a woman in law enforcement and you work really hard and you don't make any waves, it takes twice as long to become accepted. But God help you if you have even *one* disgruntled person along the way.

Bad things happen to police officers. Period. Male or female. Maybe some women get it rougher in one unit and some men get it rougher in another unit. But in order to do this job and do it well, you have to love what you are. I love being a cop. But I'm ready to retire. It's not because I'm not proud of what I do, it's just that . . . maybe I'm tired. Maybe I'm tired.

We take it and we take it and we take it. We're *such* good sports. Finally, you get to the point where you say, "No. I don't want to be a good sport anymore."

I spent a lot of years working undercover in Narcotics. Then I was in the Major Case Squad for about eight years. Unfortunately, there was a dinosaur in the squad. He would call me "the skirt" or "the broad" and even worse. He was constantly on my back. He wasn't my immediate supervisor for the first four years. He was just another supervisor in the squad, but he'd always do something to sabotage me; he always finagled some way of keeping me out of things. My sergeant got promoted and I had to work for this man. It was my worst nightmare.

He had a Nazi flag on his desk. He had a German Youth knife collection. We had a Jewish captain. And when this captain was absent, he'd say, "Where's Murray the Socks Salesman?" "Where's the kike?" He subscribed to the old ways of beating up prisoners, thinking nothing of putting their heads in toilet bowls. I mean, he's not the nicest person. Not my kind of cop.

In December of '83, he's my supervisor and I get promoted to detective second grade. I now made as much money as he made. I go to the ceremony, I'm in full uniform, my family's there—he says to me, "Kiss your overtime goodbye. Nobody's gonna make more money than me this year."

He called me a "cunt broad" in front of the squad. I wasn't there. I had been elected every year as the union delegate—I was the first female union representative to the Detective Endowment Association. I had been a delegate from 1972 through 1985. I was chosen every year. He comes in one day, I was at a union meeting, and he says to the guys sitting around the office: "What kind of men would allow a cunt broad to be their delegate?" One of the guys brought the story back to me. And I went nuts.

He was sabotaging my cases. I would turn a case folder in. He would pull out one of the reports and then yell at me for not doing that report. What he was doing was keeping a list; every time he did this, he made an entry: "Had to admonish her"; "Instructed her to do the report." He did this to me twice. I thought, "One of the guys is screwing with my paperwork." So I went to the analyst who the paperwork had to go through—"Are you screwing with my paperwork?" He said no; he didn't know what was happening. "Well, then, what the hell is happening between your desk and his?"

Then I started keeping copies of my reports. So when he'd say I didn't do the report, I would show it to him. One time, he told me the captain was looking for this report. I went down to the Arrest and Crime Coding Unit, where all the reports would go into the computer for statistics. I went down there and pulled the copy—the captain had signed it! I brought it to the captain: "Captain, you wanted to see this report." The captain didn't know what I was talking about.

One night, I went past the sergeant's desk. The drawer was open. He had just yelled at me that day for not having a report. There was my report in his desk, and he had this list of reprimands. What he was planning on doing—I was scheduled to go to the FBI Academy—this was June; I was scheduled to go there from September 30 to December. My evaluation was due the first of December. What he was planning on was giving me a substandard evaluation—I would be demoted in rank, I would now not make more money than him, and I wouldn't be there to defend myself. That was the plan. He was a very cunning man.

But he met his match because I made a decision that I was going to fight him to the end. And there was a sacrifice attached to that. Because after that, my name was mud. Once I made the complaint, I was finished.

First, I went to the boss, the lieutenant, and I reported him. "I'll look into it." Then I hear him and the lieutenant conspiring: "Don't worry about it. It'll be okay." So I thought, "I'm not gonna get any help from the lieutenant. I'm not gonna get any help from the new captain because he's got the captain's ear."

So I played dirty. I went in to him with a tape recorder in my pocket, closed the door, sat down, and said, "We've got to talk." He had been warned that I was capable of taping. For the first fifteen minutes of the conversation, he was like an altar boy. "Oh, Mary, I really don't know why we're having a problem. I always treat you well. You're a *very good* detective. Are you in the changes?"

Well, like most people, they can't hold that character very long. I just kept at him like I would a suspect on the street trying to break him for a homicide. Until finally he blew it. He lost it. "I called you—I didn't call you a *cunt* broad. I called you a *fuckin'* broad. And I can do that anytime I want." And on and on he goes on tape. For about thirty minutes. If he had been willing to work it out, I probably would have dropped the whole complaint. But there was no working anything out with this man.

I went back to the lieutenant and I said, "Well, I got the evidence I need because I taped him." I made the complaint official with the in-house EEOC.

What they did to me after that—it's unbelievable. They harassed me, they kept tabs on me, they followed me. I went to the FBI Academy, they went after my partner, he had to retire. They hurt me through my partner because my partner and I were very close.

I came back from the FBI Academy, I didn't have a partner, I had nobody to work with, nobody *would* work with me because they were afraid I was being followed by IAD. And no one is so pure they can escape the IAD [Internal Affairs Division]—I mean, you could take five minutes longer on your meals and they got you.

They upheld the code of silence. That's exactly what they did. It was "Mary, you're a cop! How could you do this to a brother officer?" I said, "Wait a minute. Try this. I am a cop. How could he do this to *me?*"

We went through the department investigation and they found him guilty of harassment over a prolonged period of time. And the only reason they found him guilty was they had the tape. Because they sabotaged the investigation. They screwed up the questions, they asked the questions of the wrong people, they mixed up the places and times. I found out that the sergeant who was supervising the investigation out of EEOC was a business partner of the lieutenant I reported it to.

The bottom line was they gave him a three-day command discipline. And he had something like thirty-five days on the books, comp time, so it didn't even cost him anything. And I was expected, then, to go back and work for him. I said, "He's still gonna be my boss!" "Well, he got instruction and he's not gonna do it again."

I asked for a transfer back to Narcotics. In going back, it meant I was never going to make detective first grade, I had to give up being a hostage negotiator, I had to give up being a union delegate, I had to give up a department car and a parking permit which allowed me to park almost anywhere I wanted in the city, anytime I wanted. This cost me a lot. Plus, leaving the most prestigious unit in the Police Department and taking a transfer back in my career path gave the idea that *I* was wrong. And this son of a bitch was getting to stay. Five months after I went back to Narcotics, I find out that this man did not even get the command discipline.

If I hadn't spent so many years in undercover, in community isolation, in Police Department isolation, I never would have made it. I was taught from my very birth on the job that you're out there and you're alone. Because when you were undercover, the uniformed officers didn't know who you were; you carried no ID. Your name wasn't even in the Central Personnel computer files. You had a different identity. Your neighbors weren't allowed to know what you did for a living. So you were really isolated.

I did that for so many years that when they isolated me because of the discrimination suit, something I really believed in, they weren't able to break me. But it took everything inside of me to do it.

One thing I always used to say to myself when I would think about the frustration—I'd be laying there on the bed, thinking, "This is the loneliest job I ever had." I've never had more friends and acquaintances in all my life, but I am alone. With my problems, I am alone. And I thought, "No matter what happens, I am either going to go up alone or go down alone." And it's the loneliest job in the world.

The code is everywhere. No matter what, even if you know something is wrong, you're supposed to cover it up rather than confront anybody. You just don't admit anything's wrong. You don't tell on the others. You don't rat on them.

I have a very bad taste in my mouth for anything to do with the federal EEO, or anything like that, because sometimes the ones you *go* to are part of the problem. In DEA [Drug Enforcement Agency] the guy that was in charge of the EEO board got forty-five days off for sexually harassing an agent—yet he was the head of the EEO board for the district. And do you know they didn't take him off that board, even after he got the forty-five days, until we had a headquarters inspection? Up till the day *before* the inspection, they had not removed him as head of the EEO board.

In ATF [Bureau of Alcohol, Tobacco, and Firearms], they had a Mexican male that was supposed to provide the answers to harassment, he was head of EEO for that office— and he was one of the biggest violators.

Example being, I was having problems with one of the redneck males. This male agent called up a friend of mine who was an agent, he happened to be a friend of mine, a black agent, and asked him if he was sleeping with me. This still goes on.

I have a picture on my desk—I have a girlfriend that has a baby; she had been at my house and I was holding her baby and I keep the picture on my desk. I came in one day and found a note stuck on the picture: "Whose baby is this?" This redneck who stuck the note on my picture was also the guy that asked my friend if I was sleeping with him, and I also found out he was listening to my phone calls.

So it got to a point where I finally had to go to the EEO guy to see if we could settle this in-house. What he did—it's supposed to be handled discreetly. But he waited until we had a district meeting, which means all the ATF agents are there for in-training. He called myself and the other individual out in front of everybody; he pulled us out into the hallway to talk to us about the problem. And he says, "Well, we'll keep this between ourselves. No one else has to know." By the end of that afternoon, tell me what happened. *Everybody knew.*

I was ostracized after that to the point that—"Be careful. Sue will file an EEO on you." Even though everyone knew it was his problem, the one it came back on was me. It doesn't matter whether the other guy is guilty or not—you filed it.

So. I will never ever . . . I have a very bad taste in my mouth. The very things that are supposed to help us . . .

For you to go to EEO, you have to have no other option. And even then, most women will not—they'll take things that we have no business taking rather than go because they know what it means for them to go to EEO.

Another horror story. A female DEA agent. Her boyfriend was killed in his car by a car thief while she was on the phone with him. She's in shock to the point where afterwards she's supposed to be receiving help. And yet the guy that's supposed to be the trauma counselor is visiting her house, showing up at odd hours, touching her, and making her feel uncomfortable. She's a brand-new agent, no prior law enforcement.

THE CODE

I'm trying to explain to her, "Anything that makes you uncomfortable is sexual harassment." Yet remember, this is the guy that has to evaluate her to allow her to come back on duty. She was afraid to say or do anything because he can say with a stroke of the pen that she is not mentally fit.

Now, tell me. Is there something wrong with this picture?

EPILOGUE: THE ALLEY

Do you know that I just had to answer that alley thing again? This guy I'm seeing. We got into this long discussion one night about policewomen. He's carrying on about how could this one woman who had been a *fool* in the station, an idiot, possibly defend herself in a fight. And I thought, "Oh, my God, please tell me that this alley is not coming up again." And here it is. And here it is. It's the alley again. Here it is, twenty years later, the alley. That guy is still in that alley.

If I ever meet him, I'm gonna say, "I want to shake your hand. I've known you for twenty years. I've been defending you and getting you and falling in love with you for twenty years. Let me shake your hand."

CONTRIBUTING OFFICERS

LIEUTENANT CAROL ABORN, Los Angeles Police Department, Assistant Watch Commander, Communications Division. Aborn joined the LAPD in July 1983 and, after graduating from the Academy in January 1984, worked an undercover assignment for the Administrative Vice Division until November 1984. She was then assigned to Hollenbeck Patrol. In September 1985, Aborn went to the Planning and Research Division, was selected for a special assignment with the Support Services Bureau in January 1987, was assigned to the Police Commission in March 1988, and transferred to the Office of Operations in March 1989. Aborn was promoted to sergeant in January 1990 and was assigned to Hollywood Patrol until 1991, spent two months in Southwest Patrol, and was selected for another assignment with Support Services Bureau. In September 1992, Aborn was assigned to the Communications Division. Aborn served as President of the Los Angeles Women Police Officers' Association from March 1992 through March 1993. Aborn was promoted to lieutenant in June 1994.

OFFICER ELIZABETH ALLEN, Seattle Police Department, South Precinct. Allen has been a Seattle PD patrol officer since 1982 and has served on all three patrol shifts. Besides patrol, Allen's assignments have included collecting criminal information on gangs and working the Bicycle Patrol (1989 through 1991). Allen served in

Media Relations for six months in 1992 and six months in 1994.

DETECTIVE LATRICIA ALLEN, St. Louis Police Department, Vice/Narcotics Division, SCAT (Street Corner Apprehension Team). Allen was commissioned to the St. Louis PD on January 3, 1989, and was assigned to patrol in the Fifth District (known as the "Bloody Fifth" for its high crime rate). In January 1991, Allen was detached to Narcotics and, in May 1991, formally assigned as a detective to Narcotics. At the time, the St. Louis PD, Narcotics Division, worked with the FBI, DEA, ATF, the Department of Agriculture, and the Department of the Treasury in an operation targeting the selling of food stamps for narcotics, guns, and money. Allen was the sole undercover buyer in this operation. She was assigned to the long-term investigations undercover unit of Narcotics from October 1991 to July 1992 and was assigned to SCAT in July 1992. Allen is a member of the National Organization of Black Women in Law Enforcement and the St. Louis Police Officers Association.

SERGEANT GIOVANNA ALVAREZ, San Jose Police Department, Bureau of Investigations, Assaults Unit. Alvarez spent two years on patrol after joining the San Jose PD in 1976. Alvarez worked as a rape decoy in 1979. She then served in the Canine Unit for two and a half years, the first woman in the department ever to work Canine. Alvarez returned to patrol in 1981. Alvarez served as a training officer from 1982 to 1985. In 1988, she was assigned to the Detective Bureau, where she served in the Fraud Unit. In 1991, Alvarez returned to patrol. In May 1992, she was promoted to sergeant. Alvarez was reassigned to the Detective Bureau and joined the Assaults Unit in March 1992.

PATROL SPECIALIST KATHERINE AMBROSE, Chicago Police Department, Third District. Ambrose joined the CPD in 1976 and was assigned to the Third District. Ambrose has served on patrol in one of Chicago's highest crime areas for nineteen years.

CAPTAIN ADONNA AMOROSO, San Jose Police Department, Bureau of Field Operations. Amoroso was hired by the San Jose PD in April 1976 and assigned to patrol in 1977, working nights on the East Side and South Side. In 1979, Amoroso transferred to the Burglary Suppression Unit (now called Narcotics and Covert Investigations), where she worked undercover in sting operations and later in the Pawn Detail. In 1983, Amoroso went back to patrol, became an FTO (Field Training Officer), and was promoted to sergeant in the Patrol Division in 1984, heading teams on the East Side and West Side. In 1987, Amoroso became a supervisor-investigator in the Robbery Unit, the first woman ever assigned to Robbery in the San Jose PD. Amoroso went to the Narcotics Unit in 1988. She was promoted to lieutenant in 1989 and returned to the Patrol Division. Amoroso worked in the Street Crimes Unit, which includes robbery stings, prostitution stings, and surveillances, at the street level, from 1991 to July 1992. Amoroso was then assigned to the Detective Division, Assaults Unit, in July 1992. She was promoted to captain and transferred to the Bureau of Field Operations in October 1993. Amoroso served as President of the San Jose Women's Police Officers' Association from 1984 to 1989. Amoroso was the recipient of the 1981 Outstanding Police Duty Award (for a sting operation) and the Medal of Valor in 1979 (for her work in a rape decoy operation).

YOUTH OFFICER KIM ANDERSON, Chicago Police Department, Area Five. Anderson joined the Chicago PD in 1974 and was assigned to the Youth Division, where she served until 1980. Anderson has served as a hostage negotiator (she was one of the CPD's first seven women negotiators) from the inception of the Hostage/Barricaded/Terrorist Unit in 1979. Anderson held assignments within the Organized Crime Division's Gangs, Narcotics, Prostitution, and Gambling units and the Intelligence Section from 1980 to 1983. She was detailed to the Chicago Terrorist Task Force from 1983 to 1985. Anderson has been an Area Five Youth Officer since 1985.

ASSISTANT COMMISSIONER CAROLEN BAILEY, Minnesota Department of Public Safety, St. Paul, Minnesota. Bailey joined the St. Paul Police Department in 1961 as a policewoman (investigator) assigned to the Juvenile Division and served until November 1963. In 1964, Bailey transferred to the Sex-Robbery Unit, where she worked as an investigator. In 1966, she was assigned as an investigator to the Sex-Homicide Unit, where she served for five years. In 1971, Bailey was promoted to sergeant, working in the Sex-Homicide-Robbery Unit for fifteen years. After her promotion to lieutenant in 1985, Bailey was assigned to the Patrol Division, Northwest Team. In May 1987, she transferred to the Vice Unit, where she served as Unit Commander for one year. From May 1988 to February 1991, she was the Unit Commander in the Volunteer Services/Special Events Unit. Bailey retired from the St. Paul Police Department in February 1991. In 1992, Bailey was appointed Assistant Commissioner, Minnesota Department of Public Safety. Bailey's service has included working on the Minnesota Program for Victims of Sexual Assault, the Minnesota Advisory Council on Battered Women, the Minnesota Advisory Council on Child Abuse and Neglect (1969–1985), serving as President and holding other board offices for the Minnesota Association of Women Police (1972–1975), acting as a consultant for the National Center for Women Policy Studies, Washington, D.C. (1976–1977), for the National Victim/Witness Center, Washington, D.C. (1977–1979), and for the National Institute of Policing, U.S. Department of Justice (1978–1980). Bailey was President of the International Association of Women Police (IAWP) from 1980 to 1982 and served as Executive Director of the IAWP from September 1988 through September 1991.

LIEUTENANT WANDA BARKLEY, Seattle Police Department, West Precinct. Barkley joined the Seattle PD in February 1980 and spent seven years on patrol in the North Precinct. During this time, Barkley spent two summers in the Mounted Unit (1986 and 1987) and six months, from fall 1987 to March 1988, as an instructor in the Driver's Safety

Unit. After Barkley's promotion to sergeant in 1988, she became the facilities coordinator in the Inspectional Services Division for the repair and upkeep of all department facilities. In 1990, Barkley spent six months as a patrol supervisor in the North Precinct. She served as a sergeant in a Community Police Team from 1991 through March 1992 in North. Later that year, she was promoted to lieutenant and went to the Internal Investigations Section. Barkley transferred to the West Precinct in August 1993. Barkley graduated from the Northwestern University Traffic Institute School of Police Staff and Command in 1994.

UNDERSHERIFF CINDY BARRETTE, Iron County Sheriff's Department, Iron County, Michigan. Barrette joined the Sheriff's Department in 1978 as a Deputy Sheriff and served there till 1983. From 1983 until 1992, Barrette worked as a sergeant for the Twin City (Caspian and Stambaugh, Michigan) Police Department. In 1992, Barrette returned to the Iron County Sheriff's Department as Undersheriff.

SERGEANT JOAN BIEBEL, Chicago Police Department, Major Accident Investigation Unit. After joining the police in 1976, Biebel worked patrol and then served on a tactical team in the Twentieth District until 1980, when she was promoted to detective, assigned to Robbery. In 1981, Biebel was assigned to Auto Theft, where she worked undercover for three years. In 1984, Biebel was promoted to sergeant and served in Traffic Enforcement until 1991, when she was assigned to Major Accident.

SERGEANT KELLY BRAITHWAITE, Chicago Police Department, Eighteenth District. Braithwaite has served on patrol since joining the CPD in 1986 and on patrol in the Thirteenth District until 1989. Braithwaite served on a tactical team from 1989 to 1994 in the Thirteenth District. She has also worked Special Employment in Cabrini-Green. In August 1994, Braithwaite was promoted to sergeant and assigned to the Eighteenth District.

DETECTIVE LILLIAN BRAXTON (RET.), New York City Police Department, Training Coordinator, Personnel Bureau. Braxton has served as President of the Committee of Police Societies for the NYPD, serves as historian for the IAWP (International Association of Women Police), has been active in NOBWLE (National Organization of Black Women in Law Enforcement), was President of the NYPD's Policewomen's Endowment Association from 1985 through 1992, and was delegate for the Detectives' Endowment Association. Braxton joined the NYPD in 1973 and worked patrol in the Forty-eighth Precinct before the "last hired-first fired" layoffs of NYPD officers in 1975. Braxton was laid off for thirty-three months, returning in 1978 to the NYPD, where she worked patrol in the North Bronx (Zone 9). Later in 1978, she was transferred to the Organized Crime Control Bureau, where she worked undercover Narcotics and trained recruits. In 1980, Braxton was transferred to the Personnel Bureau as a recruiting officer and served there till 1987. Braxton worked in the Sex Crimes Liaison Squad of the Detective Bureau from 1987 to 1989, teaching police officers techniques in Sex Crimes Investigators courses and monitoring cases involving victims of sex crimes and child abuse. Braxton was promoted to detective in 1988. She returned to the Personnel Bureau in 1989, serving as the Training Coordinator until her retirement from the NYPD in 1994. Braxton now serves as Director of the newly formed national organization Law Enforcement Support Foundation of America, which helps male and female police officers with non-line-of-duty illnesses and injuries.

OFFICER TRICIA BRAXTON, New York City Police Department, Twentieth Precinct. Officer Braxton joined the NYPD in June 1992. Part of her training included six months with the Community Policing Training Unit, during which time she worked in various precincts in the city. Braxton has been assigned to patrol in the Twentieth Precinct since her graduation from the Academy, the same precinct in which her mother, Lieutenant Lillian Braxton, once worked. Officer Braxton wears her mother's badge.

OFFICER BARBARA BREWSTER, San Francisco Police Department, Crime Prevention Company/Tactical. The Tactical Unit encompasses SWAT, crowd control, training officers in crowd control and undercover decoy work. Brewster is a twenty-year veteran of the SFPD, part of the second San Francisco Police Academy class with women recruits trained as patrol officers. She was trained at three different stations, Northern, Ingleside, and Park, before being assigned to patrol at Taraval Station in 1976. Brewster then served a sixty-day tour of duty in Narcotics and served on surveillance in Homicide. In 1977, Brewster returned to Taraval Station, where she sometimes worked a one-person car. Later that year she was recruited by the Street Crimes Unit and trained in decoy work for what was then called the Crime Specific Task Force. Brewster has been with the Crime Prevention Company/Tactical (the unit has also been called the Crime Specific Task Force, the Crime Suppression Unit, and the Headquarters/Special Operations Group/Tactical) for eighteen years.

DETECTIVE FIRST GRADE KATHLEEN BURKE (RET.), New York City Police Department. Burke joined the NYPD in 1968 and was assigned to the 103rd Precinct (South Jamaica) as a policewoman. Burke joined the Narcotics Division in 1969 and worked undercover in a variety of capacities, including a citywide narcotics undercover investigation in the New York City public schools from 1969 to 1970. Burke was promoted to detective in 1971 and stayed in Narcotics. In 1974, she left undercover and became a narcotics investigator with a Narcotics Field Team. In 1977, she was transferred to Missing Persons and later assigned to the Major Case Squad, where she served until 1985, when she was assigned to the Organized Crime Task Force. Burke was promoted in 1983 to detective second grade and to detective first grade in 1991. In 1986, Burke was shot on-duty and was reassigned in May 1988 on restricted duty to the Narcotics Division, where she was involved with computer tracking of repeat offenders. Burke retired on disability in 1991. Burke now teaches Post-Traumatic Stress Survival Training to police throughout the U.S. She was President of the International Association of Women Police from 1988 to 1991. Burke is president of a Fraternal Order of Police lodge in New York City.

MOTOR OFFICER BRENDA BURROWS, Seattle Police Department, Metropolitan Division, Traffic Section, Motorcycle Unit. After joining the force in 1980, Burrows spent eight years on patrol, in West Precinct for five years and North Precinct for three years. Burrows has served with the Traffic Section of the Motorcycle Unit since 1988. She is one of two women motorcycle officers out of a forty-person unit. Burrows is a member of the International Association of Women Police.

DEPUTY ROBIN CAREY, Carson Station, Los Angeles County Sheriff's Department. After joining the Sheriff's Department in 1986, Carey worked the Women's Jail from late 1986 through 1987, when she was transferred to Carson Station. From 1987 to the end of 1989, she was on patrol in a one-person car. Carey now serves as the Traffic Investigator for Carson Station, investigating major collisions that occur in L.A. involving civilians and also collisions involving deputies.

SERGEANT PATSY CHAPMAN, Houston Police Department, Emergency Communications Division. Chapman, originally from Michigan, joined the Houston PD in 1981 and was assigned to patrol in the Southeast Substation, which has a reputation as one of the most diverse and busy districts in Houston. From 1985 to May 1990, she worked in the Vice Division, specializing in undercover prostitution and narcotics work. A former Miss Olympia, Chapman taught Defensive Tactics at the Houston Police Academy from May 1990 to 1992 before being assigned, in August 1992, to the Public Integrity Review Group, which investigates criminal complaints alleged against city employees outside the Police Department. In February 1994, Chapman transferred to the Emergency Communications Division.

SERGEANT ROBIN CLARK, Seattle Police Department, Patrol Division, East Precinct. Clark joined the SPD in 1980 and worked as a patrol officer in East Precinct for five years. In January 1985, Clark was assigned as a detective to the Sex Crimes Unit (now Special Assault Unit), where she served from 1985 to 1987. Clark was a detective with the Green River Task Force from 1987 to 1989 and in Personnel, Background Investigations in the latter part of 1989. In January 1990, she was promoted to sergeant and assigned to South Precinct. She was transferred to East Precinct in 1991. Clark served in the Special Activities Unit from April 1993 to June 1994, when she returned to East Precinct.

LIEUTENANT CAROL CONRY, New York City Police Department, Internal Affairs Bureau. Conry joined the NYPD in June 1973 and was assigned in November to the 75 Precinct in Brooklyn. Conry was the third woman to work the 75. In 1974, she joined the Narcotics Division of OCCB, the Organized Crime Control Bureau. In June 1975, Conry was laid off, during New York's fiscal crisis, under the "last hired-first fired" provision, for two and a half years. In December 1977, Conry went back on patrol, in the 70 Precinct, also in Brooklyn, and, in 1978, joined the SCRU Unit (Senior Citizens Robbery Unit), where she served as a decoy, dressing as an elderly woman in order to arrest predators of senior citizens by getting mugged herself. In November 1981, Conry was transferred into the Detective Bureau as an investigator and worked in the 61 Detective Squad (Brooklyn) and the 72 Detective Squad. Conry was promoted to detective in December 1982 and was transferred to the Brooklyn District Attorney's Squad. Conry was promoted to sergeant in December 1983, went to the 61 Precinct in Brooklyn as a sergeant for six months, and returned to the Brooklyn DA's Squad, where she served for the next eight years. Conry received a merit promotion in July 1989 to Supervisor, Detective Squad. In May 1991, she was promoted to lieutenant and went to the 88 Precinct (Brooklyn North) as the Integrity Control Officer. Conry was transferred to the Field Internal Affairs Unit in October

1991, which was consolidated into the Internal Affairs Bureau in 1993.

SERGEANT BARBARA DAVIS, San Francisco Police Department, Public Affairs Director. Davis joined the SFPD in July 1975; after graduation from the Academy, she worked patrol in Ingleside, Mission, and Richmond stations. In 1977, Davis was assigned to Vice and worked undercover, plainclothes detail, as a prostitute decoy; she also worked undercover for gambling and massage-parlor operations. In 1978, Davis joined a special surveillance detail for the Homicide Unit. Later in 1978, she served in the Communications/Dispatch Division. Davis was a training officer (tac officer) at the Police Academy from 1979 to 1985. After being promoted to Inspector in 1985, Davis was assigned to the Bureau of Inspectors. She was promoted to the post of noncivil service lieutenant in 1989 and, as a temporary lieutenant, worked Narcotics, Patrol, and General Work Investigations Detail, which handles crimes against persons, including domestic violence, harassment threats, stalking, batteries, assaults, kidnapping, arson, and fugitives. Davis attended the FBI National Academy in Quantico, Virginia, from January 1994 to April 1994 and returned to the SFPD as the Director of Public Affairs.

POLICE OFFICER KATHLEEN DEADY, New York City Police Department, Manhattan South TNT (Tactical Narcotics Team), Narcotics Division, OCCB (Organized Crime Control Bureau). Deady joined the NYPD in July 1984. Her first assignment, from December 1984 to July 1985, was to a Neighborhood Stabilization Unit (NSU), which covered four precincts in Brooklyn South. Deady then went to patrol in the Sixth Precinct (Greenwich Village) until June 1993, when she was transferred to TNT.

SERGEANT DOREEN DEAN, Philadelphia Police Department, Taxi Enforcement Unit. Dean joined the Philadelphia PD in 1984 and was assigned as a patrol officer to South Division, Seventeenth District. In 1985, Dean joined a special detail in Prostitution called the "John Squad," where she served for the next three and a half years. In

1988, the John Squad was transferred to the Vice Unit. Dean served in the Gambling Squad from 1988 to 1991. In 1991, she was promoted to sergeant and assigned to the First District. Dean was transferred to the Taxi Enforcement Unit in 1993. Dean has served on the executive board of the National Organization of Black Women in Law Enforcement at both the regional and national level.

DETECTIVE ANITA DICKASON, Dallas Police Department, Narcotics. In 1982, Dickason joined the Collin County (Texas) Sheriff's Department as a reserve deputy sheriff. In 1988, she joined the Dallas Police Department and was assigned to patrol in the Northeast Substation. Dickason served on patrol till July 1993, when she was promoted to senior corporal and reassigned to the Narcotics Division as a detective specializing in street-level buying and executing search warrants. Dickason also teaches Defensive Tactics, including Spontaneous Knife Defense and Baton Training, at the Collin County Community College Law Enforcement Academy, which serves multiple law enforcement agencies in the northern section of Texas.

SERGEANT/DETECTIVE MARIE DONAHUE, Boston Police Department, Day Supervisor, Sexual Assault Unit. Donahue joined the force in 1973. In 1974, she was assigned to patrol in South Boston, concentrating on the busing problems/near riots at South Boston High School. Donahue became the first woman assigned to the Mounted Unit in 1975 and served in it for five years. In 1979, she transferred to Vehicle Patrol in Area A. In 1983, while serving in the Security Detail for the mayor, Donahue designed a proposal for a citywide Sexual Assault Unit, which was accepted by the City Council. Donahue served in this unit, which she founded in 1984, for the next three years. She was promoted to detective in 1984. Donahue was asked to go to the Homicide Unit in 1987 and was one of the first two women assigned there. She was promoted to sergeant in 1988 and assigned to Roxbury as a patrol supervisor. In 1991, Donahue returned to the Sexual Assault Unit.

OFFICER TERRY DUFFY, Seattle Police Department, North Precinct, Community Police Team. Duffy joined the Seattle PD in 1979 and has been posted, primarily in the North Precinct, to work various assignments, including the ACT Team (Anti-Crime Team), Harbor Patrol, Traffic, and Mountain Bike Patrol.

CAPTAIN MARGARET FAHY, Executive Officer, New York City Police Department, Ninety-fourth Precinct. Fahy became an NYPD officer in September 1974 and was assigned to patrol in the Seventeenth Precinct, Manhattan. Following the 1975 layoff of police, Fahy returned in August 1976 and worked patrol in Queens, Brooklyn, Bronx, and Manhattan. Fahy then transferred to the Thirteenth Precinct (Manhattan), patrol. From June 1981 until November 1984, Fahy served as an instructor in Police Science at the Police Academy. Fahy was promoted to sergeant in September 1983 and was promoted to lieutenant in May 1985. She was assigned to the 66 Precinct as a lieutenant and then to Health Services Division, Personnel Bureau, until October 1990, when she transferred to the 77 Precinct as a captain (Fahy was promoted to captain in November 1989). In March 1993, Fahy came to the 94 Precinct. Fahy is a member of the Emerald Society and the Policewomen's Endowment Association.

DETECTIVE LISA FENKNER, Seattle Police Department, Crime Prevention Division, Retail Theft Program. After joining the force in August 1987, Fenkner worked patrol until May 1990, when she was assigned to Crime Prevention Division, Commercial Security Section, to facilitate the Retail Theft Program.

SERGEANT RETA FIELDS, New York City Police Department, Community Policing Supervisor, Seventy-ninth Precinct. Fields graduated from the NYPD Academy in December 1981, went to her training unit at the Thirteenth Precinct for six months, and in June 1982 was assigned to the Ninety-fourth Precinct patrol. In 1984, she was promoted to sergeant and assigned to the Seventy-seventh Precinct.

Since September 1986, Fields has served in the Seventy-ninth Precinct.

OFFICER JAYE FLETCHER, Chicago Police Department, Research and Development Division. Fletcher joined the CPD in 1972 as a policewoman in the Youth Division. In 1974, she was one of the first women to volunteer for patrol duty and was assigned to the Sixteenth District, where she served through 1979. From 1979 to 1984, Fletcher worked as a public information officer in the Office of News Affairs. Fletcher took a leave of absence to act as press secretary for Richard J. Brzeczek's Republican State's Attorney campaign. In 1985, Fletcher returned to the CPD and was assigned as Women's Lock-up Keeper in the Twenty-fifth District. In November 1993, she went to Research and Development as a staff writer. Fletcher has written several upcoming true crime books.

SERGEANT/INSPECTOR JENNIFER FORRESTER, San Francisco Police Department, Investigations Bureau, Fencing Detail. Forrester joined the SFPD in 1977 as a clerk. In December 1980, she formally joined the force as a police officer and was assigned to Park Station from 1981 to 1986. Forrester worked as a chief's aide to Commander Isaiah Nelson from 1987 to 1989. She was transferred to the Northern Station in 1990 and was promoted to sergeant and transferred to the Investigations Bureau the same year, where she has served in Robbery, Burglary, Fraud, the Operations Center, and the DA's Office. In 1994, Forrester transferred to the Fencing Detail.

OFFICER MOLLY FULLERTON, Seattle Police Department, Narcotics Section. Fullerton joined the Seattle Police Department in January 1986 and worked patrol in South Precinct for five and a half years before being assigned, in July 1991, to the Crime Prevention Division, Commercial Security Section. Fullerton transferred to Narcotics in August 1992.

DETECTIVE DONNA GAVIN, Boston Police Department, Sexual Assault Unit. Gavin joined the Boston Police Department in 1986 and was assigned to patrol in Area E. In 1987, Gavin transferred to Area D as a patrol officer. In 1990, she served as Area D's Domestic Violence Officer, doing follow-up on assaults on women and men and, in particular, following cases in which the violence progressed, helping the victims through the court system. Gavin was promoted to detective in 1991 and was assigned to the Sexual Assault Unit. Gavin is on the executive board of the Boston Police Detectives Benevolent Society.

OFFICER CARLA GRUBISIC, Chicago Police Department, Organized Crime Division, Narcotics Section. Grubisic joined the force in 1986 and was assigned to patrol in the Twenty-first District. In April 1990, Grubisic transferred to Narcotics.

OFFICER PEGGY GUICE, Chicago Police Department, Third District. After joining the CPD in 1986, Guice trained in the Third District and was assigned to the Eighteenth District, patrol. In 1988, she returned to the Third District, worked patrol for a few months, and then worked in the district Review Office before being assigned to the Mayor's Detail, Detached Services. In 1989, she returned to the Third District, patrol. From 1990 to 1994, she served on a Third District tactical team. In April 1994, Guice was assigned to the School Car, Third District.

SERGEANT BEVERLY HALL, St. Paul Police Department, Juvenile Unit. Hall also serves as Coordinator, Hostage Negotiation Team. Hall joined the St. Paul PD in 1979. From March 1980 through June 1986, she worked patrol on the East Side, midnights. Hall served as a Field Training Officer from 1983 to 1985 and served a six-month rotation in the Street Crimes Unit, working undercover Narcotics and Vice. In June 1986, Hall was promoted to sergeant and assigned to citywide Narcotics until December 1987. She returned to patrol as a supervisor until January 1989. Hall was then assigned, as executive sergeant, to the Communications Center. In June 1991, she transferred to the Internal Affairs Unit. She also became a hostage negotiator in 1991 and, since December 1992, has served as the Coordinator of the Hostage Negotiation Team. In January 1993, Hall joined the Special Investigations Unit and, in August 1993, the Juvenile Unit. She has served on the board of the Minnesota Association of Women Police since 1982, was President (1982–1986) and Past President (1986–1988), and served until 1993 as Recording Secretary. In 1993, she attended and graduated from the FBI National Academy in Quantico, Virginia. Hall served on the board of the International Association of Women Police as the Region VII Coordinator from 1988 to 1994.

CAPTAIN DIANE HARBER (RET.), Los Angeles Police Department. Harber joined the LAPD in 1957 and was assigned to the Los Angeles County Jail. She served for many years in Seventy-seventh Juvenile, which includes South Central. Harber serves as a consultant with the Women's Advisory Board to the Los Angeles Police Commission.

CHIEF PENNY HARRINGTON, Portland Police Bureau, retired Chief of Police. Harrington became the first woman police chief of a major police force in the U.S. in 1985. She joined the Portland Police Bureau and was assigned to the Women's Protective Division in 1964. In 1970, she transferred to the Planning and Research Division. In February 1972, Harrington was promoted to detective. She became the first woman in the Portland PB to attain the rank of sergeant, in July 1972; was assigned to the Women's Protective Division for a month; then assigned to CRISS (Columbia Regional Information Sharing System) to develop the Police Department's computer system; and next assigned to the Radio Division to develop the Police Department's computerized dispatch system. In 1975, Harrington was assigned to the North Precinct. In 1977, she was promoted to lieutenant (the Portland PB's first woman lieutenant), stayed as a patrol lieutenant in North Precinct for six months, and then served in the Planning and Research Division for three years. In 1980, Harrington was promoted to captain and assigned to Personnel Division. In 1982, she was assigned to patrol as the Precinct Commander in East Precinct. Harrington was appointed Police Chief in January

1985. She retired from the police in 1986. Harrington was appointed to the Webster Commission after the L.A. riots in 1992 and was appointed cochair of the Women's Advisory Council to the Los Angeles Police Commission in May 1992, serving until November 1993. In June 1994, Harrington was appointed by the Los Angeles Police Commission to the Police Commission Gender Equity Task Force. Harrington heads her own consulting firm on Women in the Workplace. She joined the state bar Office of Investigations in 1988 and serves as special assistant to the director. Harrington is a member of the International Association of Women Police.

OFFICER MARY HEFFERNAN, San Francisco Police Department, Operations Center. Heffernan joined the force in November 1975 and was among the first sixty women hired as patrol officers by the SFPD. After the Academy, Heffernan trained three weeks consecutively at Park, Mission, and Taraval stations. Her first permanent assignment was to the Northern Station, where she worked patrol from 1976 to 1981. While at the Northern Station, she was detailed to Vice for two months. She was then assigned to the Muni Detail from 1981 to 1985, with a detail to the Psychiatric Liaison Unit for five months. In 1987, she transferred to the Patrol Bureau Task Force. In December 1987, she was assigned to Communications, where she served until 1989. In 1989, Heffernan transferred to the Operations Center.

LIEUTENANT MARIANE HEISLER, Portland Police Bureau, Central Precinct. Heisler joined what was then the Women's Protective Division as a policewoman in March 1968. She was promoted to detective in 1973 and to sergeant in 1974. Between 1974 and 1982, Heisler worked as a uniformed patrol sergeant in East Precinct, served in the Traffic Division, was a sergeant in charge of the passing of the dispatch system (Bureau of Emergency Communications) from police to civilian control, and was a sergeant/investigator in the Internal Affairs Division. Heisler was promoted to lieutenant in 1982 and served in the Training Division, coordinating the training for the officers, was operations manager for the Bureau of Emergency Communications (BOEC) in 1983, became the day shift lieutenant for the East Precinct in 1984 and acting captain of the precinct from May 1984 through the end of the year, and Commander of the Crime Prevention Division in 1985. Heisler served as Fleet Manager, which included running the Telephone Report Writing Unit, Court Coordinators' Office, and Prosecution Liaison Office and obtaining and outfitting police vehicles from October 1986 to 1988. She was then assigned to the Internal Affairs Division. In 1990, Heisler transferred to the Central Precinct.

OFFICER VIRGINIA HILL, Philadelphia Police Department, Juvenile Aid Division, Missing Persons Unit. Hill joined the Philadelphia PD in March 1978 but was not assigned to patrol until 1980 due to the 1979 fiscal crisis. In 1980, Hill was assigned to the Fourteenth District, where she worked patrol. In October 1981, she was trained as a missing persons investigator and used this training while doing patrol work in West and South. In 1983, Hill joined the Missing Persons Unit.

OFFICER ADRIENNE HILLIARD, Philadelphia Police Department, Sex Crimes Unit. Hilliard joined the force in December 1979 and worked patrol from 1980 through 1985 in the Seventeenth District, South Philadelphia. From 1986 to 1989, Hilliard investigated juvenile crimes in the Juvenile Aid Division. From 1989 to the present, she has served as an investigator in the Sex Crimes Unit. Hilliard is a member of the National Organization of Black Women in Law Enforcement (NOBWLE), the Guardian Civic League in Philadelphia, and the Fraternal Order of Police.

OFFICER LISA HOLMES, Boston Police Department, Area B. Holmes joined the Boston PD in 1983 as a cadet and was hired as a patrol officer in 1985, when she was assigned to Area B. She served in the Power Patrol, targeting narcotics dealers and gang members through undercover work, from 1987 to 1990. Holmes worked in the Gang Unit from 1990 to 1993. In 1993, she returned to patrol in Area B. Holmes has received the Police Department Medal of Honor, the Boston Police Relief Association Memorial Award, and the Thomas F. Sullivan Award.

DETECTIVE FIRST GRADE PEGGY HOPKINS (RET.), New York City Police Department. Hopkins was appointed an NYPD policewoman in July 1967 and was assigned, in 1968, to the Seventy-eighth Precinct as a matron under the old Policewoman's Bureau. Hopkins was transferred to the Division of Licenses in July 1968 and served there through June 1971. She served in the Deputy Commissioner of Trials Office until January 1973, when she was detailed to the Rape Squad as the first female officer assigned to this squad in the city of New York. In late 1973, Hopkins was assigned to the Brooklyn Sex Crimes Squad, where she investigated first-degree rapes, sodomy, and sexual abuse. She was promoted to detective in July 1977 (although she had been doing investigative work in the Detective Bureau as an investigator for almost five years) and assigned to the Detective Bureau's Property Recovery Squad, Special Investigations Division, in charge of inspecting pawnshops and secondhand dealers. Hopkins also served with the Kidnap Task Force during this period. She was transferred to patrol in the Seventy-sixth Precinct (Red Hook) in 1975 during the fiscal crisis. Hopkins returned to the Detective Bureau, Property Recovery, in early 1976. In 1978, Property Recovery merged with the Bond and Forgery Squad, and Hopkins was assigned the investigation of white-collar crime. In 1980, the Special Frauds Squad, including the Property Recovery, Bond and Forgery, and Pickpocket and Confidence squads, was formed, with Detective Hopkins investigating all types of crimes in all three specialties as a senior detective until her retirement in November 1989. In December 1983, Hopkins was promoted to detective second grade. In December 1987, Hopkins became detective first grade, the highest rank of detective in the NYPD.

LIEUTENANT JOANNE HUNT, Seattle Police Department, Special Patrol Unit/Emergency Response Team. Hunt was a police officer with the University of Washington from May 1973 to October 1975. She joined the Seattle PD as one of the first women patrol officers in 1975 and was assigned to the East Precinct. Hunt worked the East Precinct for four years and then spent a year in the West Precinct. In 1980, after her promotion to sergeant, she worked in Internal Investigations, in Patrol, and was an administrative aide to an assistant chief. She was promoted to lieutenant in 1984 and assigned to the Traffic Section, where she headed the Enforcement Unit until 1986 and commanded the Motorcycle Unit until 1988. Hunt then became the Illness and Personnel Accountability Lieutenant. From mid-1989 through 1990, Hunt was the Director-in-Charge of the Integrated Police Planning Group for the 1990 Goodwill Games. Throughout 1991 and for the first two months of 1992, Hunt served in patrol, East Precinct, as a watch commander. Hunt was assigned to the Seattle SWAT Team in March 1992.

SERGEANT JUANITA JOHNSON, Chicago Police Department, Identification Section, Administrative Bureau. Johnson is a twenty-two-year veteran of the CPD and was one of the first women sergeants to work in the field. After joining in 1973 as a policewoman, Johnson was assigned to Area Two Youth Division until 1974 and, while still serving in Area Two Youth, was selected to be a training officer for the pilot program on rape investigations. From the end of 1974 until 1979, Johnson served in the Youth Division Special Investigations Unit, primarily targeting narcotics in and around high schools. Johnson was involved in computerizing data in the Narcotics and Gang Crimes Unit from 1979 to 1981, when she was promoted to sergeant and was assigned to patrol, Fourth District. From 1985 to 1989, Johnson served as administrative aide to the Deputy Superintendent of Investigative Services. In November 1989, she was reassigned to the Fourth District. She transferred to the Identification Section in July 1992. Johnson has an M.B.A. in Human Resources Management and is a CPA. Johnson is a member of the Chicago Police Sergeants Association, the Illinois Police Association, and the Coalition of Law Enforcement Officers (CLEO).

DETECTIVE REGINA JOSEPH, Dallas Police Department, Auto Theft Division. Joseph joined the Dallas PD in 1988 and served in North Central Patrol from 1988 to 1990 as a police officer, when she was transferred to the Dispatch Office as a police dispatcher. In 1992, Joseph joined Auto Theft.

LIEUTENANT KATHY KAJARI, Chicago Police Department, Sixteenth District. Kajari joined the CPD in 1972. After serving two years as a policewoman in the Youth Division, Kajari volunteered for patrol duty in 1974 and was sent to the Sixteenth District. In 1980, she was appointed Director of News Affairs, where she served for the next four years. In February 1985, Kajari went to the Twenty-fifth District, Lockup. Kajari was promoted to sergeant in 1985, assigned to the Twentieth District. From 1988 to 1990, Kajari served as the Twentieth's Neighborhood Relations Sergeant. In 1991, Kajari was promoted to lieutenant and transferred to the Seventeenth District, where she served until early 1993, when she became a tactical team lieutenant in the Twentieth District. In October 1993, Kajari transferred to the Sixteenth District.

LIEUTENANT HELEN KIDDER (RET.), Los Angeles Police Department. Kidder, who joined the LAPD in 1968, spent four months in Juvenile before being assigned to the jail in November 1968. In 1969, Kidder was assigned to the Criminal Conspiracy Section, which investigated militant activities in L.A. (including the Black Panthers), and spent the next ten years there. During that time, she became the first female bomb technician on the LAPD and a bomb investigation expert. In addition to being trained at Redstone, Kidder attended the FBI National Academy in Quantico, Virginia (one of the LAPD's first two women to attend) during this period. In February 1979, she was assigned to Northeast Homicide, the first woman in the LAPD to be formally assigned to Homicide. From mid-1981 to September 1982, she served in Burglary. Kidder then served in Internal Affairs from 1982 to 1986, the first woman of detective rank assigned there. Kidder became the first female advocate within Internal Affairs in the LAPD. During the 1984 Olympics, she served as the watch commander at the Bomb Management Center. In 1986, Kidder was assigned to Watts Homicide. Kidder was promoted to Detective III that year and became the first female detective/coordinator at the bureau level. Kidder was also promoted to lieutenant in July 1986 and was assigned to Venice Patrol, the first female supervisor there. In 1987, she went to West L.A. station. She became the Department Recruiter, a commanding officer, responsible for recruitment, affirmative action, EEO issues, and discrimination investigations in 1988. In 1989, she was asked to return as a commander to the Criminal Conspiracy Section. In January 1992, Kidder retired from the LAPD.

LIEUTENANT RITA KNECHT, Los Angeles Police Department, Employee Relations Section, Office of Chief of Police. Knecht graduated from the Police Academy in July 1967, was assigned to Central Juvenile Division, and was then rotated to the jail. In 1968, she was transferred to Northeast Detective Division, where she worked Sex Crimes, Missing Children, and Pre-Delinquent Children. Although women could not be assigned to Homicide at that time, Knecht's partner and Knecht were often used as backup in Homicide. In 1971, Knecht was promoted to detective. In 1972, Knecht transferred, as Detective II, to Hollywood Division, where she served on the Sex Crimes team of Juvenile Section. Knecht went to Hollenbeck Division in 1973. In 1975, she was assigned to Robbery/Homicide Division, where she was assigned to the Rape Detail. In 1976, Knecht worked on a Task Force within Robbery/Homicide that concentrated on a pattern of homicides and rapes of elderly women. Knecht and the other woman working this West Side Rapist Task Force were the first two women in the LAPD ever assigned to a task force. In 1977, Knecht designed and taught the LAPD's first training seminar on sex crimes investigation and was the third woman from LAPD to attend the FBI National Academy. For a period of time in 1977 and 1978, Knecht served on the Hillside Strangler Task Force. Later in 1978, after a promotion to Detective III, Knecht transferred to the Southeast Division, where she was in charge of a Juvenile Unit. She was promoted to lieutenant in 1982 and sent to Northeast Patrol Division. In April 1986, Knecht transferred to Central Patrol Division, where she served until August 1986, when she was selected to be adjutant to Bernard Parks (now the LAPD's assistant chief), then Commander in Charge of the Support Services Bureau. Knecht also served as adjutant when Parks was appointed Deputy Chief. Knecht was instrumental in establishing a Sexual Assaults Investigators School within the LAPD. In 1990, she joined the Internal Affairs Group, where she served as Advocate and Officer-in-Charge of the Advocate Section. Knecht transferred in January 1994 to the Employee Relations Section.

OFFICER DOROTHY KNUDSON, Chicago Police Department, Eleventh District. Knudson joined the CPD in March 1990 (she was class commander in the Academy due to her top academic standing) and was assigned to the Twenty-third District, patrol. Knudson was assigned to the Eleventh District, patrol, in 1991. She was appointed to the Advisory Committee on Gay and Lesbian Issues, part of the Neighborhood Relations Division for the Chicago Police Department, in July 1991. Knudson is cofounder of the Lesbian and Gay Police Association.

SERGEANT CHRISTINE KOLMAN, Chicago Police Department, Nineteenth District, detailed to the Police Academy, where she teaches and implements CAPS, Community Alternative Policing Strategy. Kolman joined the force in February 1974 and was assigned to Area Six, Youth Division, till 1975, when she joined the Special Investigations Unit, when it was first formed. In 1979, SIU merged with the Narcotics and Gang Crimes Unit and Kolman served there for a year, making street buys and busts, and then was detailed to DEA through 1983. Kolman worked in Narcotics, Administration, from 1984 to 1986. From 1986 to 1988, she was detailed to DEA Airport Detail, Drug Profiling. In 1988, Kolman was promoted to sergeant and assigned to the Twenty-fourth District. In 1991, she joined the newly formed Random Drug Testing Unit. Kolman transferred to the Nineteenth in 1993 and was detailed in 1994 to Research and Development for the CAPS program at its inception and, in mid-1994, was detailed to the Academy to implement and teach CAPS. Kolman attended the Northwestern University Traffic Institute in 1991. Kolman is a member of the International Association of Women Police, the International Association of Narcotics Enforcement Officers, and the Fraternal Order of Police.

ASSISTANT CHIEF PATRICIA LAMPHERE, Seattle Police Department, Field Support Bureau. Lamphere joined the SPD in 1967 and was assigned, as a policewoman in the old Policewomen's Bureau, to the Juvenile Bureau. In 1968, Lamphere was transferred to Narcotics and worked undercover, primarily making buys, for the next six years. She was promoted to detective in 1970. Lamphere was assigned to the Check Forgery Unit in 1974 and worked undercover targeting forgers. In 1975, she transferred to Crimes Against Persons and served in the Special Assault Unit for four years, until joining the Officer Friendly School Program in 1979. Lamphere was promoted to sergeant in 1979 and went to Traffic. In 1982, she went to patrol, serving both as a sector sergeant and as a watch commander. She transferred to Personnel in 1984. She was promoted out of Personnel, as number one on the captain's list, in 1986, and went to Vice as a captain for the next three years. At the end of 1988, she was promoted to the exempt rank of major. In March 1992, Lamphere was promoted to Assistant Chief.

OFFICER MARYANNE LOWMAN, San Francisco Police Department, Investigations Bureau, Crime Scene Investigations Unit. Lowman was a police cadet at eighteen and became a station officer, one of the first women to work the Men's Jail, in 1975. Lowman became a police officer in 1977, was trained at Mission Station, and was assigned to Northern Station, where she worked patrol until 1981, when she transferred to the Muni Transit Division. In 1989, she transferred to the Operations Center. Lowman was assigned to the Crime Scene Investigations Unit in 1990.

PATROL SERGEANT PATRICIA MCCONNELL, Winnetka Police Department, Winnetka, Illinois. McConnell joined the Winnetka PD in 1978 as a patrol officer. In 1986, she was promoted to sergeant. McConnell attended Northwestern University's School of Staff and Command in 1987. From 1988 through 1993, McConnell served as the Investigations Unit Commander. In 1995, she received a master's degree in Management.

SERGEANT GILLIAN E. MCLAUGHLIN, Chicago Police Department, Patrol Division, Neighborhood Relations, Eighteenth District. McLaughlin joined the CPD in 1974 and was one of the first women in the pilot patrol program in Chicago, assigned to the Sixteenth District until May 1975. McLaughlin was the first woman assigned to the Mounted Unit and served there till 1980, with an assignment to the Mass Transit Unit, working as a decoy in the pickpocket detail in 1979. In 1980, McLaughlin was promoted to detective, working in Area Five Burglary until 1983, Area Four Violent Crimes until 1985, and Area Five Violent Crimes until 1988. In 1988, McLaughlin was promoted to sergeant and was assigned to the Eighteenth District, working a patrol car for two and a half years. McLaughlin became the Neighborhood Relations Sergeant in the Eighteenth District in 1991. McLaughlin attended the FBI Academy in Quantico, Virginia, in 1994.

OFFICER JENNIFER MCLEAN, Seattle Police Department, West Precinct. McLean joined the Seattle PD in 1986 and has worked patrol since then, with details to the Anti-Crime Team (ACT) and the Narcotics Section. McLean has also served in the Mountain Bike Patrol.

SERGEANT ROSE MCMAHON, Seattle Police Department, South Precinct. McMahon has served in patrol since joining the Seattle PD in 1979. Until 1992, she worked in West Precinct and North Precinct. In 1992, she became part of the Community Police Team, working with city agencies and community groups in North Seattle on chronic problems affecting the community. McMahon was promoted to sergeant in May 1994 and assigned to South Precinct.

McMahon is a member of the International Association of Women Police.

DETECTIVE II JOAN MCNAMARA, Los Angeles Police Department, Narcotics Group. After joining the LAPD in June 1982, McNamara was assigned to Hollenbeck Division (East Los Angeles) patrol. In 1983, she was transferred to the Communications Center. McNamara was assigned to the Report Writing Unit in 1984. In 1985, she transferred to Newton Division (South Central L.A.), where she worked for six and a half years. In 1991, McNamara was promoted to detective and joined the Narcotics Group.

SERGEANT/INSPECTOR ANGELA MARTIN, San Francisco Police Department, Inspector's Bureau, Sexual Assault Detail. Martin joined the SFPD in 1980 and was assigned to Southern Police Station patrol. While serving at Southern, Martin was detailed to Narcotics, working both in San Francisco and out of town, and the Patrol Bureau Task Force. She was promoted to sergeant in 1985 and assigned to Richmond Station (Martin was the first female sergeant in Richmond). In 1986, Martin transferred to the Inspector's Bureau, where she has served in the Juvenile Division, Fencing Detail, and the Sexual Assault Detail. Martin is a member of Officers for Justice and the San Francisco Police Officers Association.

DEPUTY GAIL MILLS, Harris County Sheriff's Department, Houston, Texas, Identification Division, Crime Scene Unit. Mills is a forensic artist and crime scene investigator with the Sheriff's Department. She joined the Harris County Sheriff's Department in September 1982, was assigned to Detention (Harris County Jail), attended the Harris County Sheriff's Academy in 1983, and transferred to the Identification Division in 1984.

SERGEANT CAROL MINAKAMI, Seattle Police Department, Emergency Response Team. Minakami joined the Seattle PD in 1977 and worked patrol in the South Precinct until 1985. In 1985, Minakami attained the rank of detective and was assigned to the Special Assault Unit, where she worked on cases involving child abuse and sexual abuse of children. From 1987 to 1989, Minakami, who at the time had more than twenty years of karate training, was an instructor of Defensive Tactics and Physical Training in the Washington State Criminal Justice Training Academy. In 1989, she was assigned to the SWAT Team as a marksman. Minakami was promoted to sergeant in January 1992.

ASSISTANT COMMISSIONER OF PUBLIC SAFETY DEBORAH L. MONTGOMERY, Minnesota Department of Public Safety, St. Paul, Minnesota. Montgomery was the first female hired on patrol by the St. Paul Police Department in 1975 and was assigned to the Rice Street Station in 1976. Montgomery worked patrol there from 1976 to November 1987. During this time, she also worked in the schools as an Officer Friendly. In 1987, Montgomery was promoted to sergeant and assigned to the Juvenile Division. In 1989, she returned to Rice Street as a supervising sergeant. In 1990, she was appointed Assistant Commissioner of Public Safety. Montgomery serves on the board of the National Organization of Black Law Enforcement Executives (NOBLE) and is a member of the National Organization of Black Women in Law Enforcement (NOBWLE). Montgomery was the Regional Coordinator of the International Association of Women in Police from 1984 to 1990, has served as President of the NAACP Youth Branch, and is a national board member of the NAACP.

DETECTIVE SUZANNE MOORE, Seattle Police Department, Crimes Against Persons Section, Robbery Unit. Moore joined the Seattle PD in October 1983 and was a patrol officer five and a half years, with assignments to ACT (Anti-Crime Team), Vice, and the Harbor Patrol until February 1989, when she was assigned to the Vice Unit as a detective. In February 1990, she transferred to the Burglary Unit, serving in the Pro-Active Burglary Squad. In June 1990, the Seattle PD formed a Gang Task Force and Moore transferred to the newly enhanced Gang Unit in July 1990. Moore transferred to Robbery in March 1994.

* * *

OFFICER MARGARET MORRISSEY, Chicago Police Department, Thirteenth District. Morrissey joined the force in 1986, worked a beat car in Thirteen until 1991, when she was assigned to the district tactical team. Morrissey also has worked the CTA Mass Transit on Special Employment.

DEPUTY CHIEF JILL S. MUNCY, Dallas Police Department, Special Operations Division. Muncy joined the Dallas PD in 1976 and spent fourteen years on patrol, as an officer and supervisor. After completing the Dallas PD's nine-month training, Muncy was assigned, in May 1977, to Northeast Patrol Bureau (now Northeast Operations Division). In 1979, she was sent to the Vice Division as the first woman on the Dallas PD assigned as a female undercover decoy prostitute. Muncy was promoted to sergeant in December 1980 and was assigned, as the first female supervising sergeant, to the Southeast Patrol Bureau. In April 1983, after a six-month assignment to Internal Affairs, she attained the rank of lieutenant. Muncy completed advanced training at the Southern Police Institute in Louisville, Kentucky, in 1983. From 1983 to 1990, she served as a patrol lieutenant in the Northeast, North Central, and Southeast divisions. In 1990, she was assigned to the Internal Audit Unit. In 1991, she taught the Response Continuum and Levels of Force courses in the Critical Incident School at the Dallas Police Academy. Muncy served as a lieutenant on a newly constituted Violence Crimes Task Force in 1991 before being named Deputy Chief of the Internal Affairs Division in October 1991. In September 1993, she transferred to Southeast Patrol Division, where she served until February 1994, when she transferred to the Special Operations Division.

OFFICER DOROTHY NOLAN, Chicago Police Department, Detective Division, Administration. Nolan joined the force in March 1976 and was assigned to First District patrol. She worked a beat car until 1979, when she was assigned to a tactical unit in the First District. In 1982, Nolan asked for and was assigned to foot patrol, becoming the first woman officer on foot patrol in Chicago, working there for the next four years. In 1986, she was assigned to Timekeeping and Review inside the district. She returned to a tactical unit in the First District in 1987 and, later that year, was assigned to be the Assistant Secretary of the district and then became the Secretary to the Deputy Chief of a patrol area. In 1988, Nolan joined the Detective Division.

LIEUTENANT LINDA O'BRIEN, Metro-Dade Police Department, Media Relations, Miami. O'Brien joined the force in July 1973 and was assigned to Liberty City road patrol in 1974. She was promoted to detective at the end of 1975 and assigned to the Sexual Battery Unit in the Homicide Bureau in 1976. She transferred to Homicide itself in 1979, the third woman ever to work Homicide, and served there until 1982. In 1983, O'Brien was promoted to sergeant and sent to the Southwest District. In 1984, she was assigned to the Internal Affairs Bureau. O'Brien transferred to Media Relations in 1987 and was promoted to lieutenant in 1992.

SPECIAL AGENT BURDENA (BIRDIE) PASENELLI, Federal Bureau of Investigation, Assistant Director, Finance Division, Washington, D.C. Pasenelli serves as the FBI's chief financial officer. She was among the first twenty women to join the FBI in 1973, after the bureau opened up the special agent position to women on May 1, 1972. She was the first woman in FBI history to serve in the positions of Assistant Special Agent in Charge of a field office, Special Agent in Charge of a field office, and Assistant Director in Charge of one of the FBI's major divisions. Before she became an FBI agent, Pasenelli had a career with the Seattle Police Department, which she joined in February 1969. There Pasenelli was assigned to the Juvenile Division of the Detective Bureau, where she served until 1971, when she became an instructor at the Police Academy. In 1972, Pasenelli was promoted to detective and assigned to the Personnel Division. Later that year, she was among the first women police allowed to take the sergeant's exam. Pasenelli left the Seattle PD prior to promotion. In January 1973, she joined the FBI. Her first assignment, in 1974, was to Sacramento, California, where she served for a year and a half. In 1976, Pasenelli was transferred to Kenosha, Wisconsin. In 1984, having attained the rank of Senior Resident Agent, Pasenelli was transferred to Washington, D.C., as a Supervisory Special Agent. Here she worked first in the Personnel Division and then in the Inspections Staff, with responsibilities across the U.S. In 1987, Pasenelli was transferred to San Diego, where she served two years as a Supervisory Special Agent, White Collar Crime. In 1989, she became an Assistant Special Agent in Charge in Houston, White Collar Crime. In 1992, she was selected to be Special Agent in Charge of the FBI's Alaska office. In October 1993, she was named Assistant Director of the FBI's Finance Division, overseeing the bureau's $2 billion annual budget. On January 1, 1994, she assumed her responsibilities as the FBI's chief financial director. Pasenelli is the first woman in the history of the FBI to achieve this rank.

OFFICER JOAN PATRICI, Cleveland Police Department, Sixth District. Patrici joined the Cleveland PD in June 1988 and was assigned to the Fifth District. In 1990, she became a Field Training Officer. In 1991, Patrici was assigned to the Sixth District.

MAJOR DIANE PAULL, District Commander, Metro-Dade Police Department (Sheriff's Department), Cutler Ridge District, Miami. Paull was hired by the Sheriff's Department in December 1974. After she completed her training, her first assignment was on the road in District Three (then Midwest District, now Doral District). In 1977, Paull became a detective in the General Investigation Unit. She was promoted to sergeant in 1979 and worked in the Internal Affairs Section for the next four years. She made lieutenant in December 1983 and was assigned to Cutler Ridge, serving as a road lieutenant, also called a "platoon commander." In 1987, Paull became a General Investigation Unit commander in Kendall District, where she served until she was promoted to captain in June 1990. Paull was captain of the Metro-Dade Police Airport District from

1990 to October 1991, when she was named Bureau Commander of the Physical Offenses Bureau, which supervised Robbery and Sexual Battery. In March 1992, she was promoted to major and returned to the Airport District as a district commander. In July 1993, she transferred to the Cutler Ridge District. Paull is a member of the International Association of Women Police.

SERGEANT LINDA PIERCE, Seattle Police Department, Mounted Patrol Unit. Pierce joined the Seattle PD in 1981 and served in patrol in South Precinct for the next seven years. In 1988, Pierce worked on policies and procedures in the Inspectional Services Division. She was promoted to sergeant in January 1989 and served until 1991 in the Crime Prevention Division. She returned to the Patrol Division, East Precinct, in September 1991. In January 1993, Pierce was assigned to the Mounted Patrol Unit.

COMMANDER ROBERTA REDDICK (RET.), SERGEANT, Los Angeles Police Department, Commander of Police, Compton, California. Reddick joined the LAPD on September 16, 1947, as a policewoman, serving her probationary year in the city jail and in Juvenile Patrol and in February 1949 in the Seventy-seventh Street Division (Watts area), Youth Services Program (the Deputy Auxiliary Police), working with children. In October 1950, Reddick transferred to the Juvenile Division, where she worked as a juvenile investigator until June 1965. From then until her retirement, she worked Public Information and Community Relations Administration. Reddick retired from the LAPD in March 1968 at the rank of sergeant (which she attained in 1966). In 1971, she joined the L.A. Community Colleges as a police officer. In 1974, she joined the L.A. City Attorney's office as a hearing officer, prefiling criminal hearings. In 1976, she was invited by the Chief of Police in Compton, a former LAPD captain, to come to the Compton Police Department as an exempt status commanding officer. In 1976, Reddick joined the Compton PD as an inspector, serving as Commander of Police. Reddick became Acting Chief of Police for a month in 1978, the first woman to be appointed acting chief of police in the West. In 1980, Reddick became

Assistant City Manager in Compton. She retired from the Compton PD in October 1980. Commander Reddick is a charter member of NOBLE (National Organization of Black Law Enforcement Executives), formed in 1977, and serves on the Women's Advisory Council to the Los Angeles Police Department Commission.

YOUTH OFFICER LINDA REITER, Chicago Police Department, Area Five. Reiter came on the force in 1982, worked patrol in the Eighteenth District for seven years, including work in Operation Angel (decoy prostitution) and female search in Cabrini-Green, until her promotion to youth officer in 1989. In 1991, Reiter was assigned to the Crime Car, which responds to notifications from the Child Abuse Hot Line, which pertains to the physical and sexual abuse of children.

DETECTIVE KELLY ROBERTSON, Los Angeles Police Department, Narcotics Group, South Bureau, Field Enforcement Section (FES). Robertson joined the LAPD in 1988. Her first assignment was to Newton Division, South Central. Robertson served, as a P I [Patrol I] and a P II [Patrol II], in South Central, on patrol. For two months in 1989 Robertson worked the Juvenile Car, which specializes in child abuse calls, providing liaisons with the detectives and working with gang members and anything to do with juveniles and/or schools. In late 1989, Robertson was assigned to Venice Beach (Pacific Division), where she served on patrol until 1991. During her time in Venice Beach, Robertson became a field training officer and was assigned to the Oakwood Task Force, which specializes in gang activity and narcotics. In September 1991, she was assigned to the Chief's Office, where she worked for the Assistant Chief. Robertson was an instructor with the Training Division for seven months in 1993–1994. She was promoted to detective in 1994 and assigned to Narcotics. Robertson is a member of the California Narcotics Officers Association, the International Association of Women Police, and the California branch of IAWP. Off-duty, Robertson teaches Physical Training and Self-

Defense at the Fullerton Training Academy in Fullerton, California, and is the Academy's Cultural Diversity Coordinator.

DETECTIVE STEPHANIE ROUNDTREE, Philadelphia Police Department, Organized Crimes and Intelligence Unit. Roundtree joined the Philadelphia PD in March 1982 and was assigned to the Thirty-ninth Police District, patrol, until April 1989, when she was assigned to the Civil Affairs Division. Roundtree was promoted to detective in 1991 and assigned to the North Detective Field Division. In March 1994, she transferred to Organized Crimes. Roundtree is the Philadelphia chapter President of the National Organization of Black Women in Law Enforcement (NOBWLE) and a member of the Fraternal Order of Police, Lodge 5.

CRIMINAL INVESTIGATOR/DEPUTY U.S. MARSHAL RIKI ROUSE, U.S. Marshals Service, Houston, Texas. Rouse joined the Sheriff's Department in Galveston in 1985 and served in the Jail Section (Galveston County Jail) for four months and then the Warrant Division until October 1989, when she was reassigned to the Galveston County Jail, Women's Section. In December 1989, Rouse transferred into patrol. In 1990, she joined the U.S. Marshals Service. After a five-month training, Rouse's first assignment was to the Corpus Christi Suboffice, Criminal Section. In October 1990, Rouse was assigned to the Houston Office, Criminal Section. In January 1991, she went to the Civil Section and worked Seized Assets. Rouse served in the Enforcement Section from July 1991 through November 1992, when she transferred back to the Criminal Section. In July 1993, Rouse returned to Civil Section, Seized Assets.

LIEUTENANT PAT SANCHEZ, Dallas Police Department, Central Patrol. Sanchez joined the Dallas PD in 1974 and was assigned to Central Patrol. From 1976 through 1977, she worked Narcotics. In 1978, she returned to Central Patrol. Sanchez was promoted to sergeant in 1979 and assigned to the Report Division. Sanchez returned to Central Patrol as a sergeant in 1980. At the end of 1981, she was promoted to lieutenant and assigned to the Report Division. From 1984 to 1989, Sanchez transferred to Central Patrol. She went to the Investigative Division in Central Division, specializing in burglaries and thefts, in 1989. In 1991, she transferred to the Investigative Division in North Central Division. In 1993, she became a lieutenant in the Internal Audit Unit. Sanchez returned to Central Patrol in 1994.

SERGEANT SHERRY SCHLUETER, Broward County Sheriff's Office, Fort Lauderdale, Florida. Schlueter is founder and squad supervisor of the Animal Abuse Squad, supervisor of the Mounted Patrol Squad, and law enforcement coordinator for the Sheriff's Posse, Broward County, Inc. Prior to joining the BSO in 1979, Schlueter was an animal cruelty investigative agent for the Humane Society of Broward County. Schlueter proposed the formation of an animal abuse investigation unit in 1978, was hired by the BSO for that purpose in 1979, and was assigned to road patrol until 1982. In March 1982, she created the Animal Abuse Unit (now Animal Abuse Squad) and served as a one-person investigative unit for all of Broward County until 1986. She was promoted to sergeant in late 1986. In 1987, the Animal Abuse Unit expanded to include two detectives working full-time under Schlueter. In 1990, Schlueter, at the sheriff's request, was responsible for helping draft a proposal to create the Mounted Patrol Squad. During this time, she served as Co-Commander of the Airborne/Surface Rescue Team, in addition to becoming the coordinator for the Sheriff's Posse. Schlueter is not only involved in law enforcement, but she is an animal rights activist and environmental activist and is considered a national expert in the field of animal abuse investigation.

DEPUTY COMMISSIONER OF TRAINING ELSIE SCOTT, PH.D., New York City Police Department. Scott is the highest-ranking sworn civilian in the NYPD. Before joining the NYPD, Scott served as Executive Director of the National Organization of Black Law Enforcement Executives (NOBLE) in Washington, D.C., from 1986 to 1991 and was a program manager for NOBLE from 1983 to 1986. She was an Urban Studies Assistant Professor at Howard University from 1981 to 1983. From 1979 to 1980, she was Assistant Professor of Criminal Justice at North Carolina Central University. Her doctorate is in Political Science from Atlanta University. Scott was sworn in as Deputy Commissioner in January 1991.

DETECTIVE MARILYN SCHULZ, Portland Police Bureau, Detective Division. Schulz was among the first three women hired to work patrol on the Portland PB in 1973. She worked patrol for four years, was promoted to detective in 1977, and has served in Homicide, Fraud, Internal Investigations, and Sex Crimes as a detective. Schulz served as the Detective Division's polygrapher/interviewer/interrogator from 1989 to 1993. Since 1993, Schulz has served at Central Precinct as a detective.

SPECIAL AGENT DEBORAH SIBILA, Drug Enforcement Administration (DEA), Houston, HIDTA (High-Intensity Drug Trafficking Area) Task Force. From 1985 to 1986, Sibila served as a special agent for the Defense Investigative Service, doing background investigations for DOD (Department of Defense). Sibila joined the Bureau of Alcohol, Tobacco, and Firearms (ATF) in 1987 and worked as a special agent with ATF for four years, serving on the Arson Task Force, investigating cause and origin for a year, conducting firearms investigations for a year and a half, and, finally, working with the Organized Crime Drug Enforcement Task Force, which investigates complex conspiracies. In 1991, Sibila transferred to DEA, investigating federal narcotics-related offenses. She served as the President of Texas Women in Law Enforcement from 1991 to 1993 and is currently on the Board of Directors. Sibila is a member of the International Association of Women Police and the Texas Narcotics Officers Association.

SERGEANT CAROL SLETNER, Roseville, Minnesota, Police Department. Sletner joined the Roseville PD in 1982 and was on patrol from 1982 to 1988. She served as School

Liaison Officer from January 1989 until the summer of 1991, when she was appointed Juvenile Officer. In 1992, she was promoted to sergeant of patrol. Sletner is a member of the Minnesota Association of Women Police and the International Association of Women Police and is President of the Minnesota Juvenile Officers Association.

SENIOR CORPORAL MONICA MENDIZABAL SMITH, Dallas Police Department, Detective, Child Abuse Unit. Smith was a member of the Congregation School Sisters of Notre Dame before becoming a police officer. She joined the Dallas PD in March 1976 and worked in the Central Patrol Division until 1981. She was promoted to detective in the Investigation Section, Burglary and Theft, in 1981. Smith transferred to the Child Abuse Unit in August 1994. Smith has served as the elected President of the Dallas Police Association since 1988.

OFFICER THERESA SMITH, Seattle Police Department, North Precinct, patrol. After joining the Seattle PD in February 1986, Smith was assigned to patrol in South Precinct. She spent two summers (1988 and 1989) on Bicycle Patrol and went to North Precinct patrol in 1990. In May 1991, she became part of the Anti-Crime Team; in May 1993, she returned to Bicycle Patrol for the summer of 1993. Smith returned to patrol in the fall of 1993.

LIEUTENANT DIANN STANTON, Broward County Sheriff's Office, Fort Lauderdale, Executive Officer, Civil Division. Stanton was the first woman assigned to road patrol in the city of Lauderdale Lakes Police Department in Broward County in 1975. In September 1976, just before the city of Lauderdale Lakes contracted with the Broward County Sheriff's Office for police service, Stanton was assigned to the Criminal Investigations Division as a detective. In 1977, Lauderdale Lakes formally contracted with the Broward County Sheriff's Office for police service and Stanton became a BCSO deputy sheriff on road patrol. Stanton was detailed to the Organized Crime Division in August 1977 to work with the Gambling Squad. She was promoted to sergeant in April 1980 and served with the Organized Crime Division until February 1981. While in Organized Crime, Stanton was in an officer-in-charge capacity and a first-line supervisor for the multi-agency Narcotics Squad. Stanton was reassigned to road patrol in 1981. In the fall of 1982, she was transferred to the Internal Affairs Division. She was assigned to road patrol, District One, in early 1984. In the spring of 1985, Stanton was transferred to the Fort Lauderdale International Airport for six weeks and then was reassigned to road patrol in District One. In late 1985, she was assigned to a DUI Task Force within the Special Operations Group, where she served until June 1986. She was promoted to lieutenant in February 1986 and assigned to road patrol, District Three, as shift commander in June 1986. Stanton became the commander of the Communications Division in September 1987. During her tenure as commander of Communications, she was detached to attend the Southern Police Institute Administrative Officers Course at the University of Louisville from February through May 1989. Upon her return, she was assigned to the Mayor's Office as administrative assistant until November 1989. Stanton returned to uniform patrol in District One as a shift commander until early 1991, when she was assigned as unit commander to the Community Involvement Division. In January 1993, she was transferred to the Civil Division. Stanton is a member of the International Association of Women Police and belongs to the Alumni Association for the Southern Police Institute.

RANGER (SERGEANT) CHERYL STEADMAN, Texas Rangers, Houston. In 1993, Steadman was one of the first two women hired as Texas Rangers. Steadman joined the Department of Public Safety, Texas State Police, in 1984 as a trooper and worked in the Driver's License Service from 1984 to 1986. Steadman served from 1986 to 1993 in the Texas State Police, Highway Patrol, before becoming a Texas Ranger on August 1, 1993.

CAPTAIN JOYCE STEPHEN, New York City Police Department, Manhattan North. Stephen joined the NYPD in 1981. After being trained in the Forty-eighth Precinct, her first assignment, in January 1982, was to the Forty-sixth Precinct (Bronx), where she worked patrol. In December 1983, Stephen was assigned to the Police Academy as an instructor in Police Science. She was promoted to sergeant in November 1985 and was transferred to the Applicant Processing Section. In April 1987, Stephen was assigned to the Chief of Patrol's Office, where she headed the Rotation Tow Program (handling abandoned vehicles) for New York City until December 1987, when she transferred to Employee Relations. Stephen was promoted to lieutenant in June 1989. In 1994, Stephen was promoted to captain and assigned to Manhattan North.

DETECTIVE JULIA TAFALLA, Dallas Police Department, Crimes Against Persons Division, Homicide Unit. Tafalla joined the Dallas PD in 1976. Her first assignment was to the Northwest Division, patrol. Tafalla and her female partner were assigned a beat of their own in 1977. Tafalla was the first woman assigned to Parkland Hospital in 1978. In 1980, she returned to patrol in the Northwest Division. During this time, she was trained as a physical evidence officer and processed property crime scenes in addition to working patrol. In 1981, when Tafalla was promoted to detective, she became the first woman assigned to the Burglary and Theft Unit. In 1984, Tafalla became the first woman assigned to Auto Theft, where she worked until 1991, when she was assigned to Homicide. Tafalla is a member of Texas Women in Law Enforcement.

SERGEANT CYNTHIA TALLMAN, Seattle Police Department, Homicide Unit. Tallman became a Seattle police officer in 1979 and worked patrol in the West and North precincts for the next five years. In 1984, she was promoted to sergeant and assigned to the Internal Investigations Section. Starting in 1985, Tallman worked as an aide to the Assistant Chief for the Administrative Services Bureau. In 1987, she returned to patrol as a patrol sergeant. From 1988 to 1990, Tallman supervised the Anti-Crime Team (ACT), a specialized unit for serving search warrants, primarily on crack houses. Tallman returned to North Precinct as a patrol sergeant in 1990 and in September 1991 was assigned to the Commercial Security Section. Tallman transferred to the Robbery Unit in 1993 and to Homicide in May 1994.

INSPECTOR JULIA THOMPSON (RET.), New York City Police Department. Thompson was one of the first women to be hired as a patrol officer for the NYPD, in June 1973; she was assigned to the 60 Precinct (Brooklyn and Coney Island). During the fiscal crisis of 1975, Thompson and the other "last hired–first fired" NYPD personnel were laid off for twenty-one months, during which time she worked for the Manhattan District Attorney's Office as an investigator. In 1977, Thompson was rehired and returned to patrol, this time in the 84 Precinct. She was detailed to the Senior Citizens Robbery Unit (SCRU) as a decoy later in 1977. Thompson was promoted to sergeant in 1979 and returned to patrol, this time in the 67 Precinct. She worked in the Internal Affairs Division from 1980 to 1981, when she transferred to the Office of Equal Employment Opportunity. In 1983, she was promoted to lieutenant and assigned to the CCRB (Civilian Complaint Review Board), where she did investigations, planning, and implemented computerized on-line report-taking for the department. Thompson went back to patrol in 1984, in the 9 Precinct, for a few months and then was assigned to the Manhattan Court Division. In June 1985, she was promoted to captain and became the executive officer, second in command, at the 6 Precinct. Thompson got her own command in the 76 Precinct, serving there from 1986 to 1987. She was promoted to deputy inspector in October 1987 and transferred back to the 6 Precinct as the commander. In 1989, Thompson attained the rank of inspector and became the commanding officer of the Eighteenth Division (encompassing six precincts, including the Rockaways, LaGuardia Airport, and Jamaica), the first woman in the history of the NYPD to command a division. At her retirement in 1993, Thompson was the highest-ranking woman in the NYPD.

LIEUTENANT NELLIE TORRES, New York City Police Department, Chief of Personnel's Office, Staff Services Section. Torres joined the NYPD as a civilian in 1979, working 911 and then radio dispatch. Torres became a sworn NYPD officer later in 1979 and was assigned to the Seventeenth Precinct, where she worked patrol from 1980 to 1982. From June 1982 to January 1983, she was assigned to the Police Academy as an instructor in Police Science. Torres returned to the Seventeenth Precinct in 1983 and was reassigned to the Academy in 1984, where she taught until 1987. She was promoted to sergeant in 1987 and assigned to the Eighty-first Precinct (Brooklyn). In late 1987, Torres was transferred to the Detective Bureau, where she commanded the Sex Crimes Unit until 1992. She was promoted to lieutenant in 1992 and served in the Ninetieth Precinct. In 1993, Torres was assigned to the Staff Services Section.

SERGEANT PAULA TREHEY, Illinois State Police, District 03 Investigations, General Assignment. Trehey joined the Illinois Bureau of Investigation in September 1974. (The IBI merged with the Illinois State Police in 1977.) Trehey (promoted to sergeant in 1980) was a narcotics investigator until 1981. Since 1981, she has served as an investigator in General Criminal, Financial Fraud, Medicaid Fraud, Internal Investigations, Race Track, and Child Abuse and Exploitation. Trehey has also served as a recruiter for the Illinois State Police. From 1990 through 1993, Trehey was president of Illinois Women in Law Enforcement and is a member of the International Association of Women Police.

SENIOR CRIMINAL INVESTIGATOR DEBBIE WATERFIELD, San Francisco District Attorney's Office, Bureau of Investigations, currently assigned to Major Crimes. Waterfield joined the DA's Office in 1976. She was assigned to the Jonestown People's Temple case from the end of 1976 to 1977. During her career, Waterfield has worked General Criminal Investigations, being assigned to Juvenile, Gangs, and White Collar Crime/Consumer Fraud, and has worked with the SFPD, in virtually every bureau, on major cases, specializing in sexual assault and child abuse. Waterfield is a member of the National Organization of Black Law Enforcement Executives (NOBLE), the Officers for Justice (San Francisco) chapter, the National Black

Police Association, and the International Police Association.

SENIOR CORRECTION OFFICER PATRICIA WATSON, New Jersey State Department of Corrections. Watson has served in the Department of Corrections since 1979, in the Garden State Processing Center (formerly the Yarville Youth Correctional Processing Center).

ASSISTANT CHIEF ROBERTA WEBBER, Portland Police Bureau, Operations Branch. Webber joined the Portland Police Bureau in July 1971 and was assigned to what was then the Women's Protective Division; in 1974, she transferred to the Drug and Vice Division, undercover, for eight months. In 1975, she was promoted to detective and assigned first to Juvenile Felonies and then to Sex Crimes. She was promoted to sergeant in February 1977 and was transferred to North Precinct; in September 1977, she was assigned to the Detective Division as a detective sergeant. In December 1979, Webber was transferred to the Drug and Vice Division as a sergeant. She was promoted to lieutenant in April 1980 and transferred to the Chief's Office as the aide to the Deputy Chief of Patrol Branch. In 1982, she was transferred to the East Precinct as a lieutenant. Webber was assigned to a special project on annexation in February 1984. In April 1984, she was promoted to captain and assigned to the Patrol Support Division (overseeing the Mounted Patrol Unit, the Canine Unit, and the Street Crimes Unit). Webber was put in charge of the Personnel Division from February 1985 to October 1986, when she was transferred to the Records Division. In March 1987, she was made commander in charge of Central Precinct, a position she held until May 1989, when she was promoted to Deputy Chief, in charge of the Services Branch. In November 1990, she was made captain of the Detective Division. In August 1992, she was promoted to commander of North Precinct. Webber was promoted to Deputy Chief of Operations in July 1993 and promoted to Assistant Chief July 1, 1994. Webber is a life member of the International

Association of Women Police and a member of the Oregon Association of Women Police.

TROOPER SUE WEBSTER, Michigan State Police. Webster became a state trooper in 1977. Her career in the state police has included postings in Paw Paw, St. Clair, New Buffalo, and Iron River. Webster was assigned as an instructor to the Michigan State Police Training Academy for the 109th Recruit School for four months in 1994.

OFFICER CHRISTINE WIGGS, Philadelphia Police Department, Human Resource Bureau. After joining the Philadelphia PD in November 1988, Wiggs was assigned to the Fourteenth District, where she worked the street until December 1990, when she was appointed administrative assistant to the Chief Inspector of the Patrol Bureau. In 1992, Wiggs became the administrative assistant to the Chief Inspector of the Human Resource Bureau.

SERGEANT BARBARA WILSON, Seattle Police Department, North Precinct. Wilson joined the Seattle PD in 1983 and worked patrol until her promotion to sergeant in June 1991, when she was assigned to Internal Investigations. Wilson returned to North Precinct as a patrol sergeant in 1992.

OFFICER PAMELA WILSON, Boston Police Department, Area A-1. Wilson joined the Boston Police Department in 1986. She has worked as a patrol officer in Area A since June 1986.

YOUTH OFFICER MARIAN WROBEL (RET.), Chicago Police Department. Wrobel joined the Chicago PD in 1947 as a policewoman, assigned to the Summerdale District until 1951. She did considerable undercover work citywide for Homicide, Burglary, Robbery, and the Confidence sections. Wrobel also served in the Eighteenth District, the Nineteenth District, and the Area Six Youth Division. Wrobel retired from the force in 1980.

* * *

DETECTIVE DONNA YOUNG, Chicago Police Department, Area Five, Detective Division. Young joined the Chicago police in May 1975 and was in the first coed class at the Police Academy. Young was first assigned to patrol in the Nineteenth (now Twenty-third) District. In 1976, she was assigned to the new Nineteenth District (Western and Belmont) and served in patrol for the next three years. In 1979, Young was the first woman in the CPD assigned to the Canine Unit, where she served until 1987. In April of that year, she was promoted to detective and assigned to Auto Theft. In 1990, she transferred to Property Crimes, where she specializes in con artists and con games. Young is a member of the International Association of Women Police and Illinois Women in Law Enforcement and served as the latter organization's parliamentarian from 1990 through 1993.

THE MOST EXCITING NONFICTION
COMES FROM POCKET BOOKS